The Sales Manager's Book of Marketing Planning

DAVID W. CRAVENS

DOW JONES-IRWIN, INC.   Homewood, Illinois   60430

This publication is designed to provide accurate and
authoritative information in regard to the subject matter
covered. It is sold with the understanding that the
publisher is not engaged in rendering legal, accounting, or
other professional service. If legal advice or other expert
assistance is required, the services of a competent
professional person should be sought.

*From a Declaration of Principles jointly adopted by a Committee
of the American Bar Association and a Committee of Publishers.*

ISBN 0-87094-419-3

Library of Congress Catalog Card No. 83–70858

Printed in the United States of America

1 2 3 4 5 6 7 8 9 0 K 0 9 8 7 6 5 4 3

Preface

Marketing planning will be essential to survival and growth of companies in the rapidly changing business environment of the 1980s. To a much greater degree than in the past company strategies are being driven by forces in the marketplace. Analyzing market behavior and adjusting strategies to changing conditions require a hands-on approach to marketing planning. Decision-based planning has become increasingly critical due to the need to frequently alter strategies for products and markets. Seat-of-the-pants approaches to sales and marketing management are ineffective in the current environment.

This book provides practicing managers with a guide to marketing planning. Developed around a step-by-step approach to marketing planning, the book serves two primary purposes. First, it offers executives who already have established approaches to marketing planning a basis for evaluating and refining the approaches. Second, the book contains a practical set of guidelines for implementing formal marketing planning in companies that want to start a planning program. Each chapter is concluded with a checklist that can be used to review your own marketing planning approach.

The intended reader is the manager who wants a complete yet concise and practical guide to developing and using a marketing plan. It is particularly useful for sales managers who are interested in expanding their knowledge of marketing planning. It should also be of interest to chief executives, marketing researchers, advertising specialists, salespeople seeking management positions, and other executives who want to increase their understanding of marketing planning.

You are an essential part of the planning approach presented in the book. The success of the marketing planning guidelines in your organization depends upon your knowledge of and experience with the market environment in which you operate. Many important marketing planning questions and issues are considered in the book. Obtaining answers to these questions requires a detailed understanding of your particular business environment.

Finally, I have drawn from the contributions and experiences of many different people and organizations. While space does permit thanking each contributor, a special note of appreciation is extended to all. Although the final result is my responsibility, the many contributions of others were vital to accomplishing the product.

David W. Cravens

Contents

1. Marketing planning. **1**

Customer satisfaction: *A good listener. Heeding the consumer. Marketing information. Strategies for meeting needs.* Strategic planning and marketing: *Importance of planning. Strategic planning.* Marketing planning: *Analyzing markets. Market targeting. Marketing objectives and positioning. Product/service planning. Distribution and pricing plans. Sales and advertising plans. Financial analysis for marketing plans. Moving from plans to action. Tracking marketing performance.*

2. Coordinating business and marketing plans **19**

Corporate mission and objectives: *Corporate development alternatives. Deciding corporate mission.* Business composition: *Establishing business boundaries. Forming business units.* Approaches to analysis. Business unit strategy: *Finding a competitive advantage. Composition of the business plan. Marketing's role in business planning.*

3. Analyzing markets **43**

Defining product-markets: *What is a product-market? Some differences in terms. Considerations in forming product-markets.* Analyzing product-markets: *Customer profiles. Size and growth estimates. Industry and distribution analyses. Key competitors. Marketing strategy guidelines. Strengths and limitations of the approach.*

4. Market targeting **63**

What are the options? *Mass strategy. Niche strategy.* Finding and describing niches: *Forming niches. Experience and available information. Research-based approaches. Describing the niches.* Evaluating target market alternatives. Selecting a target market strategy: *Product-market characteristics. Company characteristics. Other considerations.*

5. Marketing objectives and positioning **85**

Integrating corporate and marketing strategies. Setting marketing objectives: *Relevant and consistent objectives. Clear guide to accomplishment. Objectives and people.* Choosing a positioning strategy: *Programming decisions. Factors affecting program strategy.* Position analysis: *Management judgment. Customer research. Test marketing.*

6. Product/service planning **109**

Strategic role of product decisions: *Impact upon other decisions. Marketing's role in product planning.* What is a product strategy? *Product strategy defined. Setting priorities.* New product planning: *Finding ideas. Evaluation. Organizing for new product planning. A new product application.* Managing existing products: *Strategic options.*

7. Distribution planning **133**

Strategic role of distribution: *Reaching target markets. Distribution functions.* Strategic alternatives: *Type of channel arrangement. Distribution intensity. Channel configuration decision.* Selecting a channel strategy: *Strategic analysis. Strategy at different channel levels.*

8. Price planning **153**

Guide to price planning: *Product and distribution strategies.* Price analysis: *Product-market analysis. Cost analysis. Competitor analysis. Legal and ethical considerations. How much flexibility exists?* Price strategy determination: *Price as an instrument of strategy. Selecting a strategy. Pricing objectives.* Establishing policies and structure: *Product relation-*

ships and price structure. Special considerations. Determining specific prices.

9. **Advertising and sales planning** **173**

Developing a promotion strategy: *Communications objectives. Mix of communications components.* Advertising and sales promotion strategy: *Role, objectives, and budget for advertising. Creative strategy. Media/ programming strategy. Implementation and management.* Selling strategy: *Role and objectives. Size and deployment decisions. Sales force management and control.* Selecting a promotion strategy.

10. **Moving from plans to action** **201**

Financial analysis: *Marketing's influence on financial performance. Some analysis issues. Illustrative ROI analysis. Financial analyses and forecasts.* An illustration. Short-term plans and implementation: *Planning cycle and frequency. The short-term marketing plan.* Designing the marketing organization: *Design considerations. Functional organizations. Product organizations. Market organizations. Combination approaches.*

11. **Tracking marketing performance** **225**

Building an evaluation program. The marketing audit: *Plans and performance criteria.* Setting up a tracking program. Information, analysis, and action: *Opportunities and performance gaps. Determining strategic action.*

Index **239**

1

Marketing planning

The turbulent business environment in the United States and throughout the world is unprecedented in the experiences of most executives. This exciting new challenge that sales and marketing managers face has never been greater in the history of business practice. The 1980s mark the beginning of a new era for business decision makers. There is a shift toward much greater emphasis upon planning and the more active participation of sales and marketing professionals in both corporate and marketing planning. Three major forces are reshaping the role of marketing in many organizations, making it far more demanding than in the past.

☐ Rapid changes in markets are creating opportunities and threats by altering the attractiveness of markets and causing pressures for quick and correct strategic response. In many companies survival is the name of the game. We need only look back at the 1970s to appreciate the importance of understanding markets for products and services and the need for prompt attention to the changing needs and wants of customers. Polaroid Corporation's unsuccessful entry in 1977 into the instant movie market illustrates the importance of identifying the real needs and wants of customers and matching them with appropriate product offerings. People did not want to pay a premium price for instant movies whose quality did not measure up to conventional film.

☐ Top management is placing far more emphasis than in the past upon sales and marketing capabilities as a way of strengthening the competitive position of the business. While management of firms like General Electric and Procter & Gamble have long recognized the key role of these decisions, many small and medium-sized firms, and even giants like American Telephone & Telegraph, are currently directing much more attention toward marketing strategy.

☐ Finally, there is a clear recognition that meeting customer needs and wants is the responsibility of all of the people in the organization, not just those assigned to the sales department. Management must mold all activities into a businesswide effort aimed at customer satisfaction.

Sales operations form the core of the marketing efforts of many companies. The role and importance of sales management and other marketing professionals are rapidly expanding in many firms to include their active participation in marketing planning. Additionally, sales managers must plan and manage sales operations as a coordinated part of the marketing strategy of the business. Meeting this new role will require sales and marketing professionals to expand their planning capabilities.

Many managers cite marketing planning as one of their most difficult and frustrating assignments. Others question its usefulness. Virtually all managers are concerned about the time needed for planning. While planning is challenging, it need not be frustrating. And since planning is decision making, its usefulness is not really an issue. The reason managers are on the payroll is to make decisions. Thus, the real issue is not whether to plan but rather how well do we do it. Marketing planning is not a routine activity that can be easily dispensed with. One perplexing problem many executives encounter in planning is deciding what to include in the plan. Often too much is included. Following a proven step-by-step approach in marketing planning will enable most executives to improve the speed of preparation, reduce the length, and increase the effectiveness of their marketing plans. The key, of course, is making the right decisions, and no planning approach can eliminate this responsibility.

Planning is not report preparation by a group of staff people. Managers plan. In this book we shall present an action-oriented and practical approach to marketing planning and illustrate how it can be applied in many different business environments. Representing over two decades of development, with applications in a wide range of firms, the approach is built around the decisions that management must make to satisfy customer needs and wants. Properly applied, it gets results.

This chapter sets the stage for the remainder of the book by first examining what a marketing orientation is all about and considering how adopting it will lead to customer satisfaction. Next, we illustrate the importance of planning to business survival and prosperity, discussing several reasons why strategies fail. Finally, a step-by-step approach to marketing planning is outlined and illustrated. The remaining chapters of the book examine each of these marketing planning steps.

CUSTOMER SATISFACTION

If people do not want or need your product or service, they will not buy it. This is what a *marketing orientation* is all about! It applies to toothpaste, industrial cranes, financial services, or any other product or service. It is important in your business. This approach to marketing consists of three simple, yet critical, cornerstones. Let's review them:

☐ Start with customer needs and wants as the basis of business purpose. Management must identify these needs and wants and then decide which ones to try to satisfy.

☐ Next, we must determine how to satisfy customer needs and wants. This is the responsibility of all members of the enterprise, not just those assigned to selling.

☐ Finally, meeting our objectives is the result of delivering customer satisfaction.

This simple, yet critical, logic is at the heart of business success. While a marketing orientation represents nothing really new to executives and its commonsense guides are clear, surprisingly, many businesses have never put this approach into practice.

Applying the marketing orientation is a continuing activity. Plans must be developed, implemented, and evaluated to assure that customers are satisfied. We cannot identify customer needs and wants at one point and expect them to never change. Determining these needs is not always easy. Management must be ready to adapt to changing conditions which may generate new opportunities and problems. Once identified, choosing an effective business strategy is a major challenge for management. Well-planned and executed business plans do not always result in the levels of performance expected by management and so management must continue making changes until satisfactory performance is reached. Let's examine a company that has built an impressive performance record for many decades in delivering customer satisfaction.

A good listener[1]

Building the business using a marketing orientation has been profitable for Procter & Gamble. Following its guidelines has resulted in impressive performance for more than a century. An aggressive competitor, the firm's sales and marketing professionals are second to none in experience and ability in the use of such marketing techniques as market research and test marketing. P&G has performed well in highly competitive, mature product-markets.

Heeding the consumer

Following a marketing orientation goes back in P&G's history to 1879, when a factory worker made a mistake. A mixing machine for soap ran too long and resulted in a frothy concoction. The workman and his supervisor decided to go ahead and distribute the mixture. Buyers discovered when they used the soap that it floated in water. Consumers wanted more of the soap, and management traced it back to the over-mixed batch. The result was Ivory soap. While making mistakes is not what a marketing orientation is all about, the incident demonstrates P&G's early awareness of the importance of listening to its customers. Today, this sensitivity to customer needs and wants has been incorporated into an early warning system. In 1980 the company received upward of 250,000 calls and letters from customers (one half seeking information, one sixth praises, and one third complaints). By the end of 1980 all of P&G's 80 brands had a toll-free number on the package or label. The company received some 500,000 calls in 1981.

Marketing information

Management does not depend only upon consumer-initiated feedback. In 1980 P&G conducted nearly 1,000 consumer studies involving phone or home interviews with some 1.5 million people. The studies are used to measure consumer satisfaction with P&G products, to test names and packaging designs, and to explore other important marketing and product design questions. Some even analyze people's consumption habits, such as how they wash clothes, prepare meals, wash dishes, and perform other household tasks. Research data are circulated monthly to every major segment of the company where the findings are studied for their implications for sales and marketing, advertising, manufacturing, and research and development operations. For example, Cheer detergent is the result of a research finding which indicated that the average household's laundry loads increased in the 1960s from 6.4 to 7.6 a week and the average wash temperature dropped 15 degrees. The cause was synthetic fabrics and new blends which presented different washing problems. Cheer was developed to meet these needs by allowing several fabric types to be washed together.

Strategies for meeting needs

P&G's management knows how to translate feedback from the marketplace into marketing action by continually watching for new trends in tastes, needs, environment, and living habits. They carefully study the competition. New product programs and those for existing brands are planned in detail, launched, and then evaluated on a regular basis. Some critics argue that P&G buys market position with huge advertising and promotional expenditures. The firm's $650 million expenditure on advertising did place P&G at the top of all firms in 1980. While advertising is an important part of the marketing plans used to position P&G brands against competition, the key to a long string of company successes is management's ability to figure out what consumers want and to put the entire company behind an effort to satisfy people's needs and wants. P&G's well-trained professional sales force is a key factor in the company's strong distribution network.

Sometimes mistakes are made. For example, a roll of disposable, detergent-filled paper dishclothes with fabric-like characteristics failed. The product, called Fling, was market tested in 1963 and ultimately dropped. P&G's most recent disaster was its Rely tampon, which was withdrawn from the market in 1980, due to an apparent health hazard, at a cost of over $75 million. While the research and testing for Rely were impressive, the efforts did not guarantee success. Nevertheless, P&G's extensive research, planning, and sound implementation have, in the balance, paid off for the company.

Our look at P&G illustrates three important points concerning adoption of a marketing orientation. To find and hold a strong position against competitors, management must study the marketplace, build a corporate team to serve customer needs and wants, and be ready to respond to the inevitable forces of change.

STRATEGIC PLANNING AND MARKETING

Often we can learn as much by analyzing mistakes as by studying the successes of business firms. In this book the corporate and marketing plans of a variety of companies are examined to illustrate successful and unsuccessful planning decisions. My purpose is not to praise or criticize the management of any company. Rather, their experiences can assist other firms to develop successful plans for capitalizing upon opportunities and avoiding threats. Some companies that are in trouble today may be very successful in the future, and vice versa. Let's examine the Singer Company with two objectives in mind. First, the illustration shows the important role of sound planning in successful corporate performance. Second, as you consider Singer's strategic errors, note, in particular, how marketing decisions had an important influence upon corporate performance.

Importance of planning

The Singer Company is widely recognized throughout the world as the largest manufacturer of sewing machines. Sales in 1981 were over $3 billion. Essentially no sales growth occurred throughout the 1970s after taking inflation into account. Profit performance was even worse. The company entered the 1980s facing an uncertain future after more than a decade of problems including a slowdown in the growth of the sewing market, intense competition, several unsuccessful diversification moves, and some huge write-offs. Strong financial performance in the 1960s had generated large cash flows from sewing machine sales. But recognizing the slow growth implications of a mature home sewing market and facing intense competition from the Japanese, management decided to diversify into other areas.

Too much too fast. As you analyze companies such as Procter & Gamble, General Mills, United Technologies, and others, you will see a logical reason for their movements into new business areas. In contrast, Singer's management plunged the company into product diversifications with apparently limited analysis of market trends, competitive strengths, and the strategic attractiveness of each diversification to the company. As shown in Exhibit 1–1, in the mid-1960s, the company launched over a score of acquisitions that included business machines, audio equipment, heating and air-conditioning equipment, furniture, water meters, valves, aerospace gear, electronics, housing, and even a mail-order house and a credit bank in Germany![2] There was no cohesiveness to the new business units. Hastily acquired in the 60s and 70s, many were no longer in the company's business portfolio by 1980, although a few of the remaining businesses were doing well. While movement away from sewing products was necessary, the fit of many of these acquisitions into Singer's business portfolio is questionable. They represented new technologies, unfamiliar markets, different marketing and distribution methods, and many other new experiences. Huge demands were made upon management's talents and Singer's financial resources. Bringing any one of the new businesses into Singer's operations would have been a challenge for a management team not experienced in managing a diversified corporation. David Packard, co-founder and chairman of the Hewlett-Packard Company, emphasizes the importance of selectivity:

Exhibit 1–1
Singer Company diversifications

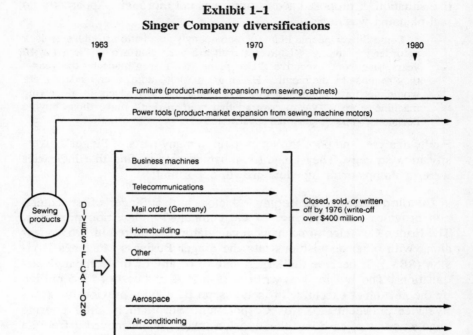

There is one piece of advice a friend gave me early in the game which I think is very important: that more businesses die of indigestion than of starvation. This simply says that a lot of people take on more than they're able to and they get into trouble.[3]

Sound business planning requires deciding what priorities to place upon a firm's various business areas including, in some instances, eliminating products or choosing not to serve certain markets. Few if any firms are successful in meeting everyone's needs. Management must make a realistic assessment of the available capabilities and resources for serving the markets of interest to the firm.

No strategic planning. Interestingly, the only two diversification areas linked to Singer's original sewing business were furniture (from sewing cabinet know-how) and power tools (from sewing machine motor experience). Analysis of the market attractiveness and the competitive situation of proposed acquisitions was not thorough. Apparently no real planning was done:

> Some Singer people blame the company's acquisition troubles on lack of orderly planning. "I haven't seen a 5-year plan around here for 10 years," says one executive. "Our plans aren't even made by the year—they're made by the month." Had more market studies been made, Singer would not have attempted to sell TV and audio products in its sewing machine stores. "We discovered that women don't make those buying decisions," one Singer man says ruefully.[4]

Faulty analyses and poor timing crop up in many parts of Singer's diversification strategy. They bought companies only to find that industries were in slumps or facing slow growth opportunities.

Building business strategies. A close look at Singer's first acquisition provides more evidence of the company's indigestion problems. The Friden Co. (electromechanical calculators), acquired in 1963, grew along with other acquisitions into the Singer Business Machines Division (SBM). It became the largest failure of any of the company's acquisitions. The division was written off in 1975 at a cost of $385 million by the new chief executive officer, Joseph B. Flavin, previously executive vice president at Xerox Corporation.[5] Surprisingly, after pouring huge amounts of cash into this division, management moved it from an obsolete technology position to first position in the electronic cash register market, and then lost this position in 1975 to the National Cash Register Company. The problem is as noted:

> While most of Singer's other woes stem from an acquisition program unsupported by controls, SBM's problems came from a succession of marketing men and engineers who headed the division but who could not blend the marketing and engineering functions successfully as they converted their products from electromechanical to electronic operation.[6]

Although the division never made money, it was strongly positioned in two large growth markets—point-of-sale electronic cash registers and small business computers. If top management had not been so preoccupied with the company's various businesses, this division might have been turned around.

In mid-1982 the company's common stock was selling at $12 per share, down from an all-time high of $100. Singer offers convincing evidence of the dangers in faulty planning, limited market opportunity evaluations, poor implementation, and inadequate management control. The company's future will be heavily dependent upon the performance of its nonsewing products, including power tools, furniture, meters, industrial air conditioning, and aerospace products. These successful divisions more than doubled their operating income from 1975 to 1979 on a 33 percent sales boost.[7]

Strategic planning

The Singer illustration shows the perils of poor planning, indicating the need for close involvement by sales and marketing professionals. Strategic planning is a continuing activity consisting of:

☐ Analyzing business performance and identifying future opportunities and threats.
☐ Determining corporate mission, objectives, and strategies.
☐ Setting objectives and developing strategies for each unit of the business.
☐ Implementing, managing, and adjusting mission and strategies to achieve corporate and business unit objectives.

Business analysis.   Assessments must be made of present and future performance of the firm in the market areas that it serves. Business analysis may also include evaluating opportunities outside the present scope of the business. A corporation that is comprised of two or more business activities (e.g., sewing products and power tools) should be managed as a portfolio of business units, each reflecting its unique future attractiveness to the firm. The planner studies the composition of the business, product and market interrelationships among the units and pinpoints future threats and opportunities. Both financial and market analysis skills are essential in performing these analyses.

Corporate mission and objectives.   Mission and objectives provide guidelines for planning throughout the business. Corporate mission is what the management wants it to be and what available resources will allow the company to be. For example, Bell & Howell defines corporate purpose to be a leading supplier of information systems throughout the world. Mission determination involves deciding the product and market areas to be pursued by the firm. While changes in mission are not made frequently, adjustments to new conditions may be necessary.

Business unit objectives and plans.   Strategic planning in the 1970s caused many changes in corporations, including acquisitions, divestments, and setting different performance goals for business units. Some business units face slow growth, while others may offer exciting future opportunities. A firm's strength over competition will also vary between business areas. Thus, business planning activities should indicate how financial resources are to be allocated among units and management's expectations regarding financial and market performance for each business unit. Business unit objectives set the stage for developing plans for each business unit. These plans include marketing, financial, operations, and other supporting activities.

Implementing and managing strategies. Plans must lead to actions, and long-term plans must be translated into short-term (e.g., annual) budgets and operating plans. Sales and marketing executives are involved in business planning in three important ways: (1) they participate in planning for the enterprise; (2) they serve with other functional managers as members of the business unit planning team; and (3) they develop and execute marketing plans for the business unit. Let's examine how marketing fits into business planning.

MARKETING PLANNING

Steve Harrell, former manager of planning for GE's Housewares and Audio Business Division and now head of strategic planning at Black & Decker, describes marketing's role in planning at General Electric:

> . . . the marketing manager is the most significant functional contributor to the strategic planning process, with a leadership role in defining the business mission; analysis of the environmental, competitive, and business situations; developing objectives, goals, and strategies; and defining product, market, distribution, and quality plans to implement the business's strategies. This involvement extends to the development of programs and operating plans that are fully linked with the strategic plan.[8]

Marketing's business planning responsibility includes: (1) participating in corporate analysis and strategy formulation as described by Harrell and (2) development of marketing plans in accordance with corporate priorities. Since these two areas are closely interrelated, we need to examine marketing's role and functions in both areas.

Exhibit 1–2
How to prepare the marketing plan

1. Coordinate business and marketing plans.
2. Analyze market opportunities.
3. Select market target(s).
4. Determine market objectives and positioning plan.
5. Product plans.
6. Distribution and pricing plans.
7. Sales and advertising plans.
8. Financial analysis for marketing plans.
9. Move from plans to action.
10. Track marketing performance.

A 10-step approach to marketing planning is shown in Exhibit 1–2. The first step ties together corporate and marketing plans. Since company mission, objectives, and business strategy were just discussed, we shall examine each of the remaining nine steps.

Analyzing markets

Correctly defining markets is necessary in order to analyze them and forecast future trends. To refer to the Toronto market, the United Kingdom market, or some other geographical area that contains people and organizations with all kinds of needs and wants, is not very useful in planning. To properly define a market there must be people (or organizations) with specific needs and wants, one or more products that can satisfy the needs, and the people must be willing and able to purchase the product that satisfies their needs and wants. Thus, we shall use the designation *product-market* since it is more descriptive than market.

Analyzing product-markets and forecasting how they will change in the future are essential to corporate and marketing planning. Decisions about entering new product-markets, how to serve existing product-markets, and when to exit are key decisions that affect the future of the firm. More so than any other area in the enterprise, sales and marketing professionals have the skills and experience essential to conduct product-market analysis, to interpret the results, and to make plans for serving product-markets.

An example will illustrate how essential product-market analysis is in developing marketing plans. The Loctite Corp., an adhesives manufacturer, introduced a successful new product in October of 1980 called Quick Metal.[9] A putty-like adhesive, the product is used to repair broken and worn machine parts. Contrary to previous new-product introductions, management went out and asked customers what they wanted in an adhesive. Six weeks of interviews were conducted with 20 equipment designers and production engineers and 40 maintenance engineers. In six months the sales of Quick Metal reached $2.2 million. Management estimated that the prior marketing approach used by the firm would have yielded only about $300,000. Other aspects of the marketing plan used for Quick Metal are discussed as we move through the remaining steps in preparing the marketing plan.

Market targeting

Once a company's product-markets have been identified and their relative importance determined, management must decide which people (or organizations) to go after in each product-market. Management may decide to serve all people in the market using a mass strategy or, alternatively, to serve one or more subgroups (niches or segments) of people in the product-market using a different marketing approach for each. The basis of forming subgroups may include the characteristics of people, their purchase and product use behavior, and/or their preferences toward products. Likewise, industrial product-market niches may be formed according to type of industry, product application, and other factors.

The target market decision was a major factor in Quick Metal's success in the market place. Contrary to the approach used for Quick Metal's predecessor, a runny green liquid called RC 601, maintenance workers were targeted instead of equipment designers. Marketing research indicated that equipment designers are often reluctant to try unproven materials. In contrast, when the equipment is down, production stops and maintenance people have the authority to buy what is needed to get production back on line. As we shall see shortly, this target market decision helped management select the marketing program appropriate to the needs of customers.

Marketing objectives and positioning

A marketing program positioning plan consists of the product to be marketed, distribution approach, pricing, sales program, and advertising program aimed at the target market. Management must first decide what is to be accomplished in the target market. Marketing objectives are often established at several levels. The corporate objectives, for which the marketing function is totally or partially responsible, indicate overall performance targets (e.g., growth, profit, human resource development, and other broad objectives). Specific objectives must be set for each target market. For example, suppose as one of its objectives a corporation wishes to double sales (in constant dollars) over the next six years. This objective must be allocated to the firm's target markets since it is unlikely that each will account for the same proportion of sales. Similarly, the profit contributions that are feasible for different market targets often vary, so this must be considered in setting objectives. For example, profit opportunities vary from one sales territory, district, or region to another. Objectives range from a very broad corporate objective to the specific objectives of a salesperson as shown in Exhibit 1–3.

After selecting the target market and formulating marketing objectives, the next step is deciding how to fit together product, distribution, pricing, and promotion plans into an integrated marketing program for each target market. Management has considerable latitude in deciding the role of each of these components. These strategies must be blended together so that sales, market share, profit contribution, and other target

Exhibit 1–3
Illustrative marketing objectives

Corporate: Achieve a net profit growth rate (in constant dollars) of 20 percent per year for the next five years.
Marketing: Maintain a marketing expense to sales ratio of 15 percent or less for 1983.
Market Target: Increase our market share in the videotape recorder product-market from 13 percent to 18 percent during the next 24 months.
Advertising: Increase consumer brand awareness in the Southeastern region from 42 percent to 50 percent by one year from now.
Salesperson: Increase our share of sales to the Apex Company from last year's 30 percent to 45 percent by the end of next year.

market objectives are met. Decisions about products, distribution channels, price, advertising, and personal selling must lead to a cohesive marketing program aimed at meeting the needs and wants of customers in the firm's target market. Designing the marketing program is essentially a positioning strategy, in that it combines marketing capabilities into a package of actions intended to position the firm against its chosen competitors to compete for the customers that comprise its target market. Management may try to offer a different marketing program than a competitor or to appear similar to a competitor. The key is deciding how to serve a target market.

Positioning should form an integrated program with each marketing component fulfilling its proper role in helping to position the firm in the target market. The result often distinguishes a company, product, or brand from its competitors due to customers' perceptions of the product or brand. The product, the method of distribution, the price, advertising, and personal selling all help to establish these perceptions, as do the marketing efforts of competitors. The real test is whether the program will deliver customer satisfaction to the firm's target market and also meet company objectives. Target market and positioning strategies are like two sides of the same coin, each dependent upon the other. Let's take a closer look at each program component.

Product/service planning

Product planning is the core of planning for the enterprise since decisions about new products, product improvements, and product drops affect the entire company from its sales force to the boardroom. Without a product or service, there is no business. The product or service forms the focal point of a positioning strategy. Distribution, prices, advertising, and personal selling are all working toward positioning the product in the eyes of the buyer. Thus, the designation *product positioning strategy* is often used. Since position can be achieved using a combination of marketing factors, such as personal selling, product positioning is normally the result of more than just the product.

In planning for Quick Metal, management started with the customer rather than first developing a product in the laboratory and then trying to figure out how to sell it. The fact that the new product was a nonmigrating thixotropic anaerobic gel with certain properties was not stressed with potential customers. Instead, the name Quick Metal stressed what the adhesive could do for the user. Of course, the research and development which came up with the new product was essential. It had to perform when needed.

Distribution and pricing plans

Distribution. Two aspects of distribution channels are critical. First, how can buyers be reached? Should marketing middlemen (e.g., wholesalers, distributors, retailers, and dealers) be used or should the firm's sales force go direct to the end users of the product or service? Going direct to the consumer using a strong sales force may be necessary for some products. Of course, personal selling is necessary with either direct marketing or working through distribution organizations.

Second, if intermediaries are to be used, then what kind of distribution channel should be developed? Since several distribution approaches may be applicable in a given situation, the proper choice is often not obvious. Once established, channels are not changed frequently so this decision is of considerable importance to the firm. For many companies a strong distribution network can be a major competitive advantage. Tandy's Radio Shack retail store network enabled the firm to gain a strong position in the small computer market. Deere & Company's farm equipment dealer network helped this firm gain the number one position in the market. Ethan Allen's independent dealer showroom network is the backbone of this firm's very successful marketing program.

Pricing. Decisions about price are influenced significantly by the mix of products offered, branding (private versus name brand), and product quality. Distribution also influences how price will work in combination with sales force and advertising programs. Management must decide:

☐ How to position price relative to competition.
☐ How active price is to be in the marketing program.
☐ The objectives that price should accomplish.
☐ What price policies should be used.

Returning to the Quick Metal illustration, Loctite has independent distributors with some 700 branches that are called upon by the company's sales force. To encourage distributors to push Quick Metal with their customers, prizes of $100 to $1,000 were given to sales contest winners. During one week of heavy promotion, daily calls were made to distributors from the home office. Pricing was aggressive at $17.75 for a 50 cc. tube, giving the manufacturer an 85 percent gross margin! One tube can eliminate 800 hours of machine downtime, so from the buyer's point of view the cost is low compared to the benefits the product provides.

Sales and advertising plans

Deciding how to use personal selling and advertising in the marketing program is the next step in the planning process. Some firms place primary emphasis on sales operations. Others allocate a major portion of the marketing budget to advertising. And many firms spend heavily on both areas. Although consumer product firms often spend more on advertising and less on personal selling and industrial products firms do just the opposite, it is dangerous to generalize. Advertising and personal selling have certain features and limitations that should be considered when deciding upon the appropriate mix between the two areas.

Loctite used an effective combination of personal selling and advertising in marketing Quick Metal. Advertising and sales promotion stressed the basic benefits provided by the product. One slogan used was "keeps machinery running until the new parts arrive." The name itself conveys important information. Selling efforts were directed toward distributors. Interestingly, sales of other Loctite products also increased during the Quick Metal campaign.

Financial analysis for marketing plans

Financial planning is an important part of marketing planning. Bottom line performance will be critical to survival in the 1980s. Familiarity with financial tools and analysis is a job requirement of sales and marketing managers and an essential capability for moving into higher level jobs. The bottom line impact of sales and other marketing decisions has become a key factor in whether these decisions are implemented. We must develop our understanding of basic financial tools so that the full financial impact of marketing plans can be evaluated.

With the exception of accounting and finance executives, most of us have difficulty with the various financial analyses, such as contribution margin, cash flow, income and break-even projections, present value, inventory turnover, and return on investment. These analyses are often essential in developing plans, and top management is asking that expense and pro forma profit and loss analyses be included in marketing plans.

Moving from plans to action

People make things happen so the marketing organization is an essential part of implementing marketing plans. Unless plans are implemented, nothing will happen. One basic rule in designing the marketing organization is that the organization should be built around the marketing plan, rather than attempting to force the plan into a predetermined organizational arrangement. Coordination of activities is essential to successful implementation of plans, both within the marketing function and with other company and business unit functions.

Specialization of marketing activities will lead to greater efficiency in performing marketing functions, and it can also provide technical depth. For example, product or application specialization in a field sales force will enable salespeople to provide consultative-type assistance to customers. Of course one of the real dangers in a highly structured and complex organization is the loss of flexibility. The organization should be adaptable to changing conditions.

No doubt by now you have detected a flaw in our discussion of desirable characteristics. Some are in conflict with each other. For example, specialization can be expensive if carried to extremes. The costs of having different sales specialists call upon the same account must be weighed against the benefits obtained from the overlapping coverage. Thus, an organizational design represents a balancing of conflicts against advantages.

Tracking marketing performance

Making decisions, implementing them, and gauging their effectiveness over time is what marketing planning is all about. Planning never stops. To be meaningful and effective, plans must contain commitments.

Evaluation is tracking performance and, when necessary, altering plans to keep performance on track. Evaluation also includes looking for new opportunities and potential threats in the future. Evaluating changing conditions in marketing planning is of critical importance:

> Any business plan that is over 12 months old in today's rapidly changing state of economic and social affairs is an extraordinarily dangerous document. At the very least, management should review all the basic assumptions and trends underlying the overall strategic plan annually. Then it should conduct a careful review of the interim progress that has been made and clearly identify the reasons for underperformance or overperformance.[10]

Evaluation is the connecting link in the marketing planning steps shown in Exhibit 1–2. Evaluation assures that planning will be a continuing management activity.

This overview sets the stage for the rest of the book. The remaining chapters are devoted to each of the marketing planning steps 2–10, following the sequence shown in Exhibit 1–2.

CONCLUDING NOTE

This book is for sales and marketing managers who want to expand their knowledge of marketing planning. Throughout the book the *how* of planning is stressed and illustrated. Guidelines for marketing planning are developed and applied. Wide use is made of how-to-do-it guides to analysis and planning. Various techniques and methods used in marketing planning are explored throughout the book to illustrate their usefulness in business analysis, product-market targeting, product positioning, new product planning, price analysis, financial planning, and many other application areas.

Before moving on to Chapter 2, two important parts of marketing planning require emphasis. The first concerns the approach and technique of planning. Our experience in applying this planning approach in many different business environments suggests its applicability in your company or business unit. Nevertheless, a note of caution is in order, and this brings us to the second aspect of marketing planning. Your business is unique. Thus, the purpose of the book is to present an approach to planning that you can apply in your business. Its application will require your insights, experience, and judgment. Our primary objective is to assist you in targeting the essential questions to be answered in preparing and managing your marketing plan. Only you can answer these questions as they apply in your particular environment.

NOTES

1. This illustration is based on material found in John A. Prestbo, "Good Listener: At Procter & Gamble, Success Is Largely Due to Heeding Consumer," *The Wall Street Journal,* April 29, 1980, pp. 1, 35.
2. "Why the Profits Vanished at Singer," *Business Week,* June 30, 1975, p. 106.
3. "Hewlett-Packard Chairman Built Company by Design, Calculator by Chance," *The AMBA Executive,* September 1977, p. 8.
4. "Why the Profits Vanished at Singer," p. 106.
5. "Flavin's Master Plan for Ailing Singer," *Business Week,* May 10, 1976, p. 66.
6. "Singer Performs Some Costly Surgery," *Business Week,* January 12, 1976, p. 30.
7. Jeffrey H. Birnbaum, "Singer Co. Starts a Severe Restructuring, Will Post Losses for 3rd Quarter and Year," *The Wall Street Journal,* October 15, 1979, p. 8.
8. Steve Harrell, speech at the Plenary Session of American Marketing Association's Educators' Meeting, Chicago, August 5, 1980.
9. This account is drawn from Bill Abrams, "Consumer-Product Techniques Help Loctite Sell to Industry," *The Wall Street Journal,* April 2, 1981, p. 29.
10. Ronald N. Paul, Neil B. Donavan, and James W. Taylor, "The Reality Gap in Strategic Planning," *Harvard Business Review,* May–June 1978, p. 129.

2

Coordinating business and marketing plans

Battered by inflation, high interest rates, resource shortages, intense competition, and worldwide instability, businesses are rapidly adopting formal planning methods as a way of positioning the enterprise to successfully cope with an uncertain future environment. And many companies that already have strategic planning programs are altering them to incorporate the advances in planning methods practices that were developed during the 1970s. An overview of business planning is shown in Exhibit 2–1. The process is a continuing one beginning with an assessment of the situation faced by a corporation. This leads to an examination of corporate mission and objectives which may, over time, be changed to respond to the findings of the situation assessment. Strategies are required to accomplish missions and objectives. These strategies are developed for the product and market areas that determine the composition of the business. An important part of planning in a firm that is made up of more than one product-market area is regular evaluation of the different business areas. These business units often have different objectives and strategies, representing a portfolio of businesses. The plan for each unit spells out what and how the unit will fulfill its assigned role in the corporation. Underlying the unit's strategic plan are functional plans for marketing, finance, operations, and other supporting areas. Strategies are then implemented and managed. Regular assessment of the strategic situation completes the cycle shown in Exhibit 2–1. In this chapter we shall examine the business planning activities shown in Exhibit 2–1 beginning with the analysis of the situation, or *situation assessment*.

A situation assessment includes analyses of environmental influences,

Exhibit 2–1
Business planning overview

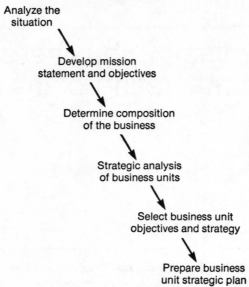

customers, competitors, and corporate capabilities and limitations. It should delineate the opportunities and threats facing the corporation. This information is then used for preparing and implementing strategic plans. Consider, for example, the Valspar Corp., which 10 years ago was a small paint manufacturer located in Minneapolis, Minnesota. The situation assessment that led to a new corporate strategy was the threat to the company's survival from national companies with efficient production operations, availability of money to support large advertising budgets, and strong brand images. Management, observing the consolidation and dropout of companies due to intense competition in the mature, low-growth paint industry, needed a strategy to cope with the industry consolidation trend. The plan that was selected after assessing the opportunities and threats facing Valspar is described in Exhibit 2–2. The major areas included in the Valspar situation assessment were product-market trends, competitor analyses, and company strengths and limitations.

CORPORATE MISSION AND OBJECTIVES

Management must decide the nature and scope of a firm's operations and then make whatever adjustments in these decisions that are neces-

Exhibit 2–2
Valspar spreads out its paint empire with strategy
of buying regional brands

What G. Heileman Brewing Co. is to beer, Valspar Corp. is to paint. At least that's the idea.

Valspar was strictly a local outfit 10 years ago, but now it's following the same strategy that transformed Heileman from a regional brewery into the nation's No. 6 beer maker.

Instead of trying to market its own brands nationally, Valspar has bought smaller paint companies and used their popular local brands to enter regional markets. Along with the new brands, Valspar has gained some of the economies of scale enjoyed by bigger rivals and additional private-label and industrial customers.

The number of companies in the mature, low-growth paint industry has dropped to 1,150 in 1979 from 1,579 in 1963, but Valspar's sales have increased to $136 million a year from $27 million in 1969. Valspar is the 10th largest paint and coatings company in the U.S. and sells its paint in most of the country.

How to compete?

Valspar's strategy is one solution to the problem facing regional companies when an industry is consolidating: how best to compete with large, national companies that use more efficient advertising and manufacturing to muscle out small firms.

A major advantage of expanding through regional acquisitions is that it's often cheaper than the advertising necessary to introduce a brand in a new region. "You're buying the affection that people have for these regional products. That's a good way of growing," says Thomas Turner of Case & Co. Management Consultants.

Heileman is a textbook example. It has thrived while other regional breweries have floundered and while some large beer makers with national brands have lost market share competing with industry leaders Anheuser-Busch Inc. and Miller Brewing Co.

Valspar's first major move came in 1970 when it merged with Minnesota Paints Inc., a private company with 1969 sales of $24.1 million. Valspar, then based in Rockford, Ill., had concentrated in Northeast and Midwest markets, and Minnesota Paints was in the upper Midwest.

Both companies assumed that going it alone would be increasingly difficult against Sherwin-Williams Inc., PPG Industries Inc., and Du Pont Co. "You can grow internally, but you can't grow fast enough," says C. Angus Wurtele, who was president of Minnesota Paints and became chairman and chief executive of Valspar in 1973.

Since then, Valspar has bought four more paint companies. The most important were Elliott Paint & Varnish Co. of Chicago in 1976 and Conchemco Inc.'s paint business in 1979. Both had strong regional brands. Elliott helped strengthen Valspar in Chicago and a few Midwestern states, and Conchemco's brands gave Valspar entries in the lower Midwest, South, and parts of the East Coast.

In addition, Mr. Wurtele says Elliott had a strong private-label business—paint made for a hardware store chain and sold as the chain's "brand"—

Exhibit 2–2 *(concluded)*

and Conchemco had industrial customers that bought paint for manufactured products.

These acquisitions have increased Valspar's share of the highly fragmented paint market to 2 percent. (Industry leader Sherwin-Williams holds 8 percent or so.) More important, Mr. Wurtele says, "We're in the top three or four companies in the markets that we're in." Over the years, Valspar has trimmed the number of brands it sells to five: Elliott, Minnesota, Valspar, Masury, and Colony.

Although the strategy has worked well, there are shortcomings. Regional companies usually don't have the bankroll to make many purchases. "We are limited in that we can only make a major acquisition every couple of years because of our size," concedes Mr. Wurtele. Valspar might have been interested in buying Dutch Boy—the brand acquired recently by Sherwin-Williams—but didn't even take a close look because it was still digesting the Conchemco paint business.

Risking disaster

One big danger is that a bad acquisition could prove to be a disaster, says Philip Kotler, a marketing professor at Northwestern University's graduate school of management. "It only makes sense to the extent you're good at takeovers," he says.

Valspar has avoided any disaster so far, though its 1973 acquisition of Phelan-Faust Paint Manufacturing Co. in St. Louis caused problems. In addition to paint plants, Phelan-Faust had about 10 retail stores that were such a drain on time and assets that Valspar finally sold them. But Valspar learned its lesson and immediately sold the retail stores that came with the Conchemco paint business.

Despite Valspar's success, an executive at a major paint company contends Valspar may be making a mistake in the long run by not concentrating on a single brand that can be advertised nationally. "In the last three or four years," he says, "the amount of dollars spent during the paint season on paint advertising has increased tremendously. I don't know what the impact will be on companies that can't participate in that advertising. It bodes ill for them, I think, during this period of consolidation."

Source: Lawrence Ingrassia, *The Wall Street Journal,* December 26, 1980, p. 9. Reprinted by permission. © Dow Jones & Co., Inc. 1980. All rights reserved.

sary over time. These choices about where the firm is going in the future, taking into account company capabilities, resources, opportunities, and problems, establish the mission of the enterprise. An illustration will demonstrate what is involved in mission determination.

By Fortune 500 standards the J. L. Clark Manufacturing Co. is small.[1] Sales were $112 million in the year ending November 1980. How has this company successfully competed with the giant manufacturers in the packaging and container industry, such as American Can

Company, Continental Group, Inc., and others? About 80 percent of sales and earnings come from packaging items. Its remaining business areas are paper and plastic tubes, business machine tapes, and industrial filters. Clark's financial performance has been strong over the past 12 years with profits increasing at nearly a 20 percent annual rate in the 5 years ending in 1979. Sales increased nearly threefold since 1970. Let's look at Clark's mission and strategy:

☐ Clark holds a leading position in several specialty packaging market niches. Internal growth plus acquisitions have enabled the company to gain all of Gillette's double-edged razor dispenser business and Johnson & Johnson's Band-Aid boxes plus a large share of container purchases for Duracell and Ray-O-Vac batteries. The firm also makes paper and metal containers for spices, foods, cleaners, polishes, drugs, and tobacco. Brand names include Avon, Sucrets, and Pepsodent.

☐ Heavy emphasis on research and development has resulted in innovative shapes and attractive designs. Management considers R&D a key to company growth.

☐ Clark has a reputation for quality work. Even sales of the firm's lithographed empty canisters have boomed in gift shops. A major program is under way to modernize plants and increase productivity.

☐ The company is in a strong financial position with a small long-term debt of about $2 million. Money is available to continue management's plans for internal growth and acquisitions to extend Clark's position in packaging.

Innovation, efficient production, and a sensitivity to customer needs and wants have helped Clark to become a market leader in several small and very specialized container markets. A market niche strategy within the huge container industry has been a central factor in shaping the mission of J. L. Clark. Selectivity in choice of market opportunities coupled with cost-effective solutions to customers' packaging problems have enabled the company to demonstrate impressive financial performance over the past decade.

Corporate development alternatives

Most companies, such as J. L. Clark, start business operations in some core business area. Success often leads to expanding into related areas and sometimes entirely new product-market areas. The major corporate development options are shown in Exhibit 2–3. There are, of course, many specific strategies and combinations of the major options.

Exhibit 2–3
Corporate development options

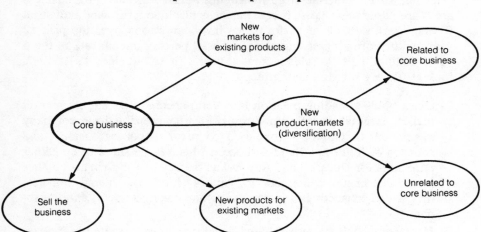

We shall examine each option to gain a better understanding of corporate expansion activities.

Core business. Many firms start out serving one product-market. The product or service may be a single product or a line of products. The initial venture is the core business as sewing products were in the case of the Singer illustration discussed in Chapter 1. This strategy, when it involves a single product-market, offers the advantages of specialization but contains the risks of being dependent upon one set of customer needs. As a corporation grows and prospers, management often decides to move into other product and market areas as shown in Exhibit 2–3.

One company that has stayed close to the core business since its founding in 1896 is Tootsie Roll Industries. "Fully 93 percent of its sales still come from the basic Tootsie Roll and its permutations, such as Tootsie Pops, Flavor Rolls, Caramel Pops, and Tootsie Squares."[2] This single-product business continues to prosper although management recognizes the risks of having all its eggs in the Tootsie Roll basket. The chief executive officer has publicly stated a desire to diversify out of the candy field. With no long-term debt and a strong cash position, the money is available. Management's criteria for an acquisition include companies in a related field located in the Midwest or East, sales from $5 million to $15 million, and a capable management willing to stay with the firm.[3]

Rarely does a firm that is successful stay with the original business; rather, at some point, it pursues one or more of the alternatives shown in Exhibit 2–3. Less dependence upon the core business is a major factor in corporate development. Of course, financial resources are necessary to expand into new areas. In some situations selling the business may offer management an attractive opportunity for expansion. For example, Entenmann's Inc., a small but highly successful bakery in the Northeast and Florida, lacked the capital needed to expand at a rate desired by its owner-managers. They sold the company in 1978 to Warner-Lambert, remaining with the company to move it toward national status.

New markets for existing products. One way to expand away from the core business is to serve other needs and wants using the same product or a similar product. The Maytag Company is a leading manufacturer of home *and commercial* laundry equipment. A. T. Cross markets its line of writing instruments to consumers and to organizations for incentives, employee recognition, and other uses. For many companies, this is a natural line of development. The strategy reduces the risks of depending upon a single market, yet it allows the use of existing technical and production capabilities. The major demands arising from this strategy are adequate resources for expansion and the capabilities for developing a new marketing strategy. Since it may be difficult to acquire a marketing capability or to turn it over to a marketing intermediary, the requirements for internal marketing strategy development should be recognized when adopting this alternative. The primary caution to be exercised is to be sure the new market opportunity is carefully evaluated as to its feasibility and attractiveness.

New products for existing markets. Another strategy for shifting away from dependence upon one product-market is to expand the product mix offered to the firm's target market. Magic Chef, the range and oven manufacturer, in 1979 added to its appliance offering by acquiring lines of washers and dryers and refrigerators and freezers. Use of common distribution channels, promotional support, and research and development are among the possible advantages of this strategy. New products can also be developed internally, although acquisition is faster. Resources are necessary to support either alternative. A disadvantage of this strategy is the continued dependence upon a particular market area, such as household appliances.

Diversification. Finally, diversification has been a popular option for corporate development by many firms. The distinction between diversification and product or market expansion is that the former involves movement into a new product-market area either by internal development or acquisition. Often the riskiest and costliest of the options shown in Exhibit 2–3, it may be attractive if existing product-market areas face slow growth, if resources for diversification are available, and if good choices are made. Diversification, once it has been success-fully implemented, offers the advantage of spreading business risks over two or more segments of business. Diversification may follow one of two avenues: (1) movement into different, yet related product-market areas or (2) building the corporation into a conglomerate that consists of unrelated product-market areas. Analysis of successful diversification strategies suggests that the following factors are often important:

1. Top management has the capabilities to manage a portfolio of busi-nesses, including a proven record of sound strategic planning. Ade-quate cash for diversification is also essential.
2. The new business areas are in attractive (fast-growing) product-markets, and business strength is high compared to competition.
3. Each business area has one or more key advantages over competing firms, such as low production costs, strong acceptance by cus-tomers, proprietary products, marketing strengths, and technical strengths.
4. The business area has good internal management and technical peo-ple who are strongly committed to the success of the business.
5. Acquisition prospects have a strong financial performance record over several years.
6. The costs of internal development or acquisition are not so high that profitable operation of the business area will be jeopardized.

Clearly, satisfying all of the above criteria is difficult, if not impossible. Nevertheless, if a new business area does not offer some distinct advan-tages in terms of these factors and other situation-specific factors, success is doubtful. Of course, each situation must be assessed to ac-count for its unique characteristics. Regardless of the advantages, move-ment into entirely new fields is often riskier than expanding into busi-ness areas related to a company's existing business activities.

Deciding corporate mission

Our examination of corporate development activities highlights the fact that corporate mission and purpose are often altered to pursue one or more of the options shown in Exhibit 2–3. Thus, early in the cor-porate planning process, the mission should be examined and a state-ment of mission developed if one does not exist, or the present statement should be reviewed and updated. The mission statement spells out what management of the corporation wants it to be, and it establishes several important guidelines for planning including:

1. The reason for the company's existence and its responsibilities to stockholders, employees, society, and various other stakeholders.
2. The customer needs and wants to be served with the firm's product or service offering (areas of product and market involvement).
3. The extent of specialization within each product-market area (e.g., deciding to offer just Tootsie Rolls versus a variety of candies).
4. The amount and types of diversification of product-markets desired by management.
5. Management's performance expectations for the company.
6. Other general guidelines for overall business strategy, such as the role of research and development in the corporation.

An overriding influence upon the mission decision is what management wants the business to be. Acknowledging the constraining nature of capabilities, resources, opportunities, and problems, management is left with much flexibility in making the decision as well as changing it in the future. Uncontrollable factors may create the need for alteration of mission. Management must decide how to solve the problem or capitalize upon an opportunity. Drucker describes the task: "Defining the purpose and mission of the business is difficult, painful, and risky. But it alone enables business to set objectives, to develop strategies, to concentrate its resources, and to go to work. It alone enables a business to be managed for performance."[4]

In addition to a mission statement, long-range objectives should be indicated so that the performance of the enterprise can be gauged. Objectives are often set for the corporation in the following areas: marketing, innovation, resources, productivity, social, and financial.[5] Examples include growth and market share expectations, human resources training and development, new product targets, return on invested capital, earning growth rates, debt limits, energy reduction objectives, and pollution standards. When corporate objectives are general, it is important that they be made more specific at lower levels in the organization. Each major business segment should also have objectives since one business area, such as Tenneco's shipbuilding business segment, is not likely to have the same objectives as, for example, the gas transmission segment would have. Objectives should be realistic and specific so that management can measure progress toward them.

BUSINESS COMPOSITION

Understanding the composition of a business is essential in both corporate and marketing planning. In single-product firms, such as Tootsie Roll Industries or Tampax, Inc., determining business composition is easy to do. In many other firms the business must be separated into parts to facilitate analysis and planning. When firms are serving multiple markets with different products, grouping similar business areas together facilitates planning. Before moving into a discussion of establishing business boundaries, we first need to identify some terms that are used to describe business composition.

As an illustration, General Mills, Inc., has been organized into five major segments: food processing (the core business); restaurants; crafts, games, and toys; apparel and accessories; and specialty retailing. Each segment, as shown in Exhibit 2–4, may consist of a few business units,

Exhibit 2–4
Illustrative levels of business composition (General Mills, Inc.)

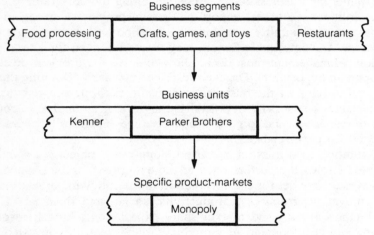

and each of the units may be composed of a few or perhaps several specific product-markets. Within the crafts, games, and toys segment one of the business units is Parker Brothers, and Monopoly is one specific product-market within the business unit. While the levels that exist in a diversified firm will depend upon the number and types of business areas involved, designations more specific than segments are needed. A business segment is typically made up of product and market activities that possess some degree of similarity, such as offering away-from-home meal services. General Mills' restaurant group (a business segment), for example, consists of Red Lobster seafood outlets, York Steak Houses, and Gallardo's Mexican restaurant chain, and a small southeastern chain called Darryl's.

Establishing business boundaries

Traditionally, product or industry designations have been used to designate the nature and scope of business operations. A company might be described as a steel processor, a candy maker, or a heavy equipment manufacturer. Use of only the product or service to establish boundaries between areas of business activity is incomplete because the end user of the product or service is excluded. There are three important dimensions to be considered in defining business activities:

1. What need or want is the enterprise attempting to meet?
2. What end-user customers does the firm want to serve?
3. What product or service offering will be used to meet the needs of customers?[6]

An example will help to illustrate each dimension. Suppose that there is need to photograph action scenes, such as a swimming race, so that the scenes can be shown in movie format. Look at the three dimensions shown in Exhibit 2–5. Notice that needs for a particular product function vary, that different end-user groups are involved, and that the need can be met using two different product offerings. By considering the three dimensions we have a useful basis for establishing business boundaries for those firms serving a range of needs with several products or services. Even in a company serving a single product-market, use of the three dimensions adds considerable direction to strategic planning by showing how other product-market categories (and the firms that serve them) must be considered in developing strategies.

As a company attempts to satisfy more and more needs by offering various products and services, it becomes more diversified. When the needs of different user groups are met with the same product or service,

Exhibit 2–5
Meeting a need to photograph and replay action scenes

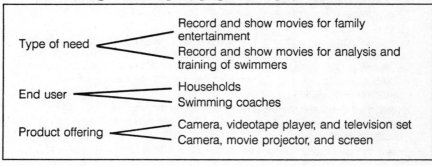

this may position a firm in more than one product-market, each requiring a different marketing strategy. So all three dimensions should be considered in defining a business and grouping together similar product-market activities.

Forming business units

Let's consider how the General Foods Corporation, a leading producer of packaged foods, has regrouped its divisional structure into strategic business units. James L. Ferguson describes how the firm's products were repositioned into menu segments:

> We started out with four divisions: Kool-Aid, Bird's Eye, Jell-O, and Post. Among the products in those four divisions, we saw five basic menu segments in addition to coffee: dessert, main meal, breakfast, beverage, and pet food. We combined these five strategic business units—SBUs—into three new divisions: main meal and dessert SBUs became the food products division; beverage and breakfast SBUs were combined into one division, and pet foods—which we considered a major growth opportunity—was put into a third division.[7]

The General Foods approach to SBU formation consists of a group of brands linked together by their natural interrelationship on the consumer's menu rather than the fact that the brands share a common manufacturing process or method of distribution. Thus, the need being satis-

Exhibit 2–6
Guidelines for forming business units

Inventory the products offered by the corporation to identify specific products, product lines, and mixes of product lines. Determine the end-user needs that each product is intended to satisfy.

Identify which products satisfy similar needs (e.g., foods for main meals). Also, determine which products satisfy the needs of more than one user group.

Form units composed of one or more products or product lines that satisfy similar needs (e.g., food preparation appliances). The products that form a planning unit should have in common major strategic features such as distribution channels, target markets, technology, and/or advertising and sales force strategies.

Determine if there are management, market, operating, or other advantages to combining two or more planning units into a division, group, or business segment.

Review the proposed scheme to determine if it offers both operational and strategic advantages. Do the potential benefits of the scheme exceed the costs?

fied is an essential factor in defining SBUs. For example, the company's main meal SBU includes frozen vegetables, instant rice, seasoned coating mix, and salad dressing mixes. While all of these are foods, several manufacturing processes are involved.

Several guidelines to use in forming business planning units are shown in Exhibit 2–6. Management, of course, has some flexibility in deciding how to divide the business into planning units. Building up from specific product market categories offers a more useful scheme in forming planning units than starting from the top and breaking it down. A note of caution is in order. Forming too many planning units can be more harmful than useful. A large number of units will require a correspondingly large number of strategies and management structures which are expensive and probably not cost effective.

APPROACHES TO ANALYSIS

Business unit evaluation essentially involves gauging how performance has been in the past, determining where we are at the present time, and forecasting the future attractiveness of the product-markets in which the business unit participates. Using this information, management must determine the future strategy of the business unit, considering the unit's opportunities, threats, strengths, and weaknesses and then compare it to other units in the corporation.

Several methods of analysis have been developed. The most popular approaches are briefly described:

☐ Product-markets grids. Using these approaches, each business unit or specific product-market is positioned on a two-way grid according to the attractiveness of the product-market(s) and the unit's business strength compared to competition. Depending upon where a unit is located on the grid, alternative strategies are indicated. Several versions of grid analysis exist, the most popular being the Boston Consulting Group portfolio approach and General Electric's screening method.

☐ Profit impact of marketing strategy (PIMS). Using a large data bank, the Strategic Planning Institute in Cambridge, Massachusetts, can analyze various strategic factors (e.g., market share) that are related to profit performance and compare a company or business unit to other firms and units in the data bank. These computerized analyses provide various diagnostic comparisons and also indicate promising strategic actions based on the results of the analyses.

Several kinds of analyses may be needed to help determine future strategies. A major distinction between the grid methods and PIMS ap-

Exhibit 2–7

Usefulness of selected methods of analysis for various planning activities

Planning activity	Portfolio analysis	Screening methods	PIMS
Comparison of business unit* with:			
Other internal units	Position on the growth-share matrix is the basis of comparison, with cash flow serving as the performance criterion.	Position on the screening grid is the basis of comparison, with ROI serving as the performance criterion.	The PIMS output provides no direct basis of comparison.
Competition	Competing units (or products) can be plotted on the matrix if market share data are available.	Placing competitive units (or products) on the screen is very difficult due to the information needed on business strength.	The PAR† and look-alikes‡ reports indicate comparative data for *groups of firms* with similar characteristics.
Present situation analysis:			
Corporation	None of the three methods is suitable on a direct basis for this purpose unless the corporation is a single-unit or single-product business. Management can form a composite assessment using the information obtained from the business unit analyses.		
Business unit	Desirability of present situation is based upon position on the matrix.	Same as portfolio analysis.	Extensive diagnostic information is provided by the various PIMS reports.
Functional areas	Not useful for this purpose.	Screening analyses for the various factors may provide some indication of functional strengths and limitations.	Some of the diagnostic information can be used to compare the unit with the data base.

Determining future strategies:			
Corporation	Provides resource allocation guidelines based on cash flow growth prospects.	Provides resource allocation guidelines based on ROI considerations.	Management can use the business unit analyses as a basis for considering overall corporate strategy.
Business unit	Indicates cash flow strategy but no specific indication of other strategic guidelines.	Strengths and weaknesses of various screening factors may suggest possible future business strategies.	The PIMS reports indicate the projected effect of several possible strategic moves and nominate an optimal strategy.
Functional areas	Not useful.	Of only limited value.	The reports are of general value in certain functional areas by highlighting strategic actions that are related to functions (e.g., product quality, market share).

*Or other appropriate units of analysis.
†PAR = Normal, or par, ROI.
‡Look alikes = Strategically similar businesses.

Source: Portions of this exhibit are based upon Derek F. Abell and John S. Hammond, *Strategic Market Planning* (Englewood Cliffs, N.J.: Prentice-Hall, 1979), p. 380.

proaches is that the grid methods can be used to examine several business units at the same time and to establish priorities for each unit. The data-based approach looks at one unit or product at a time, comparing it to the relationship established using the PIMS data bank. Thus, the former approach places more emphasis upon relative position, whereas the latter focuses upon absolute position.

In the case of the portfolio and screening methods, the major outputs are guidelines for resource allocation. These methods also indicate the relative attractiveness of different business units based on their positions on the grid. PIMS supplies several reports and analyses and has the most extensive output, followed next by the screening method and then portfolio analysis.

In Exhibit 2–7 the three methods are compared as to their usefulness in various planning activities. The methods are far more useful for indicating the nature of the actions that should be taken rather than showing what specific strategies should be adopted. Moreover, with the exception of PIMS, the strategic guidelines are primarily financial (cash flow or ROI). PIMS identifies the key determinants of ROI and cash flow but does not indicate specific strategies for improving product quality and financial performance and reducing cost. This limitation of all of the methods is understandable since it is doubtful that a method of strategic analysis will ever be developed that indicates specific future strategies. Strategic planning is far too complex and situation specific for it to be reduced to this type of treatment.

Management must consider the costs and benefits of the approaches. Each offers certain advantages and limitations. The data base underlying the PIMS studies is impressive, whereas the intuitive logic of the portfolio and screening approaches is appealing. The portfolio approach requires very little data, thus reducing its costs. The multiple-factor and data-based approaches both require a considerable amount of information in order to conduct the analyses. If a consultant is utilized this will further increase costs. Whatever the analysis method selected, it should generate information for management to use in making decisions. The methods themselves are not intended to make decisions. Some firms are using multiple approaches thus obtaining the strengths of each in various analysis activities. In fact, it is quite possible that the three approaches may eventually merge into one. Interestingly, both screening and PIMS got their start at General Electric.

Perhaps the greatest contribution of formal strategic analysis is that it raises vital questions about each unit of a business. The methods highlight the importance of developing a strategy appropriate for the opportunity and competitive situation in each business unit. Treating each business unit the same simply does not make good strategic sense. Formal analysis forces management to recognize differences in business units and to develop strategies in the best interest of total corporate performance.

Several important questions should be answered in business unit evaluation as shown in Exhibit 2–8. The use of a three- to five-year time frame is arbitrary and can be adjusted to conform with the appropriate time horizon for a particular corporation. Two important factors should be considered in selecting the time frame. First, limiting the range to one or two years is typically too short. Second, the time span should not be so far into the future that realistic projections will be impossible.

Exhibit 2–8
Key questions to be answered in business unit evaluation

What is the strategic situation of the business unit in terms of product and
  market maturity?
How has the business unit performed during the past three to five years?
How attractive will be the product-market opportunities in the next three to
  five years?
How strong is our business unit position compared to competition?
What should be the future strategy of the business unit over the next three
  to five years?

BUSINESS UNIT STRATEGY

Management must decide whether to: (1) maintain or strengthen position; (2) attempt to shift into a more desirable position; or (3) exit from a business unit. Of course as a product-market matures, strategic position may be altered due to a decline in the attractiveness of the product-market. Management must select a strategic plan for each business unit taking into account strategic position, available resources, forecasts of future competitive and market conditions, and the relative attractiveness of available opportunities. The process is described:

> . . . the end product of the strategic planning process is a future best-yield portfolio composed of individual product-market entries, taking into account risk and short-term versus long-term trade-offs. The decision of which product-market entries to include in the portfolio as well as the extent to which each should be emphasized is a most complex one to make.[8]

The real advantage in using the strategic analysis methods lies in raising such questions as how to strengthen a weak business unit or capitalize upon a strong position. Management must then decide what actions to take to reposition the business unit.

Finding a competitive advantage

The essence of both corporate and marketing strategy is finding an advantage over competition. Companies can gain competitive advantage in various ways such as:

☐ Establishing market power through market share dominance— General Motors holds this position in the U.S. automobile market.

☐ Developing new products—Xerox pioneered a new industry using this strategy as did U.S. Surgical with its line of surgical staplers.

☐ Finding a specialized niche of a product-market that can be dominated—Nucor in steel joists and J. L. Clark in specialized containers have adopted this strategy.

☐ Establishing strong distribution channels—Snap-On Tools, by concentrating on professional mechanics served by independent dealers in a van, dominates the professional market for socket wrenches and other tools.

☐ Obtaining manufacturing or operating cost advantages due to geographical location, process innovation, or other operating improvements.

☐ Developing a strong financial position for growth—Delta Air Lines' very low debt compared to other carriers illustrates this advantage in the troubled airline industry.

☐ Building a powerful consumer franchise with highly advertised brands. Chesebrough-Pond's has done this with its Health-Tex, Bass, and Ragu brands.

These are but a few of the many ways that firms establish strong positions in product-markets. As is obvious from the examples, differential advantage is gained by deciding what customer needs and wants to serve and by developing appropriate plans for meeting the needs of target customers.

Composition of the business plan

Each unit's strategy must be developed in line with the resources that top management assigns to the unit. Within the unit, priorities are often assigned according to customer category, geographical area, product line, and other units for planning. An illustration of resource allocation for an industrial equipment business unit of a diversified company is shown in Exhibit 2–9. Since this example is from an actual business unit strategic plan, details (e.g., names of products and states) have been removed to avoid disclosure. The guidelines are used by the unit's

Exhibit 2–9
An illustration of resource allocation
within a business unit

	Percent
Geographic	
1. Top eight states	70
2. Second seven states	20
3. Remaining United States,	
Canada, and other export	10
Product	
1. Top five products	80
2. Second four products	20
Dealer/customer	
1. Top 200 dealers	70
2. Next 200 dealers	20
3. Remaining dealers	10

management in product planning, manufacturing, sales force deployment, advertising, and other business unit functional planning.

A look at the composition of a strategic plan for a business unit will be useful in showing what is included in a plan. An outline for a business plan is shown in Exhibit 2–10. The key plans section of the strategic plan should be developed to meet the needs and structure of a partic-

Exhibit 2–10
Business planning guide

Corporate mission/objective/capabilities
    Corporate mission definition and description
    Objectives
    Summary of overall corporate position (strengths and limitations)

    Complete the following for each unit of the business and each major product-market within the unit.

Situation analysis
    Product-market analysis
    Industry/distribution analysis
    Analysis of key competitors
    Analysis of our strengths/limitations
    Summary of strategic opportunities and threats in the product-market
    Key assumptions underlying our strategic plan
    Major contingencies to be considered in the strategic plan

Exhibit 2–10 *(concluded)*

Target market(s) description
  The target market decision is the choice of what people or organizations in a product-market toward which a firm will aim its marketing program strategy.

  Describe each major customer/prospect group toward which a specific marketing strategy will be directed.

  Indicate priority for each target market.

Strategic plan for business unit
  Objectives
  Strategies for achieving objectives
  Key plans
    Business development
    Marketing strategy
    Operations
    Finance
    Human resources
    Other

Financial analysis and summary

Contingency plans

---

ular organization. Since our concern in the remaining chapters of the book is with the development of the marketing plan, let's look at marketing's role in building the business unit plan.

Marketing's role in business planning

Marketing's participation in business planning is illustrated in Exhibit 2–11, which is based upon the experience of the General Electric Co. While sales and marketing managers' roles in strategic planning vary from company to company, Exhibit 2–10 indicates the wide range of participation that is possible. Our examination of business planning in this chapter suggests various planning areas where the skills and experience of marketing professionals are needed.

Top management's decisions about areas of business involvement, priorities for resource allocation, and business strategies may affect the management team in two ways. First, management's decision about the future of a particular unit sets the stage for how it will be managed (e.g., for cash, growth). This may create opportunities and, in some instances, threats for the people assigned to a business unit. Second, traditional

Exhibit 2–11
Illustrative role of marketing management in business unit planning

Planning activity	Marketing's role
Mission determination	Key participant with the strategic planner and SBU manager.
Environmental assessment (economic, political, customer, regulatory trends)	Primary contributor and a major beneficiary of the results.
Competitive assessment (actual and potential competitors)	Primary contributor working with the strategic planner.
Situation assessment (industry assessment and company position to·identify strengths and weaknesses)	Major contributor working with the strategic planner.
Objectives and goals	Key participant with other functional managers, including responsibility for measuring several performance indicators.
Strategies	Responsible for marketing strategy and for coordination of plans with other functional strategies.
Key plans	
1. Product/market development	Leadership role.
2. Distribution	Primary responsibility.
3. Business development*	Key supporting role with strategic planning and manufacturing responsible for implementation.
4. Quality	Leading responsibility for quality.
5. Technology	Varies according to the importance of technology to the product or service.
6. Human resources	Responsible for functional area.
7. Manufacturing/facilities	Typically, very limited involvement.

*Decisions to expand, improve, or contract the business.

Source: Based on a speech given by Stephen G. Harrell, General Electric Company, at the American Marketing Association Educator's meeting in Chicago, August 5, 1980.

organizational structures may be inadequate for managing restructured business units.

Once management decides about the future of the firm's business areas, different challenges are created. Some call for growth strategies, while others require managing cash flow and even sometimes deciding to exit from an area. Such differences in business strategies create needs for people with different kinds of experience, technical skills, and preferences. For example, a successful new venture management team may not be effective in managing a mature business unit. While some executives are effective across a wide range of strategic situations, many are not. Consider, for example, the approach taken at General Electric:

> . . . strategic objectives for the company's wide-ranging products are defined as "grow," "defend," and "harvest," depending upon the product life cycle. Now its general managers are being classified by personal style or orientation as "growers," "caretakers," and—tongue-in-cheek—as "undertakers" to match managerial type with the product's status.[9]

Perhaps each of us should be giving some thought as to what kinds of business situations we want to be part of. Top management must offer proper incentive packages to attract and hold competent executives in all areas of the business. While matching people to jobs is not a recent innovation, the increasing trend toward different treatment of business units expands the importance of the task.

CONCLUDING NOTE

We have examined the major steps in developing business plans that were shown in Exhibit 2–1. Business planning begins with the corporate situation assessment and is followed by consideration of the adequacy of corporate mission and objectives, determination of business composition, analysis of business units, setting objectives and selecting strategies for business units, fitting these strategies into plans, and then implementing and managing the strategic plans. The importance of planning has been demonstrated in various ways.

The planning process (Exhibit 2–1) generally corresponds to the approaches used in business firms and other goal-directed organizations. It demonstrates marketing's rapidly expanding role in business planning, and it provides essential guidelines to sales and marketing planners. In Chapter 3 we shall begin our discussion of marketing planning, starting with market analysis followed by target market strategy in Chapter 4. In moving through the book, consideration of the role of marketing in business planning will continue as we work toward our primary objective— the preparation and management of marketing plans.

Beginning with this chapter, each chapter will be concluded with a manager's guide or checklist that can be used to compare what you are doing in your company regarding the topics discussed in the chapter. You may decide to modify or expand some of the manager's guides to better fit your needs. The guide for Chapter 2 is shown in Exhibit 2–12.

Exhibit 2–12
Manager's guide for coordinating business and marketing plans

☐ What is the mission and objectives for our company?

☐ How is our company divided into business areas? Should we consider changing how the company is broken into parts?

☐ What is top management's game plan for our business unit?

☐ What are our objectives and strategies for carrying out top management's plans for the business unit?

☐ Are these strategies getting the results we want to achieve?

☐ Is our marketing strategy consistent with the business unit strategy? If not, what changes are needed?

NOTES

1. This illustration is based, in part, upon "Good Wrap: J. L. Clark Thrives on Packaging for Some Popular Consumer Goods," *Barron's,* October 27, 1980, pp. 40–41.

2. John Brimelow, "Toot, Toot Tootsie Roll," *Barron's,* September 17, 1979, p. 9.

3. Ibid., p. 9.

4. Peter F. Drucker, *Management* (New York: Harper & Row, 1974), p. 94.

5. Ibid., p. 100.

6. These are similar to the customer group, function, and technology dimensions recommended by Derek F. Abell and John S. Hammond, *Strategic Market Planning* (Englewood Cliffs, N.J.: Prentice-Hall, 1979), p. 392.

7. "James L. Ferguson: General Food's Super-Marketer," *MBA Executive,* March/April 1980, p. 6.

8. Harper W. Boyd, Jr., and Jean-Claude Larreche, "The Foundations of Marketing Strategy," in *The Annual Review of Marketing,* ed. Gerald Zaltman and Thomas V. Bonoma (Chicago: American Marketing Association, 1978), p. 53.

9. "Wanted: A Manager to Fit Each Strategy," *Business Week,* February 25, 1980, p. 173.

3

Analyzing markets

Tracking the effects of external influences upon product-markets including government, technology, social change, economic conditions, and nature is essential to identifying opportunities and threats for a particular company. Consider, for example, the impact upon a retail chain such as Limited Stores, Inc., of shifts in the size of the different age groups in the population. In the late 1970s management described the firm's target market as providing medium-priced fashion apparel tailored to the tastes and lifestyles of women 16 to 35 years of age.[1] Census projections of age-group shifts from 1980 to 1990 are: (1) the young adult (20–34) segment will grow by only 3 percent, and (2) the teenage (13–19) segment will actually decline by 17 percent.[2] Limited is aimed at a no-growth segment of the population. In contrast, the middle-aged segment (35–54) will grow by nearly 30 percent! This information raises some interesting strategic issues. Assuming management wants the firm to grow, should Limited try to gain greater penetration into the 16–35 segment, or should they attempt to appeal to the people who were in this segment in the 1970s, thus shifting their target market to the rapid growth 35–54 segment? Further penetration of a static market will be difficult. Following the original target age group through its life cycle will require altering the product offering and various other elements of corporate and marketing strategy.

By 1982 management's strategy for responding to the changes in the marketplace became clear. Limited's CEO announced that the chain had targeted the 20–40 age segment and was adjusting the marketing approach and lines to appeal to this group. To move the company into a

43

new segment, Limited acquired Lane Bryant, a retail chain specializing in women's special size apparel. This niche also falls into the high growth 35–54 age segment. Market analysis played a critical role in guiding the repositioning of Limited, Inc., in the marketplace.

In order for a market to exist people must have needs and wants and products or services to satisfy their needs. For example, reference to the senior citizen market must include a matching of certain needs of this group to a product or service category which can satisfy the needs. By using the designation *product-market,* both of these requirements are satisfied. Defining and analyzing product-markets underlie most, if not all, of the planning decisions that are made in a company or business unit. Corporate and marketing planners carry out several key activities concerning the firm's product-markets including:

☐ Defining product-markets.

☐ Learning about the needs and characteristics of the people/organizations within each product-market.

☐ Estimating the size of the product-market and forecasting how it will change in the future.

☐ Analyzing industry and competitive structure in the product-market to spot opportunities and avoid threats.

We begin this chapter with a discussion of how to define product-markets. Approaches to definition are described, and their strengths and limitations are evaluated. Finally, a step-by-step guide to product-market analysis is presented and its use illustrated.

DEFINING PRODUCT-MARKETS

How markets are defined has an important influence upon various planning decisions. These key questions must be answered by corporate and marketing planners:

☐ What products should be assigned to a particular business unit?

☐ How should the markets be defined for the SBU so that planning will be facilitated?

☐ What definition will be most useful in guiding market target and other marketing strategy decisions?

☐ What roles should the product and the consumer play in establishing product-market boundaries?

The definition of product-markets is the starting point in answering these and other market-related questions

We must be alert to the different decision-making needs of executives in defining and analyzing product-markets. Consider, for example, the dessert foods SBU manager at General Foods versus the Jell-O brand manager. The former is concerned with strategy from a total business unit perspective whereas the latter is occupied with marketing strategy and tactical issues for a single brand. Information needs vary substantially between these management levels and thus are important in establishing product-market definitions.

What is a product-market?

Intuitively, the idea of a product-market is easy to grasp, although, as we shall see shortly, there are some differences in the ways that analysts operationally define the term. Markets are groups of people that have the *ability* and *willingness* to buy *something* for end-use purposes.[3] Ability and willingness to buy represent demand for a product or service. People with needs and wants buy product or service benefits. Thus, a product-market is a matching of people with needs leading to demand and certain product benefits that satisfy those needs. Unless product benefits are available, only people with needs exist, not markets. Likewise, people must have demand for what product(s) can do in order for there to be product benefits of value. A product-market then is a matching of product benefits to market needs leading to demand. Thus, markets should be defined based on needs substitutability between product and brands and on differences in the ways in which people want to satisfy needs. We can define a product-market as the set of products judged to be substitutes, within those usage situations in which similar patterns of benefits are sought, and the customers for whom such usages are relevant.[4]

To illustrate the importance of understanding customer needs and the alternative ways (products and services) these needs can be met, let's consider the competitive challenge faced by Keuffel & Esser Co. For decades K&E was the leading manufacturer of slide rules and drafting and surveying equipment and supplies. While management's eye was focused on the market for slide rules and other specific products in the mid-1960s, new technology moved rapidly into the arena dominated for so long by K&E. In the 1970s hand-held calculators and small computers virtually wiped out the market for slide rules; laser technology was having a major impact upon the alignment and directional device market; and computers were taking over many drafting functions. Management finally recognized its new competitive threats, but it was almost too late. These actions were taken by Thomas R. Hye, K&E's new president:

> K&E had been marketing some 12,000 products of its own and others through a fat catalog that was the bible of the field. Hye cut out more than

one third of the items. He began distributing other makers' calculators and small computers. He restructured manufacturing, and he bought 79 percent of Laser Systems and Electronics, Inc., to get into electronics; as a result, K&E now has "Vectron"—a device that does surveying with a built-in microprocessor.[5]

Both customer needs and ways of meeting needs change. By understanding how a firm's specific products are positioned within more general product-markets, changes can be monitored and evaluated to determine whether alternate strategies and product offerings are needed. This requires that the definition of a product-market contains all relevant product categories competing for the same needs. Care should be taken to avoid establishing narrow boundaries that exclude products that are potential competitors for the same end-user needs.

Some differences in terms

While the general idea of a product-market is widely accepted, there are some differences as to how broad or narrow its definition should be. These problems can be resolved by recognizing that: (1) terms such as *generic, product,* and *brand* may convey different meanings to managers, and (2) there are different product-market levels.

The term *generic product-market* may designate a broad category of products that can satisfy a general yet similar need, such as home entertainment. Stereos, radios, TVs, and various other products fall into this category. Alternatively, the term *generic* may be used to designate all available brands of a specific product category, such as aspirin. There are also differences in the identification of brands of products. Some managers use the term *product-market* to indicate those brands that are competing for a very specific set of needs. Thus, Godiva luxury chocolates compete in a different product-market from those in which Whitman (and other less expensive chocolates) competes. This product-market definition assumes that there is one product-market level made up of brands that directly compete with each other.

If one is willing to recognize that there are different product-market levels, most of the definitional differences can be resolved. Using this basis of defining product-markets, the following levels can be established.

Generic product-market. This level includes all products or services that can satisfy a particular need, such as housing, pain relief, or temperature measurement. Since people with the same need may not choose to satisfy the need in the same manner, generic product-markets will often be heterogeneous, thus comprised of different end-user groups. This level can be designated as a class of product types that satisfy a set of generic needs.

Specific product-market. This level represents all brands of one particular product category, such as aspirin. Since all brands in a specific product category may not compete with each other, this level often contains user groups with dissimilar needs (e.g., people who want luxury apartments and those who desire economy apartments).

Brand product-market. The brands that compete form a brand product-market. In some instances, the brands may come from more than one specific product-market, such as single-family houses and condominiums.

Considerations in forming product-markets

At least three factors may affect the formation of product-markets:

1. The number of distinct uses or applications for a specific product.
2. The number of usage situations encountered by each user.
3. The number of alternatives in the users' consideration set.[6]

Product uses relate to the functions provided by the product. For example, steel can be used in many ways. A surgical skin stapler performs the single function of stapling skin together after surgery. The usage situation refers to the various types of situations in which the product may be used, such as photography for the family, a social occasion, or business situation. Finally, a buyer typically considers only a limited set of product (brand) alternatives when making a purchase decision.

When there are many uses or applications, many usage situations by each user, and many alternatives to be considered, the resulting product-market can become quite complex. At the other end of the spectrum (so few), the task of product-market definition is more straightforward. To gain a better perspective toward the task, we need to examine some of the considerations involved in forming product-market boundaries.

One key question is deciding where to start. Do we start with an SBU, attempting to decompose it into specific product-markets, or should we try to build a market structure using the three-factor classification scheme? Should we start by defining a generic product-market and then determine the specific product-market categories that are competitive with each other? It may be appropriate to give consideration to all of these viewpoints depending upon the purpose of the product-market analysis.

While we should not allow existing market or industry classification schemes to determine product-market boundaries, existing schemes should be considered. Many approaches are based upon industry guidelines and thus may not sufficiently consider types of needs and alternatives to meeting the needs. Since industry groups, government agencies, and other organizations generate a great deal of information about products and markets, it is important to attempt to utilize this information.

Another consideration is the purpose of the analysis. If management is deciding whether or not to exit from a SBU, primary emphasis may be upon financial performance and competitive position; detailed analysis of the product-market may not be necessary. Alternatively, when trying to find an attractive market niche, the depth of analysis will be much greater than in the former case.

Our objective is to provide guidelines for establishing product-market boundaries that will serve various purposes. Products and markets can be combined in various ways. It is important to form product-market boundaries in a manner that will be of value to the enterprise, allowing management to capitalize upon existing and potential opportunities and to help avoid possible threats.

ANALYZING PRODUCT-MARKETS

A complete solution to determining product-market structure should establish boundaries for product-markets, their size and composition, and the brand and/or product categories competing for the needs and wants of specific end-user groups.

Suppose management is interested in expanding the mix of products and that the present line of products meets a generic need for household cleaning functions, such as laundry and dishes. A logical expansion would be to move into a closely related generic product-market, thus gaining possible advantages through common distribution channels, advertising, sales force, and research and development. The Maytag Co. fits this situation with their line of washers, dryers, and dishwashers. In 1980 Maytag decided to add a line of products for household use in heating foods. An offer was made to acquire the Hardwich Stove Co., a maker of gas and electric ranges and microwave ovens.

Establishing product-market structure for use in evaluating possible opportunities in the food heating generic product-market can be done as shown in Exhibit 3–1. By establishing the product-market boundaries management can examine the various specific product-markets and the different brand product-markets.

The difficulty of defining product-markets will depend in part upon the range of product uses, the uses encountered by each user, and the variety of product and brand offerings. One important question is how

Exhibit 3–1
Breaking out product-market
boundaries

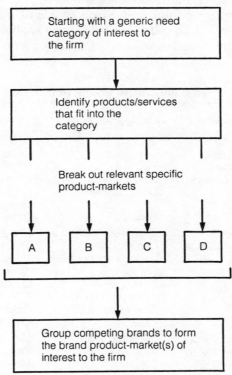

Starting with a generic need
category of interest to
the firm

Identify products/services
that fit into the
category

Break out relevant specific
product-markets

A   B   C   D

Group competing brands to form
the brand product-market(s) of
interest to the firm

broad the generic category should be since, ultimately, all products and
services fit into a generic product-market concerned with meeting human needs. Such a huge category is obviously of no value. At the other
extreme, by defining the relevant product-market as that served by a
specific product, such as microwave ovens, we exclude potentially useful information about how kitchen appliances respond to an overall
generic need.

Some judgment is involved in establishing product-market boundaries. Often, industry practices, management experience, and thoughtful
analysis of product uses will assist in defining a proper generic product-
market. Structuring industrial and other organizational product-markets
is often more straightforward than is the case in consumer product-
markets. In both industrial and consumer markets our focus is upon the
end user of the product or service—the person or organization that con-

50

sumes the product. If a firm makes haystack loaders, the customer or end user is the farmer rather than the distributor or dealer.

In Exhibit 3–2 some illustrations are shown of product-market definition using the structured approach. Since choice of the product-market boundaries is arbitrary, considerable insight and analysis may be needed in a given situation to arrive at an operationally useful definition.

Exhibit 3–2
Some illustrative product-markets

Generic level	Specific level	Brand level*
Agricultural equipment to meet the needs of farmers in the production of crops	Tractors Combines Plows Mowers Corn pickers Hay handlers Others	Allis-Chalmers Deere & Company Hesston Corp. International Harvester New Holland Massey-Ferguson Others
Financial services to meet the needs of individual investors	Life insurance Commodities Savings accounts Bonds Stocks Money market funds Real estate Others	Merrill Lynch Citicorp Travelers Aetna Chase Manhattan E. F. Hutton Golden West Others
Products to meet peoples' needs for eating away from home	Fast-food restaurants Nightclubs Cafeterias Family restaurants Others	McDonalds' Victoria Station Morrisons Cafeterias Local restaurants Others

*These brands do not compete in all of the specific product-markets shown.

Let's examine more closely the eating away from home portion of Exhibit 3–2 to see some of the definitional issues that one encounters when trying to establish product-market boundaries. There are several other ways the generic classification could have been formed, as shown in Exhibit 3–3. In our illustration (Exhibit 3–2), we focused upon the eating away from home use situation and we concentrated upon food rather than food and beverages. Several alternatives for establishing boundaries exist by using one or a combination of the categories shown in Exhibit 3–3. The important consideration is to avoid a definition that is either too narrow or too broad. For most purposes the entire block

Exhibit 3–3
Characteristics of people's generic needs for food and beverages

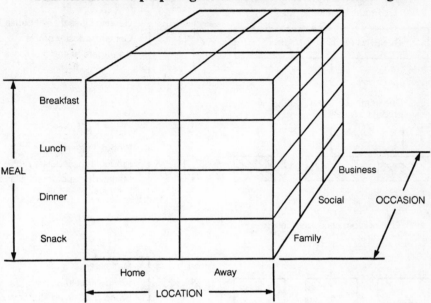

shown in Exhibit 3–3 is too broad, whereas one cell may be too restrictive if, by using it, competing products and brands are excluded.

Industry categories often fall into the specific product-market level and thus too are restrictive for use in generic definition. For example, to define product-market structure starting with candy, frozen foods, or dairy products would eliminate from consideration many competing and complementary products. Because of people's mixed needs and wants, competing products and services do not always fall into well-defined categories.

A guide to product-market analysis is shown in Exhibit 3–4. The information that can be obtained at each level of the analysis is indicated. Five kinds of information are normally obtained from an analysis. First, it is important to know as much as possible about the people/organizations that use the product. These profiles of customers are useful in designing marketing strategy and tactics. Second, management is interested in the present size of each product-market and how fast it is growing. Third, we want to learn about the firms that supply products and services at each level, including both similar types of firms (e.g., manufacturers) and those functioning at different levels in channels of

Exhibit 3–4
Guide to product-market analysis

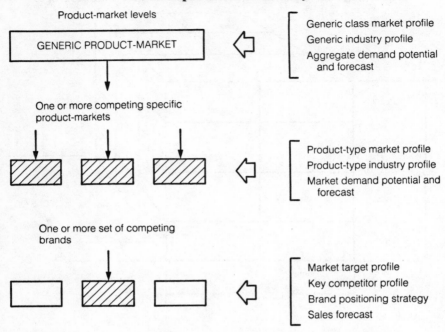

Source: Adapted from David W. Cravens, Gerald E. Hills, and Robert B. Woodruff, *Marketing Decision Making: Concepts and Strategy,* rev. ed. (Homewood, Ill.: Richard D. Irwin, 1980), p. 120.

distribution (e.g., distributors, retailers). Fourth, an assessment of major competitors is essential to guiding marketing strategy decisions. Finally, the analysis should help management decide what target market strategy to adopt and the marketing program positioning strategy to use.

Customer profiles

Since the objective of the enterprise is to meet customers' needs and wants, it is essential to learn as much about customers as possible. Answers to the following four questions will supply essential information about customers:

1. Who are the existing/potential customers?
2. What are the characteristics of the customers?

3. How do the customers decide what to buy?
4. What factors, other than customer characteristics and company marketing efforts, influence buying?

Identifying and describing the people or organizations that comprise the market for a product (questions 1 and 2) is the first step in product-market analysis. Typically, demographic and socioeconomic characteristics are used to identify potential users in generic, specific, and brand product-markets. Various characteristics, such as family size, age, income, geographical location, sex, and occupation, are often useful in identifying customers in consumer markets. A variety of factors can be used to identify end users in industrial markets including type of industry, size, location, and product application.

Many published sources of information are available for use in identifying and describing customers. Some examples include U.S. census data, trade association publications, and studies by advertising media (TV, radio, magazines). The important task is to find those characteristics that will identify potential customers. In some situations, research studies may be necessary to locate and describe potential customers. An interesting example of Kikkoman International's identification and analysis of potential customers for its soy sauce in the United States is given:

> . . . 20 years ago, when Kikkoman was first entering the U.S. market, the company's promotional efforts at home were largely confined to splashing its name on posters and flashing it out in neon lights. The company also provided free soy sauce to the huge cooking classes attended by young Japanese women about to be married (and it still does so).
>
> This low-key approach was a far cry from the mass marketing of food products in the United States. So before setting up an American subsidiary, Kikkoman took a close look at how goods are sold here. "Kikkoman studied, studied, studied marketing, marketing, marketing," says Yokio Ike, senior vice president of Yamaichi International (America) Inc., the New York subsidiary of the Japanese brokerage house.
>
> One of Kikkoman's studies found that Japanese-Americans had become so westernized in their eating habits that they no longer constituted a growing market. Therefore, the study concluded, the marketing target would have to be the American population as a whole.
>
> Another study focused on the competition. The U.S. soy sauce market, then only $1 million a year, was dominated by two brands, Chung King (now owned by R. J. Reynolds Industries Inc.) and LaChoy (now belonging to Beatrice Foods Co.). Both companies had lines of Chinese foods, which also have long employed soy sauce, and neither promoted soy sauce as anything other than a condiment for the food products. Therefore, the relatively few Americans who knew about soy sauce generally thought of it only in terms of Oriental cookery.
>
> So Kikkoman concluded that to gain a foothold—much less expand—in the United States, would entail educating Americans about soy sauce and

emphasizing its versatility. Earlier, in Japan, Kikkoman officials already had noticed that American occupation troops sprinkled soy sauce on everything from hamburgers to pork chops. And the executives' hunches were backed up by the American advertising agency that they had retained when they first decided to try cracking the U.S. market.[7]

By early 1978, Kikkoman soy sauce was the leading brand in the $20 million-a-year U.S. market. The company had been instrumental in expanding the market to its present level.

In learning how customers decide what to buy, we must analyze how buyers move through the sequence of steps leading to a decision to purchase a particular brand. People normally follow a decision process beginning with the recognition of a need, the seeking of information, identification and evaluation of alternatives, and choice of a brand. This process varies by product and situation. Some decisions that are repetitive and for which the buyer has past experience tend to be routine. One key aspect of studying how buyers buy is finding out what criteria people use in making decisions. An example of a bank's efforts to determine the criteria people use to select a financial institution is described:

> A telephone survey using a sample of 1,200 heads of household who currently had some type of savings account was conducted in order to determine the evaluation criteria used in the selection of a financial institution. Once the "ideal" profile was determined, respondents were asked to evaluate their current financial institution against the same criteria so that management could identify those needs that were not being satisfied by existing competition and could develop programs to meet those needs. The study also provided guidance in developing creative strategies by identifying important product and service areas that should be addressed when communicating with various market segments. Additionally, the image of the institution was determined to isolate areas of strength and potential improvement within current operations.

The final step in building customer profiles is to identify any external factors that may influence buying. Typically, these factors cannot be controlled by the buyer or the companies that market the product. In some instances uncontrollables may have a major impact on customers. Consider, for example, the negative influence of 17 percent interest rates on home loans that prevailed during 1981–82. Relevant external factors should be identified and their future impacts estimated. Over the past decade we have experienced various shifts in market opportunities due to environmental factors. Illustrations include the effect of gasoline prices upon the demand for automobiles, oil field services, and various other products. Another is the influence of international tensions upon the market for defense weapons.

Size and growth estimates

As shown earlier in Exhibit 3–4, there are two estimates used in product-market analysis. One is a measure of the potential that exists in a market. This is a measure of the opportunity in a product-market. Since, in most instances, an opportunity is never fully realized by the firms serving the product-market, a second measure is needed. This is a forecast of what is likely to occur for the time period under consideration. Thus, the potential represents an upper limit while the forecast normally is something less than total potential. In addition to size estimates, expected growth rates over the planning period are very useful in planning.

Industry and distribution analyses

The ways in which products and services reach end users should be identified and analyzed. Normally an analysis is conducted from the point of view of a particular firm. For example, a department store chain such as Dayton-Hudson would include other retailers in its industry analyses. Two kinds of information are needed: (1) study of the industry of which the company is a part and (2) analysis of the distribution channels that link together the various organizations serving end-users' needs and wants. Starting first with the industry analysis, the following information is needed:

□ Industry characteristics and trends, such as sales, number of firms, and growth rates.

□ Operating practices of the firms in the industry including product mix, services provided, barriers to entry, and related information.

A knowledge of distribution channels is essential to understanding and serving product-markets. While some producers go direct to their end users, many work through distribution channels. An example of the distribution channels used in the carpet industry is shown in Exhibit 3–5. Suppose that you are the sales manager for a fiber producer and are selling to carpet makers (tufters) through manufacturers' agents. By looking at other distribution approaches that are being used, important patterns and trends in serving end users can be identified. Distribution analysis can also uncover new market opportunities that are not reached via present channels of distribution. Finally by obtaining information from various distribution levels, forecasting of end-user demand is often aided. For example, by contacting retailers and contractors (Exhibit 3–5), a carpet fiber producer can gain important insights as to end-users' needs and wants (e.g., shifts in color preferences).

56

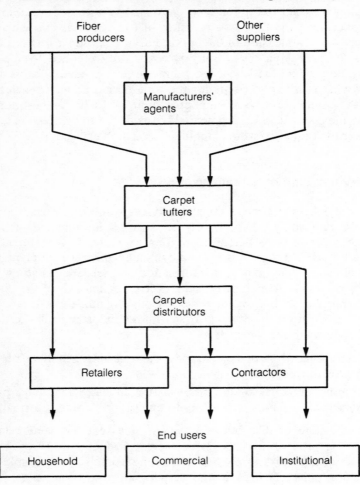

Exhibit 3–5
Illustrative distribution channels in the carpet industry

Key competitors

Normally, a company does not compete with all firms in an industry so it is necessary to find out which are key competitors. Also, if specific customer needs can be satisfied by product categories from other industries, potential competitors should be included in the analysis. Information that is obtained from a key competitor analysis often covers the following areas:

☐ Estimated overall business strength of each key competitor.

☐ Present market share and past trends.

☐ Financial strengths and performance.

☐ Management capabilities (and limitations).

☐ Technical and operating advantages (e.g., patents, low-production costs, new products).

☐ Description and assessment of marketing strategy.

Keeping up with what the competition is doing is one of management's most important responsibilities. The above information should be obtained and studied on a regular basis.

Marketing strategy guidelines

Finally, product-market analyses supply information that is needed in developing marketing strategy. For example, Kikkoman's management determined through consumer studies that, in order to gain a profitable market position for its soy sauce, it would be necessary to educate people about the product and its variety of uses. This information led to the following promotional strategy:

> Kikkoman decided to rely heavily on television advertising. Only in this way, the company believed, could its educational programs succeed. "We had to explain what soy sauce was and how to use it, and what the difference is between our soy sauce and what is made in this country and called soy sauce." Mr. Suzuki says, adding: "What goes under the name soy sauce here would never be called that in Japan."
>
> Therefore, the TV ads emphasized how Kikkoman soy is specially brewed and aged, like beer; the American brands, the ads noted correctly, are made chemically. "Add Quality; Add Kikkoman" was the slogan.
>
> Getting these points across nationwide was Kikkoman's ultimate aim. However, because of the size of the United States, the company decided to start out regionally. Its first target was San Francisco, where it based its U.S. subsidiary.
>
> In a sense, San Francisco was an easy target. Its large Japanese-American population knew about soy sauce and the Kikkoman brand. But this time, of course, the company was trying to tell not only Japanese-Americans but the rest of the population as well that soy sauce *wasn't* strictly Japanese and that Kikkoman was the premium product. (The latter claim was buttressed by a decision to price Kikkoman a few cents higher than competing brands.)
>
> While it was all a new idea for Americans, it was equally new for Kikkoman. The company, after all, was used to consumers who took its product—and its preeminence—for granted. But the Americans caught on, and so did the subsidiary. By 1959, it was ready to tackle Los

Angeles. Over the next 10 years, Kikkoman expanded very gradually on a region-by-region basis. In all cases the company used food brokers on the ground that maintaining its own sales force would cost too much; and it still uses them.[8]

Other guidelines from market analyses include target market alternatives, product requirements, pricing practices, and other inputs to selecting target markets and developing marketing programs.

Strengths and limitations of the approach

The approach to product-market analysis we have examined has some key advantages. First, it incorporates both the product and end user's needs. By using different levels of aggregation (generic, specific, and brand), products and brands are positioned within more aggregate categories thus aiding analysis of product interrelationships, distribution approaches, and various other areas (see Exhibit 3–4 above). Second, the approach offers a consistent guide to needed information regardless of the type of market being analyzed. A method of attack is provided for any situation. Finally, the approach encourages the use of various kinds of information including management judgment and experience, published data, and special research studies.

Using this method the analyst can draw from common types of information regardless of the product-market under study. Typically, market information falls into three categories: customer definition and descriptive profiles, industry and competitor analyses, and forecasts of demand. This information is needed for guiding various marketing decisions.

One of the real strengths of the approach is that it links families of product-markets into a hierarchy that can be examined at increasingly more specific levels. The premise underlying the method is that the generic product-market will be defined so that it contains all competing specific product-market categories. If only management judgment and experience are used to define the generic level, the structured approach could fail to identify a relevant product category, particularly in a complex or changing product-market situation. Thus, if not used with care, the approach may be too rigid in some instances.

The potential user should also be alert to other limitations of the approach. It is highly dependent upon how the generic product-market is defined. If it is too broad, so much information may be generated that analysis and interpretation will be difficult. Too much information can be as dangerous as not having enough. At the other extreme, very narrow product-market boundaries can result in excluding relevant competing brands. The approach, by its very nature, may create a myopic (nearsighted) tendency on the part of management. For example, even if competing product categories are included when generic product-market boundaries are established, the approach tends to focus attention within a specific supply orientation and, by doing so, fails to give adequate attention to customers' needs.

As we discussed earlier, sales and marketing managers should be cautious in interpreting the meaning of various terms used in product-market definition. A product-market does not have the same meaning for all people, so be sure that you understand how the term is being used. As we shall find in the next chapter, this same problem exists with regard to the term *market segment or niche*.

Finally, when discussing market forecasts, market share, and other aspects of market analysis it is important to be sure of the basis being used. The following discussion highlights some of the factors to be considered:

> The definition and computation of a market share figure raises three major operational problems: What measure of sales is to be used? What market are we in? Against which brands is our product competing?
>
> A company's sales may be understood as the sales of groups of product lines, of a specific brand, or even of a given size. Sales may be measured in units or dollars to incorporate size and price discrepancies among rival products. The figures may be based on order, invoices, consumer purchases, or even consumer use. Each level has a different meaning but also corresponds to the different degrees of difficulty encountered in obtaining the relevant information. In some cases, consideration should be given to deals, discounts, and concessions. These may be included in promotional expenses, but if they are offered on a continuing basis over an extended period of time, they should be deducted from the sales figure. Finally, the handling of intracompany transfers of product and services must be decided in advance.[9]

This statement shows the importance of establishing a clear definition of the product-market being analyzed.

CONCLUDING NOTE

Understanding product-markets is essential to making good marketing decisions. The activity of defining and analyzing product-markets is probably more critical to making sound planning decisions than any other activity in the enterprise. The uses of these analyses are many and varied. One of the more important viewpoints of markets is moving beyond a market definition based only on product considerations to incorporate market needs into the picture. Exhibit 3–6 contains a checklist of items that may be helpful to you in determining if you need additional information on your market(s).

In this chapter the important idea of a product-market was introduced and its implications examined. Various considerations in forming product-markets were discussed. We examined an approach to defining and analyzing product-markets. Several of its features and limitations were highlighted in our discussion. Regardless of the approach used for definition and analysis, the information shown in Exhibit 3–4 will be needed in making sales and marketing management decisions. This includes customer profiles, size and growth estimates for the product-market, industry and distribution analyses, analysis of key competitors, and marketing strategy guidelines.

Exhibit 3–6
Managers market analysis checklist

☐ Have we defined the product-markets that we are serving?
☐ Who are our existing/potential customers?
☐ What are the characteristics of our customers?
☐ How do our customers decide what to buy?
☐ What factors influence the purchase decision?
☐ How big is our market(s) and how fast is it growing?
☐ What do we know about the industry and its distribution channels?
☐ What are the strengths/limitations of our competitors?
☐ Does the above information suggest any changes in our sales and marketing programs?

NOTES

1. See The Limited Stores, Inc., *1978 Annual Report.*
2. "Decade's Boom in Prime-Age Consumers Will Offer Vast Opportunities for Business," *The Wall Street Journal,* June 26, 1980, p. 29.
3. The following discussion is based upon suggestions provided by Professor Robert B. Woodruff of the University of Tennessee, Knoxville.
4. George S. Day, Allan D. Shocker, and Rajendra K. Srivastava, "Customer-Oriented Approaches to Identifying Product-Markets," *Journal of Marketing,* 42 (Fall 1979), p. 10, published by the American Marketing Association.
5. "Staving Off Oblivion," *Forbes,* September 4, 1978, p. 94.
6. The three factors are suggested by George S. Day, "Strategic Market Analysis: A Contingency Perspective," working paper, University of Toronto, July 1979.

7. John E. Cooney, "Selling American: Top Soy Sauce Brewer in Japan Shows How to Crack U.S. Market," *The Wall Street Journal*, December 16, 1977, p. 29.
8. Ibid., p. 29.
9. Bernard Catry and Michel Chevalier, "Market Share Strategy and the Product Life Cycle," Reprinted from *Journal of Marketing*, October 1974, p. 29, published by the American Marketing Association.

4

Market targeting

When you analyze the corporate and marketing plans of successful companies, one feature stands out. Each has a target market strategy that has been a major factor in gaining a strong market position for the firm, although the actual strategies used by firms are often quite different. It is interesting that this characteristic cuts across companies in all kinds of businesses including those providing industrial and consumer products. Consider, for example, the target market strategy used by K mart Corp., the second largest nonfood retailer in the United States and one of the dramatic success stories in modern merchandising:

> Since the K mart concept was introduced in 1962, the company's sales have surged from about $500 million to $13 billion—an annual growth rate of 20 percent. Net income has climbed 23 percent a year compounded.
> K marts range in size from 40,000 to 96,000 square feet (84,000 is standard) and are sited in 48 states and in 261 of the country's 275 Standard Metropolitan Statistical Areas.
> Growth has sprung from increasingly diversified merchandising and steady store additions. For example, 180 pharmacy departments were opened in new and existing K marts last year, bringing the total of those departments to 760 as the fiscal year ended on January 31. The company also added 21 optical departments and expanded its automotive service centers. Early this year, a prototype for a "do-it-yourself" department, bringing together home improvement items, was completed.
> Last November, K mart Canada Ltd. acquired the Canadian footwear operations of SCOA Industries Inc., of Columbus, Ohio. Of the 186 SCOA retail units involved, 109 are leased departments in K mart Canada stores, the rest leased departments in other outlets or company-owned units. In the United States earlier this year, K mart acquired Furr's Cafe-

terias Inc., a Texas-based chain with annual revenues of $99 million. It paid $70.4 million in cash. . . .

One important part of the diversification program has been the establishment of shoe departments in all its U.S. units. Operated under license by a Melville Shoe Corp. division, these departments numbered 1,584 by the end of last year. K mart owns a 49 percent equity in virtually all of them. Sales ran up to $572.7 million last year, up 15.5 percent. (The company doesn't include this figure in its reported sales.). . .

In recent years, it has aimed increasingly at middle-income, home-owning, younger-to-middle-age customers—specifically, families between the ages of 25 and 44, with incomes in the $15,000–$35,000 bracket. That group is expected to grow rapidly in the 80s. Indeed, between 1977 and 1990, the number of households occupied by this segment of the middle class is projected to boom 55 percent, to 18.3 million. If that's how it turns out, K mart is ready, willing, and able to help these highly acquisitive Americans spend.

K mart has been betting on the 25-to-44-year group for a long time. Through the 70s, the company kept its focus on households and families, in the belief that once the post-World War II babies got out of college they would become typically middle income, with basically the same values as their parents and with homeownership the centerpiece of the "good life."

Despite the impact of such things as the 1973 oil embargo, the 1974–75 recession, and inflation, K mart has succeeded in establishing a strong reputation among these people for value, price, and merchandise quality.[1]

The target market decision is the choice of which people or organizations a firm will aim its marketing program toward. This decision is one of management's most demanding challenges. Should a firm attempt to serve all customers that are willing and able to buy or selectively go after one or more subgroups of customers? Gaining an understanding of a product-market is essential to making the target market decision. The steps in selecting a target market strategy are shown in Exhibit 4–1. This chapter is organized around these steps, starting with a discussion of the available options for selecting a target market strategy. Then we consider how market niches can be formed and described. Next, the important task of evaluating alternative strategies is examined and illustrated. Finally, several guidelines for choosing a target market strategy are discussed.

Exhibit 4–1
Steps in selecting a target market strategy

1. Decide how to form niches in the product-market.
2. Describe the people/organizations in each niche.
3. Evaluate target market alternatives.
4. Select a target market strategy.

WHAT ARE THE OPTIONS?

The possibilities for selecting the firm's target group of customers range from attempting to appeal to most of the people in the market (a mass market approach) to going after one or more niches (subgroups or segments) within the market. The mass and niche target market strategies are defined as:

☐ *Mass strategy.* All potential customers in a product-market are assumed to be sufficiently similar in their responsiveness to a marketing program.[2] Note that *mass* refers not to absolute size but instead to the fact that the firm is aiming one marketing program at all of the people or organizations rather than going after one or more subgroups within the product-market using a totally different or modified marketing program for each subgroup.

☐ *Niche strategy.* Using this strategy one assumes that people or organizations within a product-market will vary as to their responsiveness to any marketing program. The objective is to identify two or more subgroups within the product-market so that the people or organizations that fall into each niche will respond similarly to a marketing offer. A niche strategy can be implemented by going after a single niche or by designing a separate marketing program to appeal to each niche of interest.

Exhibit 4–2
Illustrative target market strategies

Target market strategy	Consumer products	Industrial products
Mass strategy	Kikkoman International, Inc. (soy sauce) Josten's, Inc. (high school class rings and yearbooks)	Federal Express (small package delivery service) U.S. Surgical Corporation (surgical staplers)
Single niche	Godiva Chocolatier, Inc. (luxury chocolates) Hardee's Food Systems, Inc. (fast foods)	Snap-On Tools (mechanics' hand tools) *Oil & Gas Journal* (magazine)
Multiple niches	Hart Schaffner & Marx (men's clothing) Anheuser-Busch (beer)	Quaker Chemical Company (specialty chemicals) Reliance Electric, Inc. (motors and other industrial equipment)

Since different terms are sometimes used to describe a target market strategy, a clarification is necessary. Market niche and market segment are two of the most popular designations, and we shall use them interchangeably. Several illustrative target market strategies are described in Exhibit 4–2. Let's examine each alternative to find out more about its characteristics.

Mass strategy

The founder of Federal Express Corporation, Frederick W. Smith, created a new service-market in 1971 by offering an overnight pickup and delivery service for small high-value packages. There was no reason to look for a niche. The entire service-market contained only a small, but rapidly growing, group of people and organizations with a specific need for fast delivery of valuable merchandise (e.g., documents, drawings, photographs) at acceptable prices. The weight of items transported is normally under 70 pounds. Federal's fastest-growing service is the Courier Pak, up to five pounds for under $20. The company has experienced explosive growth with sales in 1982 likely to move above $1 billion!

There was a variety of potential users for Federal's new service whose needs had not been met with existing services, such as the U.S. Postal Service. During the last decade, several firms entered this service-market including Emery Air Freight Corporation, the U.S. Postal Service's Priority Mail, and the airlines. Federal, Emery, and other major firms were using mass market strategies. As the service-market gains maturity and special needs develop for subgroups within the market, niche strategies are likely to occur. For example, the U.S. Postal Service is offering a substantially lower-priced service than Federal Express for customers wanting fast (two- to three-day small package delivery) but not requiring overnight service.

The Federal Express illustration highlights several of the conditions that often favor use of a mass target market strategy. New product-markets often contain buyers with similar needs, whereas a mature market is likely to be both larger and more complex. Often there are few competitors in a new product-market and sometimes none. U.S. Surgical Corporation had no direct competition for its line of surgical staplers for nearly a decade. The costs of serving new product-markets are also relevant. Federal decided to get into business on a scale suitable for offering services throughout the United States, which made a lot more sense than starting on a city-by-city basis since there was no way to control the customer's shipping destination. In most new product-markets and even some of those that have reached maturity, it may be difficult to identify one or more niches that can be served by a firm. In these instances, a mass approach may be the most appropriate target market strategy.

Niche strategy

Often companies appeal to only a portion of the people or organizations in a product-market. Management may identify one or more specific niches for the firm to serve. Alternatively, although no specific niche strategy has been formulated, the marketing program selected by the firm will position it in a product-market in such a way that the firm appeals to a particular subgroup within the market. The former situation is obviously preferred. Finding a niche by chance does not provide management the opportunity of evaluating different niches in terms of the revenue and cost implications associated with each. At the other extreme, the task of selecting the very best target market is often impossible due to research and analysis costs and the difficulty of estimating how the market niche will respond to marketing effort. When a niche strategy is employed it should be by design, and the underlying analysis should at least lead to selection of a promising target opportunity.

Let's consider an illustration. Snap-On Tools, a manufacturer of socket wrenches and other mechanic's tools, concentrates its efforts on the professional mechanic, thus avoiding direct competition with Sears and other retailers catering to the mass market for tools. Snap-On Tools dominates the professional niche of the product-market. The type of user (e.g., mechanics) provides the basis for segmenting this market.

Several of the same factors that lead to choice of a mass market strategy may suggest a niche strategy. For example, if the competitive intensity in a product-market is high instead of low, this may indicate that a niche strategy should be considered. Likewise, if buyers' needs and wants in a particular product-market are quite different, a niche strategy may be appropriate. For now, let us sum up the choice of a target market strategy by saying that when the various factors affecting the decision suggest a mass strategy, they often do not favor a niche strategy, and vice versa. More specific guidelines for selecting a target market strategy will be presented later in the chapter.

When following a niche strategy, a company may decide to serve more than one niche. A few niches may be selected, or a firm may move toward more intensive coverage of the product-market. The idea would be to aim a specific marketing effort at each niche that management may choose to serve. Anheuser-Busch, the leading U.S. brewer, with its multiple-brand offering, is going after several major population groups within the total product-market. Some of the groups are quite large, and there are undoubtedly people who buy more than one of the Anheuser-Busch brands. Acknowledging some overlap in population groups, the firm's target market strategy is more of a niche approach than a mass strategy since different brands, prices, distribution, and promotional approaches are involved.

Some companies have selected target market strategies which offer buyers a *variety* of products. On the surface this appears to be a niche strategy, with each product offering a different appeal. Yet these strategies are the result of giving buyers brand alternatives. When a buyer desires a brand change, a switch can be made to another brand or product version offered by the same firm. Sometimes, without conducting consumer research studies, it may be difficult to distinguish whether a firm is using a niche or a variety strategy. Offering customers different flavors or varieties of food products are illustrations of variety strategies.

FINDING AND DESCRIBING NICHES

Using a niche strategy, a company may gain worthwhile advantages over a mass approach. These advantages include higher profitability and strength over competition through better use of the firm's capabilities and resources. By selecting niches (portions) of the product-market, each containing people or organizations that exhibit some degree of similarity, management can gain greater customer responsiveness from effort expended than if the firm directs the same marketing effort to all people or organizations in the product-market. Management must somehow identify possible niches and then, for each niche of interest, determine which marketing program positioning strategy will obtain the most favorable profit contribution net of marketing costs. Since there are many ways to divide a product-market and several marketing program combinations that might be used for each niche, finding the very best (optimal) target market and marketing program strategy is probably impossible. One should first decide whether moving away from a mass strategy is advisable and, if so, what target market alternative looks attractive to management.

An important question is whether or not niching is worth doing. Since there are many ways to form niches, how does the planner make the choice? We need a basis for evaluating the worth of a particular niche scheme. There are five criteria that are useful for this purpose.[3] The first concerns the responsiveness of people to a company's efforts. Suppose that we have divided the people in a product-market into four groups, each a potential segment. If little or no variation exists between the four groups, then the way they respond (e.g., amount, frequency of purchase) to any given marketing program will be the same. If four (or any) segments actually exist in this illustration, a different marketing program strategy will work best for each group.

After meeting the first condition, the other requirements come into play. Second, it must be feasible to identify two or more different customer groups, and third, a firm must be able to aim an appropriate marketing program strategy at each target segment. Fourth, in terms of revenues generated and costs incurred, segmentation must be worth doing. Finally, the segments must exhibit adequate stability over time so that the firm's efforts via segmentation will have enough time to reach desired levels of performance. If we fail to meet the five requirements, use of a niche strategy is questionable. The ultimate criterion, of course, is performance. If a niche scheme leads to improved performance (profitability) in a product-market, then it is worthwhile. The advantage of meeting the requirements for segmentation is that we are more certain that use of the strategy will lead to improved performance.

Forming niches

First, we consider how niches can be formed and described, and then we shall turn to the task of evaluating one or more niches of interest to a particular firm.

In deciding how to form niches, there are two important issues to be considered:

1. Should niches be formed by grouping (aggregating) individuals or organizations using a buildup approach, or should this be done by breaking apart a product market?
2. What factor(s) should be used to identify niches?

With regard to the first issue, either approach can be used although following a disaggregation procedure requires that there be an established product-market. We shall concentrate our discussion upon breaking apart a given product-market. On the second issue, the factors fall into the three categories shown in Exhibit 4–3. Several examples of factors for dividing consumer and industrial or organizational product-markets are shown in Exhibit 4–4. Depending upon the situation, a single factor or a combination may be used to identify niches.

How does one select the factor(s) to use in breaking up a market into niches? Recall our earlier discussion of five niching criteria. We would like to end up with a partitioning that will satisfy the five criteria. Approaches that are used for identifying niches are: (1) management experience used in conjunction with the analysis of available information and (2) research approaches. Let's examine each approach.

Exhibit 4–3
Ways of dividing product-markets

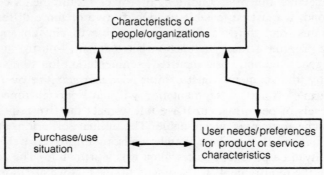

Exhibit 4–4
Illustrative factors for use in dividing product-markets

	Product-market	
Type of factor	*Consumer*	*Industrial/organizational*
Characteristics of people/ organizations	Age, sex, race Income Family size Life-cycle stage Location Lifestyle	Industry Location Size Technology Profitability Management
Puchase/use situation	Size of purchase Brand loyalty Purpose of use Purchasing approach Importance of purchase Choice criteria	Application Importance of purchase Volume Frequency of purchase Purchasing procedure Choice criteria
Users' needs and preferences for product charac- teristics	Product similarity Price preference Brand preferences Desired features Quality Application assistance	Performance requirements Assistance from supplier Brand preferences Desired features Quality Service requirements

Experience and available information

Management's knowledge of customer needs coupled with market analysis can be used to establish niches. Study of industry publications and other published information may be helpful in identifying possible ways to break up a product-market into niches. Consider, for example, the illustrative comparison of users of two beer brands shown in Exhibit 4–5. For each characteristic notice the percentage of people that are Budweiser versus Heineken users. The information was obtained from *Target Group Index,* published annually in 53 volumes. It provides a wide range of consumer characteristics, advertising media usage, and other information analyzed by product and brand usage. The information is generated from a large sample of households throughout the United States.

Exhibit 4–5
Illustrative characteristics of Budweiser and
Heineken beer users

| | Percent | |
Characteristic	Budweiser	Heineken
Age 18–54	54	69
Mid-Atlantic	26	39
Graduated college	20	29
Income $25,000 or more	20	33

Source: *Target Group Index 77,* vol. P-9 (New York: Axiom Market Research Bureau, 1977), pp. 60–61, 68–69.

A note of caution is in order. It is not difficult to find differences among the people or organizations in a product-market. There is a wide array of information available for use in forming population subgroups within product-markets. The key, of course, is whether a niche scheme establishes groups which possess different product and brand responsiveness. The more evidence of meaningful differences, the better support we have that useful niches exist. For example, referring to Exhibit 4–5, the differences in people's responsiveness to Budweiser and Heineken beers may not be captured by age, region, education, and income.

This method has some real advantages in terms of costs and ease of use. And, in particular situations, there may be a strong basis for choosing a niche scheme using this approach. This is more often the case in industrial and organizational markets, where management and salespeople have a good knowledge of user needs. Alternatively, the analysis may be a first step leading to one of the research-based approaches.

Research-based approaches

Two general research approaches have been used during the last decade or so to identify niches. The first involves establishing a measure of niche response, such as product usage rate (e.g., heavy, medium, light), and then finding one or more customer characteristics that distinguish one user group from another. The objective is to find whether or not there are differences in the people (or organizations) that fall into each predetermined niche, such as light and heavy users. The second approach requires consumer research data, which is analyzed using statistical methods to form niches. Let's refer to the former approach as predetermined niche methods and the latter as niche formation methods.

Predetermined niche analysis. In using this approach a way of forming niches is selected, and then the characteristics of users (and nonusers) are analyzed to determine if niche membership can be predicted using one or more characteristics. Factors used to establish the predetermined niches include usage rate, brand preference, frequency of purchase, or any other criteria considered important by management. Predictors of niche membership include demographic and socioeconomic characteristics; attitude, interest, and opinion information; and various other factors (see Exhibit 4-4). The intuitive logic underlying these methods is appealing.

Unfortunately, strong and distinct differences have often not been found through predetermined niche analysis. Rather, the differences in many instances have been weak and inconclusive. Nevertheless, in large, mature product-markets there has been some success in establishing user profiles based on brand preference. We should also consider that many of the more apparent niche formations have probably been achieved without extensive customer research, accomplished instead through the product-market analysis approach discussed earlier.

Niche formation research. Several research methods are being used to establish niches or segments in product-markets. Some of the more promising research techniques use consumer research data to construct perceptual maps for products and brands. These positioning studies represent one of the most active marketing research areas. Such studies are useful in selecting target market strategies and also in deciding how to position a product or brand to serve the chosen target market. Since our objective is not a comprehensive review of the methods for use in forming niches, we shall concentrate our discussion upon positioning research.

While the end result of positioning is simple to understand, its execution is demanding in terms of research skills. The following steps are typically included:

1. Selection of the product-market area to be examined.
2. Determination of the brands that fall into the product market.
3. Collection of consumer perception data for brands (and an ideal brand) obtained from a sample of people.
4. Analysis of data to form one, two, or more composite attribute dimensions, each independent of the other.
5. Preparation of a map (two-dimensional X and Y grid) of attributes on which are positioned consumer perceptions of competing brands.
6. Plotting of consumers with similar ideal preferences to see if subgroups will form.
7. Interpretation of the results as to target market and product positioning strategies.

An illustrative end result of a perceptual mapping application is shown in Exhibit 4–6. The obvious appeal of this research method is clear after studying the illustration. The technical requirements for applying the research approach and for interpreting the results are de-

Exhibit 4–6
An illustrative consumer perception map

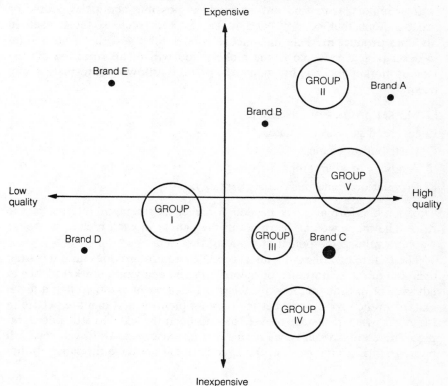

manding. There are many pitfalls along the way that require marketing research skills and experience. Nevertheless, the potential value of a properly designed and executed study can be significant.

Let's assume Exhibit 4-6 correctly represents the positioning of brands A through E. If our brand is C what does the map tell us? Niche V is a logical target market for us and III may represent a secondary target market. To appeal to group V we probably will need to change somewhat group V consumers' price perceptions of brand C. Offering another brand less expensive than C to appeal to group IV is another possible action. Of course, management should study the research results in much greater depth than we have in this brief examination. Our objective is only to show how the results might be used. Perceptual mapping, like many of the research methods for niche identification, is expensive and represents a technical challenge. When used and interpreted properly these methods offer powerful tools for management use in identifying niches.

Describing the niches

It is important to find out as much as possible about the people or organizations that occupy each niche. Factors such as those used in dividing product-markets into niches (see Exhibit 4-4) are also helpful in describing the people in the niches. You will recall from the discussion of market analysis in Chapter 3, that the following information was needed:

☐ Market profiles of customers.
☐ Size and growth estimates.
☐ Distribution channels.
☐ Analysis of key competitors.
☐ Product or brand positioning strategy.

This same information is needed for each segment of interest to the firm. The more we can learn about the people in each niche, the better we can evaluate the potential value of the niche.

The failure of Polaroid's instant movie camera provides an interesting example of the importance of identifying and analyzing market niches in advance of introducing new products. Management assumed that a niche existed in the product-market for moving pictures and that the people in the niche wanted instant movies as had been the case in still photography. There are several flaws in this line of reasoning. Unlike instant still photographs, giving persons their pictures did not have the same on-the-spot effect using an instant movie cassette. This problem, in combination with the product's high cost, low quality (compared to conventional movies), and unnecessary time utility provided to the user, resulted in a small demand for the product.[4] The one advantage, on-the-spot filming and developing, was not enough to convince people to buy the product. Would some consumer research have given management enough information to question the economic feasibility of the project? Considering the large investment that was made in the venture, extensive marketing research studies would appear essential. Several key questions should have been answered including the home movie market attractiveness, threats from videotape systems, and consumers' perceived benefits versus costs of instant movies. Such analysis would likely have shown that there was not a sufficient number of people with special needs or preferences for instant movies. Polaroid's management apparently assumed such a niche existed when, in fact, it did not materialize when the product was introduced.

After an acceptable niche scheme is adopted and the people in each niche are described, evaluation of each niche of interest to the firm should follow. We now turn to this task, which, when complete, will also assist in evaluating the usefulness of a niche formation scheme.

EVALUATING TARGET MARKET ALTERNATIVES

Target market alternatives are shown in Exhibit 4-7. The possibilities range from a mass strategy to one, more than one, or all niches. When serving several niches, the marketing program positioning strategy used for each niche may be totally different from those used in other niches, or each program may overlap to some extent with the programs used in other niches. Thus, a firm may use a unique combination of the product offering, distribution approach, price, advertising, and personal selling to serve each segment, or some of the marketing mix components may be similar (overlapping) between segments. For example, the same airline services are used to appeal to business and pleasure travelers, although different advertising and sales efforts are aimed at each niche.

Once niches are formed each one should be evaluated to accomplish three purposes:

1. Since there is often more than one marketing program that can be used for a given niche, a selection of the best alternative is necessary for each niche candidate.
2. After evaluation is complete, those niches which still look attractive as target market candidates should be ranked as to their attractiveness.

Exhibit 4–7
Alternative target market and positioning strategies

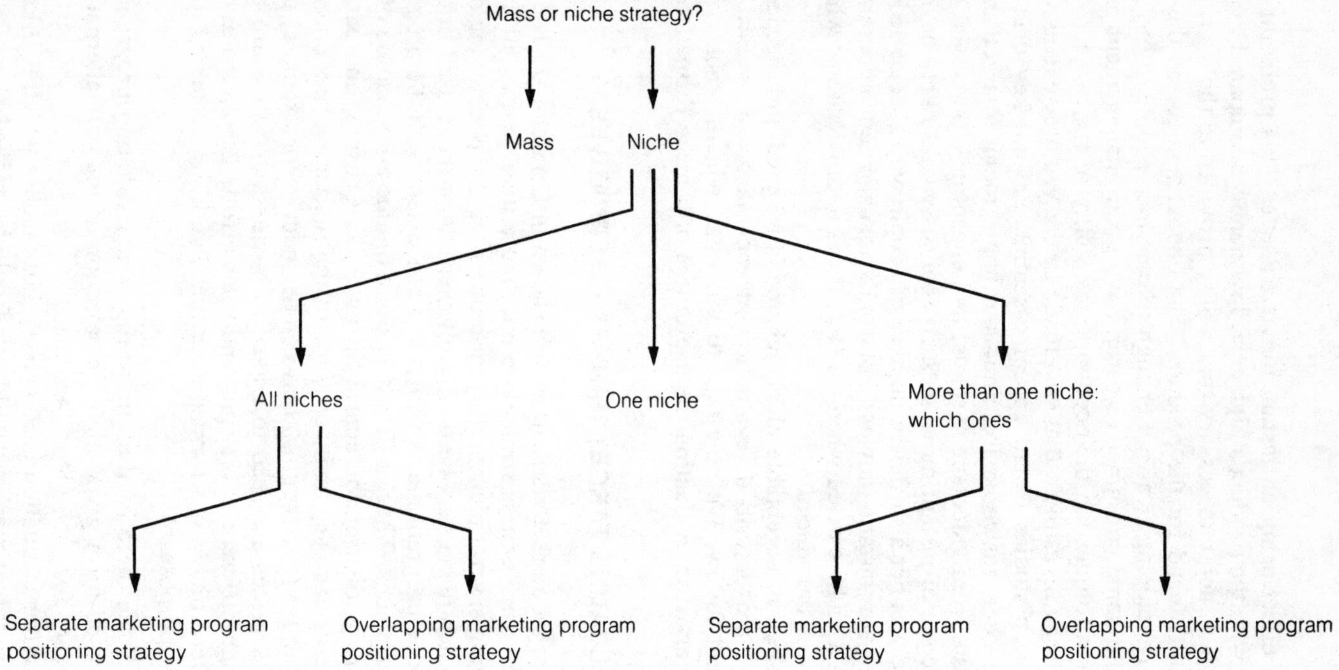

Mass or niche strategy?

- Mass
  - All niches
    - Separate marketing program positioning strategy
    - Overlapping marketing program positioning strategy
- Niche
  - One niche
  - More than one niche: which ones
    - Separate marketing program positioning strategy
    - Overlapping marketing program positioning strategy

3. Finally, management must decide if a niche strategy is better than a mass market approach.

We shall examine evaluation in the following discussion, establishing several guidelines for making the target market decision.

In evaluating a niche it is important to make two kinds of assessments. Recalling our discussion of strategic business unit screening in Chapter 2, an assessment can be made as to niche attractiveness and business strength. This will provide an evaluation relative to the market and competition for each niche. The second assessment consists of revenue, cost, and niche profit contribution projections over management's planning horizon. Since we have already discussed screening, we shall concentrate upon financial analysis of a niche.

The purpose of financial analysis is to estimate sales and costs for each niche of interest. Using this information the niche's estimated profit contribution can be determined. One major consideration is deciding how far into the future to estimate sales and costs. Management is typically interested in a comparison of market target opportunities over some planning horizon which will vary by type of firm and other factors specific to the situation. Since accurate forecasting is difficult if the projections are too far into the future, management may find it most effective to develop detailed projections two to four years ahead. Then by using the niche position evaluation plus the financial forecasts, consideration can be given to both in comparing niche opportunities. In all instances the risks and returns associated with serving a particular niche should be considered.

An illustrative niche analysis is shown in Exhibit 4–8. We have used a

Exhibit 4–8
Illustrative analysis for product-market
niche evaluation

	Niche		
	X	Y	Z
Estimated (in $ millions):			
Sales*	$10	$16	$5
Variable costs*	4	9	3
Contribution margin*	6	7	2
Market share†	60%	30%	10%
Total niche sales	$17	$53	$50
Niche position:			
Business strength	High	Medium	Low
Attractiveness‡	Medium	Low	High

*For a two-year period.
†Percent of total sales in the niche.
‡Based upon a five-year projection.

two-year period for estimating sales, costs, contribution margin, and market share. Depending upon forecasting difficulty, estimates for a longer time period may be feasible. When appropriate, estimates can be expressed as present values of future revenues and costs. Business strength in Exhibit 4–8 refers to present position. Alternatively, it can be expressed as present position and an estimated future position, based upon plans for increasing business strength. Attractiveness is typically evaluated for some future time period. In the illustration we have assumed a five-year projection. A longer period can be used depending upon the estimated life cycle of the product-market of interest.

While there should be more detailed information supporting the analysis shown in Exhibit 4–8, such as assessments of key competitors, let's use it to illustrate how niche opportunities can be ranked according to overall attractiveness. This is admittedly a subjective process since managers will vary in their weighting of estimated financial position, business strength, and niche attractiveness. Using the information in Exhibit 4–8 how would you rank niches X, Y, and Z? Unless management is ready to allocate a major chunk of resources to niche Z to build business strength, it appears to be a candidate for last place position. Yet Z has some attractive characteristics. It has the most favorable market attractiveness of the three, and estimated total niche sales are nearly equal to Y for the next two years. The big problem with Z is business strength. The key question is whether market share can be increased in Z. If not, X looks like a good prospect for top rating, followed next by Y, and Z in third position. Of course, management may decide to go after all three niches.

SELECTING A TARGET MARKET STRATEGY

Daimler-Benz, the German automobile manufacturer is one of the more successful (and envied) companies in the automobile industry. The strong performance of this luxury car manufacturer in an energy-sensitive period has been almost unbelievable. Its sales position is admittedly small in comparison to General Motors. Nevertheless, Daimler-Benz has successfully targeted a high-price, high-quality niche. Interestingly, the firm uses different marketing strategies for different product lines, as for example in heavy trucks where it has a strong worldwide market position. Daimler-Benz is a tough, innovative competitor in a highly competitive industry. Dr. Joachim Zahn, chairman of the firm, describes its passenger car target market strategy:

> "We have a special segment of passenger car production, and we are not interested in leaving it. We know it's a limited sector. We are in the *Spitzengruppe*—at the top level—with a special category of customers." He

explains, with an implied sideswipe BMW and Porsche: "Not the unreliable people: one day this car and another day a Lamborghini or whatever." Among Mercedes' most reliable customers are taxi drivers: some 75 percent of German taxis are Mercedes. In many parts of the world, the Mercedes has become the ultimate status symbol.[5]

How does a firm like Daimler-Benz decide what target market strategy to follow? We turn now to establishing some guidelines for making this decision.

Assuming that niches can be identified, management has the option of selecting one or more niches as a target market or, instead, using a mass strategy. Several factors that often affect this decision are shown in Exhibit 4–9. The zones shown are illustrative since the target market decision of a particular firm will probably not result in all of the factors falling clearly into either the mass or niche strategy zone. We shall examine each of the factors to gain a better understanding of its influence upon the target market decision.

We need to comment briefly upon the factors shown in Exhibit 4–9. First the zones shown are illustrative and are intended to indicate which strategy is more logical considering one factor at a time rather than a composite. Second, it is unlikely that all of the relevant factors in a given situation will point in the same direction (e.g., toward a mass strategy). Third, the relative importance of each factor will often vary by company situation. Finally, there are clearly exceptions to the target market strategy directions indicated in Exhibit 4–9. For example, a company may have achieved a high market share using a niche strategy, as is the case with Crest toothpaste. Our purpose is not to suggest that large firms should use mass strategies and small ones should use niche strategies. Rather, the objective is to highlight how the value of each factor (e.g., market share) is useful in guiding the target market strategy decision.

Product-market characteristics

The market that a firm decides to serve has a strong influence upon the choice of a target market strategy. When buyers' needs and wants are similar there is no real basis for establishing niches. A product-market made up of a small number of end users also argues in favor of a mass strategy, particularly if dollar purchases per buyer are small. Market complexity is another consideration, overlapping to some extent the other factors. The more complex the market situation as to competing firms, variety of product offering, variation in user needs and wants, and other factors, the more likely that a useful niche scheme can be found. Consider the U.S. Surgical Corporation, a manufacturer of sur-

Exhibit 4-9

Factors affecting the choice of a target market strategy

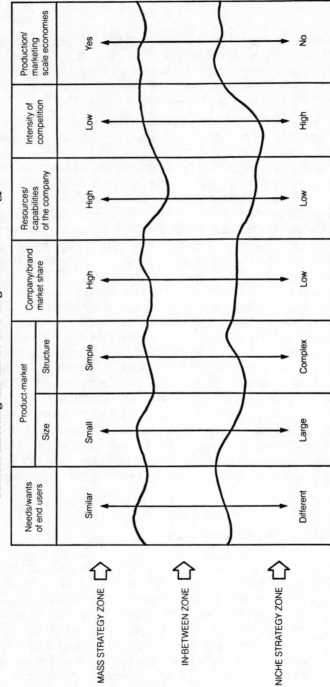

gical staplers. When the firm entered this new product-market, use of a mass target market strategy was a logical decision considering users' needs and size and lack of complexity of the market. There was no apparent way to distinguish between surgeons' needs—the number of users was small in any particular location, and U.S. Surgical had no direct competitors other than the companies supplying needles and thread.

Company characteristics

A firm's market share is an important factor in deciding what target market strategy to use. Low market share firms can often strengthen their position over competition by finding a niche where they have (or can achieve) an advantage over that competition. Strategy for low market share firms is described below:

> . . . A low share company must compete in the segments where its own strengths will be most highly valued and where its large competitors will be most unlikely to compete. Whether that strength is in the type and range of products offered, the method by which the product is produced, the cost and speed of distribution, or the credit and service arrangements is irrelevant. The important thing is that management spend its time identifying and exploiting unique segments rather than making broad assaults on entire industries.[6]

The examples of small market firms we have discussed lend strong support to this position. Also important in choosing a target market strategy are the resources and capabilities of a firm. With limited resources a niche strategy may be essential as is also the case when the firm's capabilities are in short supply.

Other considerations

Referring back to Exhibit 4–9, selection of an appropriate strategy must also take into account the number of competing firms and the capabilities of each. Intense competition often favors a niche strategy, particularly for low share firms. Finally, production and marketing scale economics may influence management in choosing a strategy. For example, the production process may require a large volume to gain cost advantages. The same may be true for marketing and distribution programs. If so, a mass strategy may be necessary in order to reach the sales volume necessary to support large-volume production.

The beer product-market demonstrates many of the characteristics that favor use of a niche strategy, and this product-market also illustrates several of the factors shown in Exhibit 4–9. Consider, for example, Anheuser-Busch, the industry giant. As shown in Exhibit 4–10, the firm is using a multiple-niche strategy, offering a wide range of price, quality, and flavor alternatives each aimed at a group of target customers. Notice that the differences in preferences of beer consumers, the company, and the competitive situation in this mature and highly competitive product-market strongly indicate a niche strategy.

Exhibit 4–10
Anheuser-Busch's target market niches

Brand	Illustrative target customers
Budweiser	Heavy beer using blue-collar males in the 20–34 age range desiring a premium-priced beer
Michelob	Socially conscious drinker, older, desiring a special taste, high-priced quality beer
Michelob Light	Calorie-conscious drinkers that desire an expensive, high-quality beer
Natural Light	Heavy beer using drinkers that are both taste conscious and calorie conscious and want a beer with popular appeal
Busch	A popular-priced beer for people interested in a special taste appeal
Classic Dark	People desiring the special taste of a dark beer
Wurzburger Hofbrau (import)	White-collar (e.g., professional, managerial) people who want the flavor and status of a European imported beer

CONCLUDING NOTE

The target market decision sets into motion the marketing plan. Choosing the right target market is a most important decision affecting the enterprise. This decision is central to properly positioning a firm in the marketplace. Sometimes a single target cannot be selected for an entire strategic business unit when the SBU contains different product-markets. Moreover, locating the firm's best differential advantage may first require detailed niche analysis. Target market decisions connect corporate and marketing planning. These decisions establish key guidelines for planning, and the target market decision provides the focus for the remaining marketing planning decisions.

When it appears feasible to identify niches in a product-market, management should consider attempting to form niches, evaluate them, and then choose between niche and mass strategies. We have developed several guidelines to assist in niche identification and evaluation. Likewise, important considerations in choosing between mass and niche strategies were discussed. While several promising methods are available for use in niche formation, the task continues to offer management a major challenge. The manager's checklist for use in your company is shown in Exhibit 4–11.

Exhibit 4–11
Manager's checklist for target market strategy

What is your company's target market?

☐ If you are not using a niche strategy, could niching improve your profits?

☐ What are the annual purchases in your target market, and what do you estimate the annual growth rate to be over the next five years?

☐ How much do you know about your target market?

1. How many people/organizations are in it?
2. What are their characteristics and locations?
3. How do they decide what to buy?

☐ Should you consider changing your target market strategy?

☐ Are there target markets you are not now serving that you should go after?

☐ Are there customers in your target market that should be dropped because costs of serving them exceed returns?

NOTES

1. Thomas N. Troxell, Jr., "K mart's Squeeze," *Barron's,* October 27, 1980, pp. 37, 44.

2. David W. Cravens, Gerald E. Hills, and Robert B. Woodruff, *Marketing Decision Making: Concepts and Strategy* (Homewood, Ill.: Richard D. Irwin, 1980), p. 171.

3. Ibid., p. 171.

4. Mitchell C. Lynch, "Instant Movies Falter: Is Polaroid's Chairman Wrong for a Change?" *The Wall Street Journal,* August 9, 1979, pp. 1, 29.

5. Barbara Ellis, "Stupid We Are Not," *Forbes,* September 3, 1979, pp. 65–66.

6. R. G. Hammermesh, M. J. Anderson, Jr., and J. E. Harris, "Strategies for Low Market Share Businesses," *Harvard Business Review,* May–June 1978, p. 98.

5
Marketing objectives and positioning

Selecting a target market strategy is only one side of the marketing equation. The remaining half is choosing the right marketing program for meeting the needs of customers in the target market and achieving the firm's marketing objectives. In this and the following four chapters we shall examine how to develop a marketing program positioning strategy. We begin in this chapter with a look at how product, distribution, price, and promotion strategies must be blended together to form an integrated marketing program.

The intense competition in the $1.5 billion fragrance (perfume, toilet water, and cologne) market illustrates the importance of selecting the right marketing program strategy. In this industry, the product and the image built via advertising are key elements in product-market positioning. The stakes are high! Only a handful of the many fragrances introduced each year are really successful. Revlon's Charlie line is one of the big winners as described below:

> But having a good fragrance is only part of the battle. The way the product is marketed is vitally important, industry executives say. As a result, when one fragrance makes it big with a successful approach, other companies are quick to try something similar.
>
> When Revlon Inc.'s Charlie was introduced in 1973, for example, the industry at first scoffed at the idea of a woman's fragrance with a masculine name. But Charlie was heavily promoted by Revlon as a scent for liberated, freewheeling women. "Charlie was for an outgoing person," says Paul P. Woolard, president of Revlon's domestic division. He describes the fragrance as "sensuous but not too far from innocent."
>
> Charlie caught on immediately with American women. Sales reached $10 million the first year, putting the product solidly in the black. Other

companies soon responded with similar appeals. Faberge Inc. brought out Babe. Coty Inc. introduced Smitty, and Max Factor came out with Call Me Maxi.

None managed to catch up to Charlie, which Revlon boasts has become the world's best-selling fragrance. Call Me Maxi, for one, floundered as a fragrance (although cosmetics under the same name did well), and soon Samuel Kalish, who had been lured from Revlon to be president of Max Factor, was out of a job. Max Factor spent $10 million in promoting Call Me Maxi. About $10 million worth was sold, but a lot was eventually returned. Buyers said it simply had an unsatisfactory scent.[1]

In this chapter we turn first to showing how marketing program strategy is linked to strategic planning for the enterprise. Next, we shall consider the important task of setting marketing objectives. This is followed by a discussion of key guidelines for building the marketing program. Finally, strategic position analysis and establishing the role of marketing program components are considered. This chapter provides an essential foundation for shaping the role and strategy of each program component, which will be covered in Chapters 6, 7, 8, and 9.

INTEGRATING CORPORATE AND MARKETING STRATEGIES

Both the corporate planner and the marketing planner must understand how corporate and marketing strategies are tied together. Hardee's Food Systems, Inc., the successful regional fast-food chain, demonstrates how these strategies have been coordinated to transform the firm into an aggressive marketing organization. Hardee's strategy is described in Exhibit 5–1. The illustration highlights several important actions that underly corporate and marketing planning:

☐ Corporate strategic analysis resulted in reshaping priorities for business units, including dismantling some previous diversification efforts.

☐ Management evaluated market opportunities which caused the firm to move out of the Northeast and instead concentrate in the Southeast.

☐ With its new growth objectives based on young adults, promotion to children has been stopped and program positioning strategy redesigned to appeal to the young adult target market.

☐ The product mix has been altered to include roast beef sandwiches and the highly successful biscuit breakfast offering. Stores have also been redesigned to strengthen their appeal to young adults.

At the center of Hardee's strategy is its marketing program positioning strategy, which has differentiated the firm against its much larger

Exhibit 5–1
Hardee's aggressive marketing drive pushes its results onto the fast track

After sitting on the back burner of the fast-food hamburger business for years, Hardee's Food Systems, Inc., is finally cooking.

Only a few years ago, the restaurant chain concentrated on small, noncompetitive markets in the South with limited potential for growth. Now it is going after McDonald's, Burger King, and Wendy's. It has added stores in big cities and new sandwiches to its menu. Sales and earnings are showing the result.

Hardee's recently reported that its earnings for the quarter ended April 30 rose 23 percent to a record $2.9 million. Revenue climbed 21 percent to $100.9 million. And analysts estimate that sales growth, adjusted for inflation, has outpaced that of Hardee's main competitors for the past year and a half.

"Hardee's has finally gotten it together," says an official at Burger King, a subsidiary of Pillsbury Co.

Demographic statistics

The man behind the transformation of Hardee's, the nation's fourth-largest fast-food hamburger chain, is chairman Jack A. Laughery, who joined the company eight years ago when it merged with a midwestern fast-food chain he headed. Mr. Laughery is known for his professionalism and hard work.

He has assembled a talented team of professional managers to run the company. Echoing their boss, they will rattle off demographic statistics with ease when explaining, for example, why Hardee's recently decided to sell off stores in the Northeast.

Mr. Laughery is also a hard-working executive. He recently had to hire an assistant just to divert his phone calls to other managers. He did find time enough last year, though, to spend a week cooking burgers and fries at a Hardee's in Iowa.

When Mr. Laughery arrived at Hardee's the company was suffering from the results of a diversification program that took the company into areas it knew nothing about, such as food processing.

One such move was the purchase of a shrimp processor that had bought a lot of shellfish just before prices collapsed. The company "got caught with shrimp bought at $3.85 a pound when prices were $2.20 a pound," recalls Leonard Rawls, former Hardee's president and currently a franchisee. Another mistake was the purchase of Honey Fried Chicken Corp., parent of the Yogi Bear Honey Fried Chicken chain, which sold chicken buckets called Boo-Boo baskets. "What the hell is a bear doing selling chicken?" Mr. Rawls now asks.

One of Mr. Laughery's first moves was to dismantle the diversification process. He also abandoned the chain's practice of almost exclusively entering small markets. Though safe from competition, the small-town market limits volume. "When we went into Oklahoma City two years ago," says Richard Sherman, senior vice president, administration, "we didn't go into all the small towns. We went right into Oklahoma City."

Exhibit 5–1 *(concluded)*

For demographic reasons, Hardee's also decided to get out of the children's market.

To appeal to more adults, Hardee's redesigned its stores into more sedate structures and added roast beef sandwiches to its menu. It also stopped promoting burgers with cartoon characters Speedy McGreedy and Gilbert Giddyup. The new ads feature a race-car driver.

The company's latest success is its biscuit breakfast, a trio of biscuit sandwiches promoted in ads showing steaming biscuits fresh out of the oven. At some stores, biscuits account for as much as 22 percent of sales. Made from scratch each morning, the biscuits are seen by consumers as high in quality, says Daniel Somers, vice president, finance and strategic planning. And, unlike eggs and pancakes, they're easily taken out. "You can buy bags of biscuits and bring them hot to the office," he says.

Sign of success

As one sure sign of success, the big three are imitating Hardee's. Burger King, McDonald's Corp., and Wendy's International Inc. are each experimenting with a biscuit breakfast. Although some think biscuits will sell only in the South, Hardee's says stepped-up advertising in northern markets is countering regional bias. Burger King, which a few months ago scoffed at biscuits as a regional product, currently believes, "let's not prejudge the appeal of the product," says a spokesman.

Hardee's turnaround also is due to financing from Imasco Ltd., the Montreal-based tobacco and food concern. Imasco has poured $30 million into Hardee's securities and owns about 44.3 percent of the company's shares. Although Imasco is interested in acquisition, it says Hardee's isn't on the menu.

Despite the changes, Hardee's remains concentrated in the Southeast and isn't about to rival the national dominance of McDonald's or Burger King anytime soon. Hardee's hopes rivals think that too. "As long as they consider us regional, they won't consider us competition," says Mr. Somers. Still, McDonald's systemwide sales of $5.3 billion dwarf Hardee's systemwide sales of $750 million. And average unit store sales at Hardee's are about half the $1 million of McDonald's.

Source: Janet Guyon, *The Wall Street Journal*, May 29, 1980, p. 18. Reprinted by permission. © Dow Jones & Co., Inc. 1980. All rights reserved.

competitors. The Hardee's example illustrates the various steps necessary in integrating corporate and marketing strategies. Notice how each of the steps shown in Exhibit 5–2 was accomplished by Hardee's management. Beginning with a candid assessment of company business operations, strategic guidelines were established, thus providing an umbrella for business unit and marketing strategies. Next, a marketing strategy was shaped beginning with the young adult target market, objectives, and a corresponding positioning strategy. Let's turn now to the

Exhibit 5–2
Integrating corporate and marketing strategies

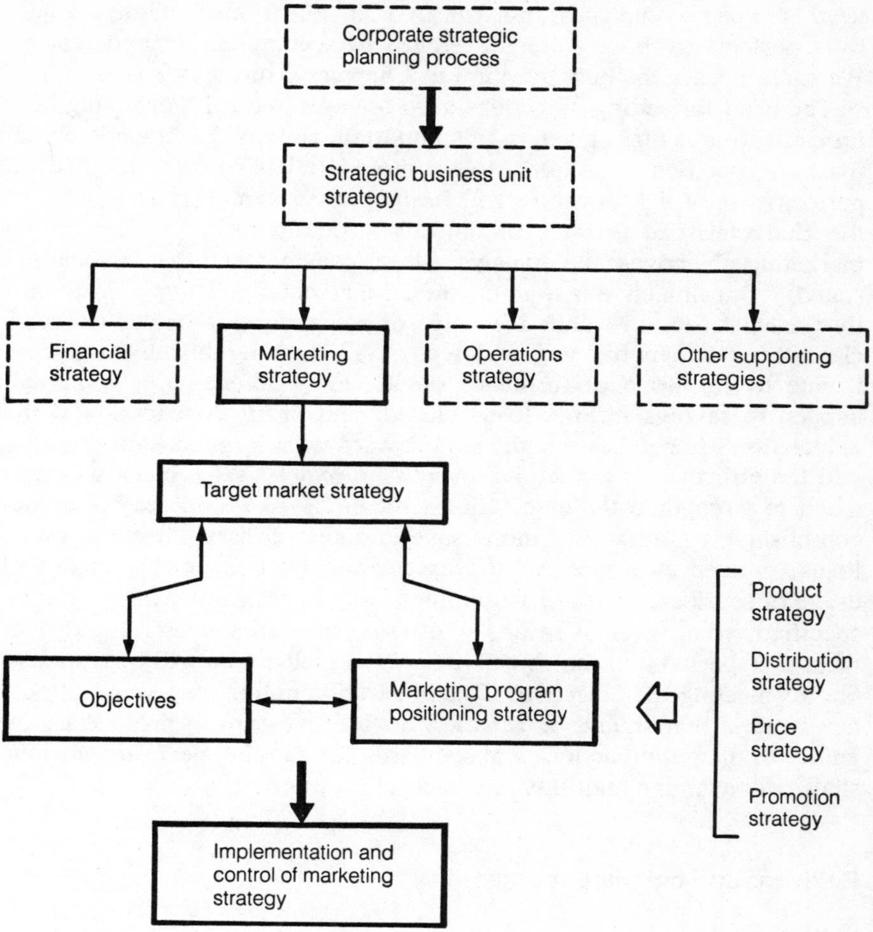

task of setting objectives and developing a marketing program position-ing strategy, both of which must be matched to the target market strategy selected by management.

SETTING MARKETING OBJECTIVES

Let's be sure we are on the same track regarding terminology. We are making no distinction between a *goal* and an *objective*. Either identifies something to be achieved by an organization or individual during a specific time period. Note that the purpose of an objective is to indicate *what* is to be accomplished, not *how* to do it. The *how* of attaining objectives pertains to those actions designed to accomplish desired results. We shall discuss the how question in Chapters 6 through 9.

The need for setting objectives is so obvious that it is surprising how little attention is often given to this important activity. Even when objectives are specified, they often do not provide a basis for tracking actual performance. An illustration will be helpful to demonstrate several of the characteristics that useful objectives should have. As one of its marketing objectives, the management of a savings and loan association stated, "Our objective is to strengthen the association's image as a family financial center." While the value of achieving this objective seems clear, the statement has several defects. Will reaching this objective contribute to corporate performance objectives? For example, what will happen to savings inflow, loans closed, and profit contribution if the association's image is strengthened? Toward what target customer group will the effort to strengthen its image be directed? What exactly does it mean to strengthen the association's image? Will this objective be accomplished by attracting more savers, more dollars of savings and loans, greater awareness of the association by consumers, increased usage of services, or what? Assuming a way of measuring image can be specified, what level of results will be considered successful and over what time period will the objective apply? Finally, who will be responsible for meeting the objective? This illustration highlights several important criteria that should be satisfied if objectives are to provide useful guides to marketing actions and standards for gauging performance. We shall now examine and illustrate each of these criteria.

Relevant and consistent objectives

The marketing function contributes to bottom-line corporate and business unit performance by generating sales and by consuming resources (e.g., advertising media expenditures). Marketing objectives should, when accomplished, meet the sales results desired by management while keeping resource consumption at levels which yield favorable contributions to profits. In linking the marketing function to corporate and business unit operations it is essential that objectives at various levels in the organization are *relevant* and *consistent*. The former refers to whether accomplishing a particular objective, such as increasing consumer awareness of a brand, will contribute to organizational performance. In other words, will achieving lower level objectives contribute to higher level objectives? The latter characteristic, consistency, is concerned with establishing marketing objectives that are consistent in their interrelationships with higher level objectives and with other objectives at the same level. For example, suppose marketing management wishes to increase sales by weeding out customers with low purchasing potential and instead decides to identify and develop a small number of prospective customers with high purchasing power. Next, suppose that a salesperson sets as one objective, increasing his/her number of accounts 20 percent by the end of 18 months. The salesperson's objective is not consistent with the higher-level objective which is aimed at selectivity rather than expanding the number of customers.

The difficult task is picking objectives that are relevant to overall performance and also consistent at the different organizational levels. An illustration will be helpful in showing the hierarchical nature of objectives. Look at Exhibit 5–3. Suppose that one channel of distribution objective is to increase by 10 percent the number of retail outlets carrying the products offered to market target A in business unit II. If this is an appropriate objective then it should contribute to meeting the sales objectives at the different levels shown in Exhibit 5–3. Yet it is entirely possible that adding more retailers will not contribute as much to sales as would increasing the assistance and support provided to the firm's existing retailers. Also, we must be sure that a particular objective does not work against other objectives. Suppose, for example, that the 10 percent increase in the number of retailers will help to meet the $20 million sales objective for market target A. But the effort needed to find, screen, and assist the new retailers will consume more in resources than will be gained in revenues over a time period considered acceptable by management.

Choosing the right objectives for products, distribution, pricing, advertising, and sales force is a demanding task. Objectives must be relevant to higher level objectives and consistent among each other. Essentially, this amounts to setting objectives at one level that will move toward achieving higher level objectives. Establishing the right interrelationships among objectives requires analysis and coordination between the managers responsible for each organizational unit.

Marketing objectives must also be consistent with the objectives of other functional units, such as finance, operations, and research and development. Suppose one of the marketing manager's distribution objectives is to reduce the percent of stock-outs (product not available to fill an order) to retailers from 15 percent (based on invoiced amounts in dollars) to 5 percent. Operations has set an objective to reduce finished goods inventory for all products by 15 percent at the end of 12 months. The two objectives may be in conflict unless the reductions are made in product categories that will not affect stock-outs. Alternatively, perhaps marketing's stock-out objective is too optimistic and will cost more than

Exhibit 5–3

Illustrative objectives at different organizational levels

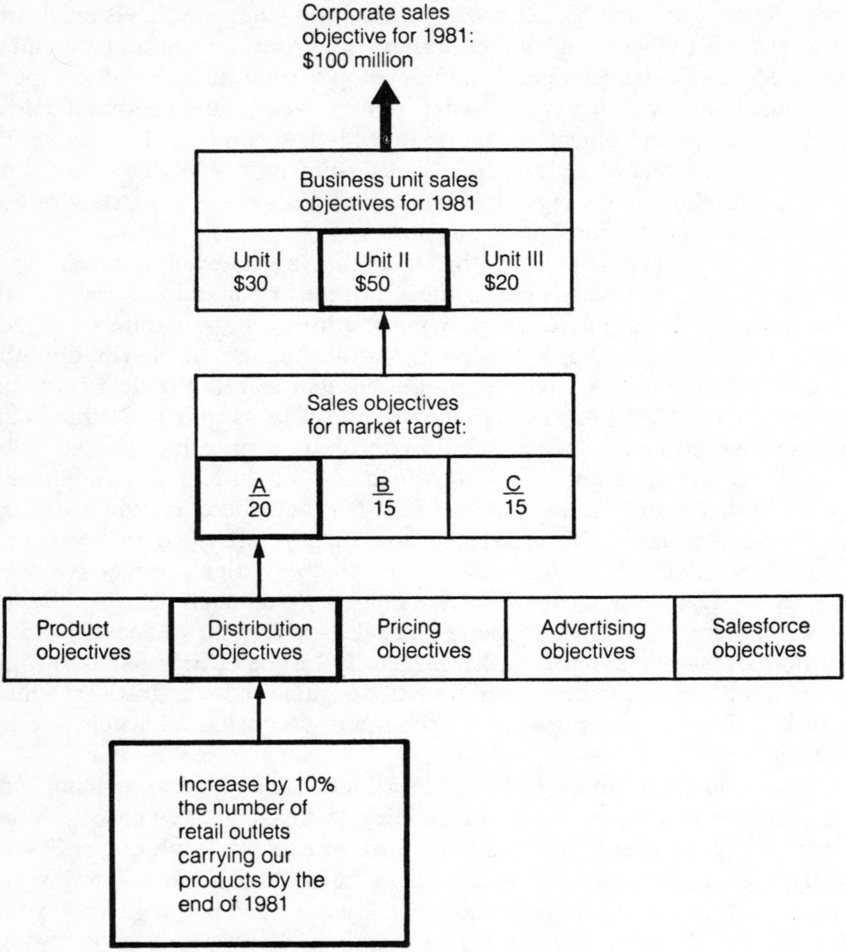

Corporate sales
objective for 1981:
$100 million

Business unit sales objectives for 1981		
Unit I $30	Unit II $50	Unit III $20

Sales objectives for market target:		
$\frac{A}{20}$	$\frac{B}{15}$	$\frac{C}{15}$

Product objectives	Distribution objectives	Pricing objectives	Advertising objectives	Salesforce objectives

Increase by 10% the number of retail outlets carrying our products by the end of 1981

the benefits to be gained by meeting it. The illustration indicates the importance of coordinating objectives between functional areas.

Since each objective must be established taking into account all other related objectives, where should the starting point be for setting objectives? Top management's objectives for the enterprise and each of the business units set key guidelines for the objectives of marketing and other organizational units. After these guidelines are determined, objectives at various management levels can be set. There are two major approaches typically used in establishing objectives. The first is a top-down approach where objectives at each level in the organization are determined based on the objectives at the next higher level. For example, referring again to Exhibit 5–3, the sales objective for business unit II of $50 million would be designated by top management, and then the SBU management would allocate the $50 million among market targets A, B, and C. The amount of give-and-take at each level will depend upon the extent of coordination and participation by the managers involved.

The second approach is more flexible than the first in that it specifically calls for participation and interaction between managers at all levels of the organization. Broad guidelines are indicated by top management, subject to inputs from other management levels. This approach involves far more participation than the first, and when properly implemented, it provides an effective method for setting objectives. Actually, the two approaches differ primarily according to the extent of flexibility and participation that is present, since in both top management must make explicit its expectations for the enterprise.

Clear guide to accomplishment

An objective is not very useful unless it indicates, when compared to actual results, what is expected to happen and the extent to which the objective has been achieved. To better understand the components of an objective, look at Exhibit 5–4. First, it is useful to indicate the type of objective (e.g., profitability) involved since this will help tie the objective to others also contributing to the same purpose. After establishing the type of objective, we should indicate what is to be accomplished and the desired level of performance as illustrated in Exhibit 5–4. Note that the objective specifies in quantitative terms what is to be done, when it is to be accomplished, and who is responsible for meeting the objective. When setting objectives, attention should also be given to how performance will be measured. This may include regular reports and analyses prepared by the firm and, when appropriate, special research studies. Finally, it is helpful to indicate key actions that, if taken, promise to improve performance over and above the level of performance specified (e.g., increasing houseware sales to more than 30 percent of total sales).

The time frame for an objective may range from a month or quarter up to a few years. Objectives extending beyond three to five years are best characterized as desired events rather than specific results targets. This, of course, will depend upon the planning horizon utilized in a particular firm.

Objectives are not of equal importance, so management should have

Exhibit 5–4
Components of an objective

Type of objective:
  Profitability
Desired level of performance:
  The manager of the health and beauty aids division of XYZ Wholesale
    Products, Inc., is responsible for increasing the percent of houseware
    sales from 25 percent to 30 percent of total sales in dollars by one
    year from now (houseware products have the highest profit margin of
    all products in the product mix).
How performance will be measured:
  Sales reports, salesperson product sales reports, and customer sales
    analyses.
Actions that will improve performance:
  Expand warehouse space.
  Increase awareness of salespersons concerning the need for a higher
    proportion of houseware sales.
  Sales incentive plan.

---

priorities regarding objectives. Since comparison of objectives is some-what like comparing apples, tomatoes, and radios, establishing the relative importance of objectives rests upon management's judgment and experience. Nevertheless, an effort should be made to indicate which objectives are critical to the performance of the enterprise and which can contribute but are not as important as those assigned a critical status. Always facing scarce resources, indicating priorities is one of management's most important responsibilities.

The Conference Board, Inc., surveyed a broad cross section of consumer and industrial products firms to determine the specific items that are covered by objectives and strategies in the marketing plans of the firms. The results of those surveys are shown in Exhibit 5–5. For most of the items covered, consumer and industrial products manufacturers are quite similar. As you might expect some of the major differences are in the areas of advertising and field sales.

Objectives and people

Two aspects of the human side of objectives are important. First, how realistic are the objectives that are established? Management must distinguish between hoped-for results and those that are actually achievable. Objectives should be realistic yet demanding. Managers, in their review of subordinates' objectives, must be alert to whether an objective is un-

Exhibit 5–5
Areas where companies specify marketing objectives and strategies

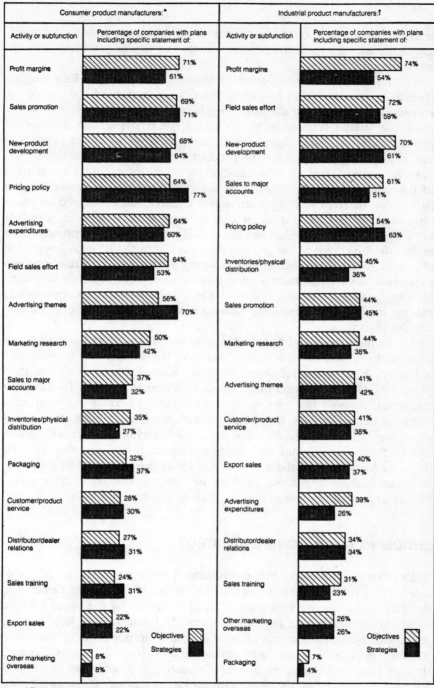

Consumer product manufacturers:*			Industrial product manufacturers:†		
Activity or subfunction	Percentage of companies with plans including specific statement of:		Activity or subfunction	Percentage of companies with plans including specific statement of:	
Profit margins	Objectives 71%	Strategies 61%	Profit margins	Objectives 74%	Strategies 54%
Sales promotion	69%	71%	Field sales effort	72%	59%
New-product development	68%	64%	New-product development	70%	61%
Pricing policy	64%	77%	Sales to major accounts	61%	51%
Advertising expenditures	64%	60%	Pricing policy	54%	63%
Field sales effort	64%	53%	Inventories/physical distribution	45%	36%
Advertising themes	56%	70%	Sales promotion	44%	45%
Marketing research	50%	42%	Marketing research	44%	38%
Sales to major accounts	37%	32%	Advertising themes	41%	42%
Inventories/physical distribution	35%	27%	Customer/product service	41%	38%
Packaging	32%	37%	Export sales	40%	37%
Customer/product service	28%	30%	Advertising expenditures	39%	26%
Distributor/dealer relations	27%	31%	Distributor/dealer relations	34%	34%
Sales training	24%	31%	Sales training	31%	23%
Export sales	22%	22%	Other marketing overseas	26%	26%
Other marketing overseas	8%	8%	Packaging	7%	4%

*Based on information provided by 98 companies.
†Based on information provided by 138 companies.

Source: David S. Hopkins, *The Marketing Plan* (New York: The Conference Board, 1981), pp. 23, 24.

realistic, achievable, or too low. Established at proper levels, objectives can serve as important motivational tools, particularly when linked to incentive programs.

Second, who is to be responsible for meeting objectives? Reaching an objective often depends upon more than one person, and the people involved may not be from the same organizational unit. This is a situation involving shared responsibility. Consider for example, the director of product planning for an agricultural equipment manufacturer. This person has responsibility for new product development, advertising and sales promotion, and all other marketing activities except management of the sales force. Who should be assigned the sales objective for the firm's line of farm loading equipment? Clearly, both the product planning director and sales director can have an impact upon the product sales objective. The alternatives are to assign them a shared objective, to assign the objective to the person they both report to, or to assign the objective to all three individuals. Coping with these interrelationships requires close coordination among those people involved. In our example, designating responsibility to all three individuals is recommended, making explicit the dependence of each director upon the others in meeting the objective.

Allocating responsibility for objectives also requires an understanding as to how much control a person has over the outcome of a particular objective. Even when an objective is not shared, its achievement may depend significantly upon uncontrollable external factors. To illustrate this point, suppose that two salespeople are judged equal in experience, competence, and motivation. The market potential in each territory is about the same. Last year's sales in the two territories were $1 million and $1.6 million. Should their sales objectives for the coming year be the same? Apparently, there are factors other than sales effort influencing sales in these territories, such as the competition. Such uncontrollable factors should be taken into account in setting objectives.

CHOOSING A POSITIONING STRATEGY

Developing product or brand positioning strategies became very popular among marketing strategists in the 1970s. We shall use *position* to designate how our marketing program is perceived by the buyer relative to the programs of our key competitors. In other words, how are we positioned against our competition with respect to our product offer, distribution approach, prices, advertising, and personal selling? Of course the key issue in developing and implementing a positioning strategy is how it is perceived by the people in our target market. If our marketing program is considered identical to one of our competitors, then we would have the same positioning strategy. Rarely if ever is this the case. Distinctions in the minds of consumers always exist between competitive offerings. Typically, the product becomes the focal point of a positioning strategy since distribution, prices, advertising, and personal selling all are working toward positioning the product in the eyes of the buyer. Thus, the designation *product positioning strategy* is often used. Since position can be achieved using a combination of marketing program factors, product positioning is the result of more than just the product.

A positioning strategy then is the design of a marketing program consisting of the following decisions:

1. The product or service offering.
2. How distribution will be accomplished.
3. Choice of a pricing strategy.
4. Selection of a promotional strategy.

These decisions represent a bundle of strategies so the objective is to form an integrated program with each of the above components fulfilling its proper role in helping to position the firm in the product-markets management chooses to serve. The result often distinguishes a company, product, or brand from its competitors due to customers' perceptions of the product or brand. The product, the method of distribution, the price, advertising, and personal selling all help to establish these perceptions, as do the marketing program actions of competitors plus other uncontrollable factors (e.g., government safety ratings of automobiles). When a positioning strategy is properly selected, the needs of the people or organizations that comprise the target market are satisfied. The essence of a good positioning strategy is one that will deliver customer satisfaction to the firm's target market and also meet corporate and marketing objectives.

Programming decisions

There are three key marketing programming decisions: (1) determining the total amount of resources to be used for the marketing program; (2) deciding how to allocate these resources among product, distribution, price, advertising, and personal selling; and (3) choosing what to do with the resources assigned to each program component. Some important characteristics of these decisions should be recognized:

☐ They are interrelated with the first constraining the second and it constraining the third.

☐ The decisions are both quantitative and qualitative in nature in that management must decide how much to spend and what to spend it on.

☐ There are many strategy alternatives that can be selected depending upon the size, deployment, and use of resources.

These characteristics add considerably to the complexity of the programming decision. How does management select an appropriate positioning strategy? Typically, it is a combination of management judgment and experience, trial and error, some experimentation (e.g., test marketing), and sometimes field research. Attempting to find the ideal positioning strategy is impossible in most situations due to the many influences that must be taken into account. Nevertheless, good strategies can be selected by following a sound analysis and evaluation process.

Factors affecting program strategy

Choice of a marketing program positioning strategy depends primarily upon the factors shown in Exhibit 5–6. The starting point is the target market that management has selected. Market opportunity analysis will supply information about the characteristics and the people/organizations in the target market. The programming task is to estimate the responsiveness of the target to alternative positioning strategies, taking into account competition, management's performance criteria (e.g., sales, market share, profit contribution), and available resources. Recall from Chapter 4 that these same factors were considered in making the target market decision. We are concerned with finding the best match between the target market and a positioning strategy.

Let's review what guidelines the target market strategy will provide us in shaping a marketing program. First of all, the characteristics and needs of our target market will give an indication of the kind of marketing program necessary to gain favorable response from the target market. For example, if the people in the target market want a high-quality product, then meeting their needs will require a marketing mix that will be perceived as providing high quality. The target market also indicates who the key competitors are. Similarly, choice of the target market will establish a feasible range for sales and market share. Finally, selection of the target market should have taken into account the firm's resource capabilities for serving the target market. Our objective in building the marketing program is to work within the guidelines established by the target market strategy.

As shown in Exhibit 5–6, the stage of the product-market life cycle also has a significant impact upon the role and importance of the different marketing program components. In moving through the introduc-

Exhibit 5-6
**Factors influencing the choice of a marketing program
positioning strategy**

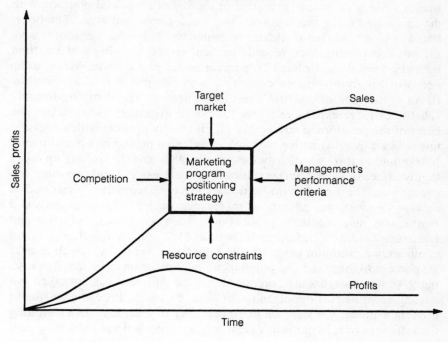

Product-market
life cycle

tory, growth, maturity, and decline stages, the roles of the mix elements often are adjusted to respond to changing conditions. Price, for example, typically declines over the life cycle of a product-market. Advertising is initially used to create new product awareness and to interest potential buyers in the öffering. At later stages advertising may stress the advantages of one brand over other competing brands.

Management's performance criteria for the product-market also have a major influence upon the marketing program positioning strategy. Depending upon priorities, emphasis may be placed upon expanding market share, holding position and generating profits, reducing the firm's commitment, or actually leaving the product-market. Each alternative calls for a quite different marketing program. If marketing management in the SBU is shaping a major growth program while top management favors a hold position, conflict is inevitable. What top management wants to do in an SBU must correspond to the positioning strategy that is selected.

Let's examine the marketing program positioning strategy used by Maker's Mark Distillery, producer of the premium-priced bourbon with the cap sealed using the distinguishing hand-dipped red wax.[2] The bourbon was first marketed in 1958, and management has built an impressive growth and performance record, particularly considering that bourbon industry sales have declined 26 percent in the past decade. Meeting the needs of bourbon drinkers desiring a superior product with a mellow flavor is the crux of the firm's business purpose. The distilling formula substitutes more expensive wheat for rye to give a smoother taste. The heart of the positioning strategy is a high-quality product with a pleasant taste placed in a distinctive package and given a prestigious brand name. Marketing is through distributors to retailers and is backed up by a highly effective sales effort conducted by the president and two other top executives. The firm has no field sales force. Advertising is targeted at newspapers; regional editions of magazines, such as *Time, Playboy,* and *Penthouse;* and specialty publications, such as *Southern Living* and *Louisville Lawyer.* The budget is small at $1.2 million a year. The brand commands a premium price—$8.75 a bottle in Kentucky, which is over 50 percent higher than the popular-priced Jim Beam bourbon. Interestingly, some observers are convinced that management has not taken full advantage of market opportunity for Maker's Mark, instead choosing to grow at a slower yet steady 8 to 10 percent per year, thus demonstrating the influence of management's performance criteria upon marketing program design.

By now you are probably ready to ask How do we know if we have developed a good positioning strategy? What criteria are used to judge the worth of a positioning strategy? Two criteria are appropriate:

1. Does the strategy yield performance results that correspond to management's expectations with regard to sales, market share, profit contribution, growth rates, and other relevant objectives?
2. To what extent does the strategy place the firm in a position that cannot be easily duplicated by competition?

Gauging the effectiveness of a marketing program strategy using specific criteria, such as market share and profitability, is more straightforward than is evaluating competitive advantage. Yet the development of a marketing program strategy that cannot be easily copied is an essential consideration. For example, the strong retail furniture dealer network developed by Ethan Allen, Inc., would require considerable resources, not to mention a long time period, to be duplicated by a competitor. In contrast, Tylenol was able to respond immediately with a price that met Datril's when the latter brand sought to gain market penetration using price.

A marketing program positioning strategy is usually developed to serve a target market with either a single product (microwave ovens) or a line of related products (kitchen appliances). Deciding which approach is best is often situation-specific depending upon such factors as the size of the product-market, characteristics of the product or service, the number of products involved, product interrelationships in the consumers' use situation, and various other considerations. For example, Procter & Gamble, Johnson & Johnson, and Chesebrough-Pond's marketing programs are oriented around particular brands, whereas firms such as General Electric and IBM use product line or combination line and brand approaches.

Exhibit 5–7
Positioning strategy overview

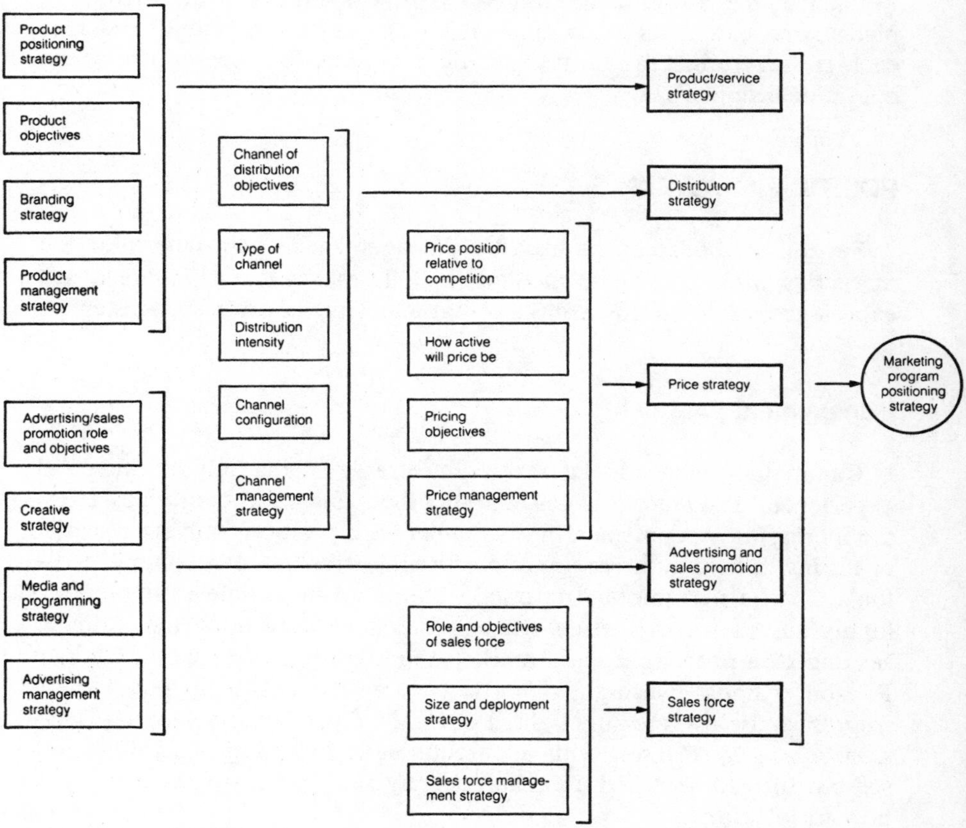

An overview of the various decisions that must be made in developing a positioning strategy is shown in Exhibit 5-7. Since these areas will be examined in depth in Chapters 6-9, our objective here is to show how they fit into the marketing plan and to indicate guidelines about what should be included in the plan. This section of the strategic plan should contain a statement of how (and why) the product mix, line, or brand is to be positioned to serve the target market. This statement should indicate:

- [ ] An overview of product strategy including how the product(s) will be positioned against competition in the product-market.
- [ ] Distribution approach to be used.
- [ ] Pricing strategy.
- [ ] Advertising strategy.
- [ ] Sales force strategy.

Each of the boxes in Exhibit 5-7 can be included in the marketing plan to the extent they are applicable. The statement should describe each strategy, objectives, and specific programs for accomplishing the operational objectives.

POSITION ANALYSIS

Several methods can be used by management to help determine the marketing program. These methods include management judgment and experience, customer research, and market testing of proposed strategies.

Management judgment

Can management select a positioning strategy using only intuition and experience? The answer is yes although the managements of many firms are increasingly supplementing judgment with position analysis research or testing to help guide program positioning strategy development. Revlon's Charlie perfume and cosmetic line is an incredible example of a highly successful marketing strategy based entirely upon the intuitive sensing of a promising mass market opportunity by one man—Charles Revson. Almost overnight, Charlie became the best-selling American fragrance. Below are highlighted several of the key positioning decisions made by Revson with apparently no supporting analysis or research. Instead he relied upon an uncanny sense of customer needs and how to fulfill them:

☐ Revson was convinced that women wanted a lifestyle product, building it around a liberated image.

☐ He sensed that women were ready for a perfume named for a man and so he gave it his name—Charlie.

☐ He had the chemist who developed Charlie formulate it over and over again until Revson was satisfied.

☐ The product was launched in 1973 with a huge promotional program built around the Charlie image.[3]

Revson's insights into consumer behavior were almost unbelievable. He seemed to know exactly what women wanted and how to provide it. In any situation a sense of the market is an essential ingredient in guiding the design of a positioning strategy. Yet by combining this feel for the market with more formal methods of position analysis, the likelihood of achieving success can be greatly enhanced. In today's complex, competitive, and changing market environment, the manager who is willing (and able) to make strategic seat-of-the-pants decisions like those made by Charles Revson represents a clear minority of decision makers. And as we saw earlier, there were several unsuccessful attempts by firms in the fragrance market to duplicate the success achieved by Charlie.

Customer research

The more management knows about customer needs and wants and how those people in the target market will respond to alternative marketing programs, the more likely a good positioning strategy can be developed. Various kinds of research studies can generate useful information for designing positioning strategies.

An illustration will be useful in showing how customer research often yields important information for strategy development. The example involves a mature, heavy apparatus industry in the United States with modest growth:

> Exhibit 5–8 shows shifting market shares of competitors in this industry over nearly 30 years. In particular, it traces the entry of a new competitor in about the 19th year, who was able to expand its market share against the dominant producer while commanding a price premium that started at 3 percent and grew to 8 percent. How did the newcomer do it?
>
> The key was management's recognition that its company's products offered significantly lower fuel consumption under extended high-speed operating conditions (see Exhibit 5–9). Traditional market segmentation

Exhibit 5–8
**Changing market shares of competitors in an industry,
selected years over 28-year period**

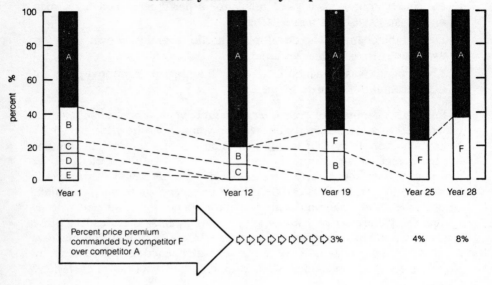

Exhibit 5–9
**Comparison of fuel consumption and speed characteristics,
two competitors' products**

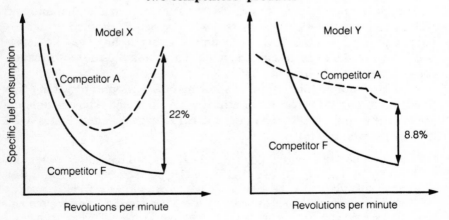

was in terms of the geographical location of major users. Instead, the new company segmented the market across all user areas in terms of types of applications where its products would offer significantly lower cost operation. It then concentrated its marketing efforts on helping users measure the difference.

The dominant competitor could not match this performance without abandoning its basic technical approach and without diluting strengths of its own other portions of the market where it still had an advantage.

An essential aspect of the smaller competitor's strategy was recognizing that it would never "take" the dominant position but that it could selectively capture a sizable portion of the market against the stronger competitor by concentrating on segments where measurable economic performance differences were in its favor.[4]

Note in this illustration the use of management judgment in combination with research and analysis of customer needs in finding a product-market niche and then developing a positioning strategy for serving the target market. Interestingly, company F was able to penetrate a mature market using a premium price strategy, building features into F's product that could not be easily duplicated by competitor A.

Obtaining relevant information about customers and prospects, analyzing it, and then developing strategies based on the information and upon management judgment is the crux of marketing planning.

Test marketing

Market testing is sometimes used for certain kinds of products to generate information about the commercial feasibility of a promising new product and to try out marketing program strategies. The decision to test market depends primarily upon the following factors:

1. How much risk and investment are associated with the venture? When both are low, launching the product without a test market may be appropriate.
2. How much of a difference is there between the manufacturing investment required for the test versus national launch? A large difference would favor a test market.
3. What are the likelihood and speed of competitive response to the product offering?
4. How do the marketing costs and risks vary with the scale of the launch?[5]

While often less than the cost of a national introduction, test marketing is nevertheless expensive. And the competitive risks of revealing one's plans must be weighed against the usefulness of test market information. The major returns from testing are risk reduction through better demand forecasts and the opportunity to fine tune marketing program strategies. Urban and Hauser indicate that "$1 million is typical for packaged goods in a one-city test market, and some firms spend $1.5 million or more."[6] And more than a few strategists are admittedly uneasy about using market test results from only one city to project national performance of a new product.

Test marketing can be used to generate two kinds of information: national forecasts and the effectiveness of alternative marketing program strategies. Both are highly dependent upon the extent to which results from one or a few test markets will provide accurate projections of a national or regional market.

CONCLUDING NOTE

Developing a marketing program positioning strategy requires the blending of product, distribution, price, advertising, and personal selling strategies. The result is a combination strategy that will achieve management's performance objectives while gaining the largest possible differential advantage over competition. Shaping this bundle of strategies is a major challenge to marketing decision makers. Our intent in this chapter has been to sort out the issues involved in marketing programming and to show how programming is linked to strategic planning of the enterprise and the other two key aspects of marketing strategy, target market selection and setting objectives. We have overviewed and illustrated the major approaches to strategic position analysis to show what methods are available to analyze alternative program positioning strategies. A checklist for evaluating your company's marketing program strategy is shown in Exhibit 5–10. Use it to review the marketing program for your target market, brand, product line, or geographical area of responsibility.

In Chapters 6, 7, 8, and 9 we shall examine each marketing program component, considering its role and function in forming a total strategy. As we move through these chapters you should keep in mind several characteristics of the marketing mix variables. They are both supplementary and complementary in nature. Some must work together to be effective, such as the need to communicate the features and availability of a new product. Other elements can, to some extent, serve as substitutes for each other. For example, pricing can be used in a promotional role through the use of promotional pricing (e.g., cents-off coupons). Each mix component may set some constraining guidelines for those decisions that remain. We have placed the mix variables in a sequence that begins with the product or service as the least constrained element.

Exhibit 5–10
Managers checklist for marketing program strategy

☐ Is your target market clearly described?
☐ Do you have objectives for each target market that are:
  Specific?
  Relevant and consistent?
☐ Does each objective provide a clear guide to accomplishment? Has the importance of each objective been established by management?
☐ Are the objectives feasible—is there a reasonable chance of meeting each objective?
☐ Are the decisions concerning products, distribution, price, advertising, and sales force coordinated, or is each decision area managed independently of the others?
☐ Who is responsible for the overall management and coordination of the marketing program?
☐ Can improvements be made in the effectiveness of the marketing program by adjusting the amount and/or the type of marketing activities?
☐ Is regular evaluation made of the effectiveness of the marketing mix? For example, are the size and effort allocations of the sales force correct?

This same sequence corresponds to the time frequency of decisions: product and distribution decisions extend over rather long time horizons compared to much shorter time spans for promotional decisions.

NOTES

1. Stanley H. Slom, "Taking Fragrances to Market Isn't Easy; Making Them Successes Is Even Harder," *The Wall Street Journal*, August 16, 1978, p. 46.
2. This illustration is based upon the article by David P. Garino, "Maker's Mark Goes against the Grain to Make Its Mark," *The Wall Street Journal*, August 1, 1980, pp. 1, 4.
3. The illustration is based upon "A Whiff of Immortality," *Forbes*, September 15, 1975, p. 36.
4. This illustration and the accompanying exhibits are reprinted from William E. Johnson, "Trade-Offs in Pricing Strategy," in *Pricing Practices and Strategies*, ed. Earl L. Bailey (New York: The Conference Board, 1978), pp. 50–51.
5. N. D. Cadbury, "When, Where, and How to Test Market," *Harvard Business Review*, May–June 1975, pp. 97–98.
6. Glen L. Urban and John R. Hauser, *Design and Marketing of New Products* (Englewood Cliffs, N.J.: Prentice-Hall, 1980), p. 419.

6

Product/service planning

Product strategy is the core of planning for the enterprise, and it plays a pivotal role in shaping marketing strategy. Management's decisions about the products to be offered are among the most important of those affecting the future of a company. No other strategic decision has such widespread impact, cutting across every functional area and affecting all levels of an organization. This key strategic role should not come as a surprise since meeting people's needs and wants with goods and services is what business is all about. To illustrate the importance of product strategy, let's examine how Japan's Matsushita has shifted from being a stodgy copycat to become a highly successful product innovator:

> Matsushita's reputation as a copycat was well deserved. Whenever a competing consumer-appliance company brought out a new product, Matsushita would rush to bring out a similar one. By selling its product for less and advertising more, Matsushita often outsold its rivals in the lucrative Japanese market.
>
> Matsushita (pronounced mott-Sooshtah) isn't playing catch-up anymore. Two years ago, after Sony Corp. had beaten Matsushita to the market with such industry breakthroughs as videotape recorders and bright-screen color televisions, Matsushita officials decided that salesmanship alone wasn't enough to stay on top of the supercompetitive world of consumer electronics. The company launched a major drive to upgrade its research and development activities, and now Matsushita ranks second to none in using innovative technology to turn out electronic gadgetry for thousands of products.
>
> The research effort has enhanced Matsushita's position as Japan's top maker of consumer electronics. It has propelled its Panasonic, Quasar, and Technics brands to prominence in United States and other world markets on products ranging from small computers to sesame-seed

grinders. It has secured the leading share of the world's home videocas-sette-recorder business. And it has built Matsushita's standing as one of the world's largest and best-managed corporations. Consider:

Consolidated sales in the fiscal year ended last November 20 increased 10 percent to the current equivalent of $8.73 billion; net income rose 14 percent to $363.1 million. In the third quarter of the current fiscal year, sales increased to a record $2.46 billion; earnings set a record of $106.8 million.[1]

In this chapter we shall consider the major product strategy decisions faced by firms like Matsushita Electric, beginning with a look at the strategic role of the product and the various decisions that form a prod-uct strategy. Product planning and management are discussed and guide-lines developed for evaluating product performance. As we move through the chapter keep in mind that the discussion applies to either products or services.

STRATEGIC ROLE OF PRODUCT DECISIONS

We emphasized in Chapter 1 the danger of taking a product-oriented approach to business. Yet without a product or service we do not have a business. Obviously, product decisions play a key role in any enterprise. Let's take a closer look at how and why product strategy occupies such an important position in a company.

Impact upon other decisions

When a chief executive officer (CEO) is asked about future plans for the enterprise, there are always some comments about products, and often new product plans dominate the discussion. Decisions about what products to offer, how they should be modified, and when to discontinue them form the core of business purpose.

While products are necessary to execute business purposes, they alone cannot guarantee business success. Products must be matched with market needs and then corporate and marketing plans developed for meeting the needs selected by management. Standard Brands' (Planters, Baby Ruth, Fleischmann's) management struggled with a bold new product strategy during the last half of the 1970s that was "designed to lift the company into the front rank of the food industry's best consumer marketers—General Mills, Beatrice, and Pillsbury—by pumping life into its established brands and by moving rapidly via acquisition and new product devleopment into the hot new segments of packaged foods."[2] Hampered by insufficient market research, strong competition, poor execution, and an antiquated marketing structure, the product strategy didn't get the job done. This experience highlights the fact that product strategies alone cannot deliver management's performance goals and must be matched with other key corporate and marketing strategies.

Most products, like people, have limited lives. This, coupled with competitive pressures and the changing needs and wants of buyers, help to explain the high priority given to product planning. Another reason for developing good product planning procedures is to reduce the high failure rate of new products. A 1979 Conference Board, Inc., study indicates that the proportion of new products that fail may be considerably less than has been cited in the past by various authorities. The research project which included surveys of 148 medium- and large-sized American manufacturers that launched major new products during the last five years found a failure rate of one in three rather than the 90 percent often cited.[3] The study also found insufficient and poor market research to be the major cause of new product failures followed by technical problems and errors in timing the introduction. All of this argues loud and clear for sound new product planning. And the stakes are high. In 1978, Standard Brands' Curtiss Division introduced the Reggie candy bar (named for baseball star Reggie Jackson). It made no money in 1979 due to advertising costs of over $30 million.[4] It was expected to be profitable in 1980.

Marketing's role in product planning

Marketing has three major contributions to make in shaping and managing corporate and SBU (strategic business unit) product strategies. First, product-market analysis is needed at all stages of product planning, providing information for matching new product ideas with consumer needs and wants. The knowledge and experience and market research methods of marketing professionals are essential in product strategy development. Product-market analysis is needed in finding and describing unmet needs, in evaluating products as they are developed and introduced, and in evaluating the performance of existing products. Various methods of product evaluation and testing are available in the marketing professional's portfolio of techniques. These tools can be used for conducting new product concept tests, product use tests, and test market planning and analysis.

Marketing's second contribution concerns product specifications. Increasingly, management is looking to marketing for the establishment of characteristics and performance features for new products. Information about customers' needs and wants must be translated into specifications for the product. For example, at General Electric, marketing is responsible for determining these specifications. Research and development needs direction as to where efforts should be concentrated. Consider the high-performance paper towel, Bolt, marketed by American Can since 1976, that "looks and performs like cloth."[5] Industry experts question the need for the performance specifications of the towel, particularly considering its price is double that of popular priced brands. The issue, of course, is whether Bolt offers more quality than consumers want and are willing to pay for.

The third contribution of marketing to product strategy is the selection of target market and program positioning strategies. Marketing management must select the best strategy for targeting and marketing the product. This positioning of product attributes to buyers' needs is often critical to the success of both new and existing products. Since the choice of product specifications and positioning are very much interrelated, marketing strategists must incorporate analysis of product positioning alternatives early into the marketing planning process. As we shall see shortly, positioning decisions may involve a single product or brand, a line of products, or a mix of product lines within a strategic business unit.

Before we examine the various decisions that make up a product strategy, let's consider how product decisions fit into the scheme of things for marketing intermediaries, such as wholesalers, distributors, and retailers. Like manufacturers, marketing intermediaries are also vitally concerned with what new products to include in their mix of products, when to expand into new product areas, and whether to eliminate products. While many of these decisions involve evaluation, selection, and dropping of products that are developed by manufacturers, some intermediaries actually develop their own new products and services. For example, financial institutions are more like intermediaries than producers. Yet many service innovations have been developed, tested, and offered commercially during the past several years, the money market funds being a case in point. Product strategies are important in any kind of business or institution concerned with meeting the needs and wants of people.

WHAT IS A PRODUCT STRATEGY?

Product strategy defined

A *product strategy* consists of:

☐ Deciding how to position a business unit's product offering (specific product, line, or mix) to serve its target market(s).

☐ Setting strategic objectives for the product offering.
☐ Selecting a branding strategy.
☐ Developing and implementing a management strategy for new and existing products.

We need to take a closer look at each part of the definition.

First, let's examine the distinction between product mix, product line, and specific product. Exhibit 6–1 shows that a product mix is deter-

Exhibit 6–1
Composition of the product mix for a strategic business unit

Specific product

Product line	1	2	3	· · ·	n
A	X		X		
B		X	X		X
C	X	X	X		X
D	X				
·					
·					
·					
M	X	X			X

mined by the number of product lines and specific products included in each line. The possibilities range from a single line and single product to various line and specific product combinations. To gain a better understanding of product mix composition, read the account of Maytag's 1980 acquisition of the Hardwick Stove Co. described in Exhibit 6–2. Maytag's product strategy is apparently to expand its offering of home appliances. Hardwick, a small, unknown firm, has limited brand identity. Continuing to operate Hardwick as a separate entity seems questionable in view of Maytag's obvious market power. Of course, depending upon the quality of Hardwick's products, some risk, may be involved in applying to them the Maytag name. This point was apparently carefully

Exhibit 6–2
Staid Maytag puts its money on stoves but may need to invest expertise, too

Something's finally cooking at Maytag Co.

After remaining aloof from the takeover game played by rival appliance makers for years, rich and conservative Maytag is making its first major acquisition—Hardwick Stove Co.

In many ways, the proposed acquisition is puzzling. Maytag is a well-known brand; Hardwick isn't. Maytag sells top-of-the-line laundry equipment and dishwashers. Hardwick's ranges are medium- and low-priced. And what little Maytag has said about its plans indicates that it won't soon put its popular name on Hardwick products.

Competitors have made acquisitions to broaden their product lines to compete with such industry giants as General Electric Co. and Whirlpool Corp. But the reason Maytag is changing its ways is that it has more money than it can spend. Its bankroll includes about $68.5 million in cash and marketable securities. "We are a debt-free company with a growing pot of cash," says John W. Cumming, vice president and controller, "and that's the climate in which we went looking for an acquisition."

A big step

Whatever the reason, it is a big step for staid Maytag, which built its reputation on solid dependability, not jazziness. Its home remains in little Newton, Iowa, where it was founded. Since it began making washers in 1907 (it started as a farm implement company in 1893), Maytag hasn't tried many new ventures. It began making clothes dryers in 1953 and dishwashers in 1966.

Maytag doesn't even like to change advertising campaigns. Many companies switch commercials from year to year. But Maytag's advertisements featuring "Old Lonely"—the Maytag repairman who has nothing to repair—have been the company's mainstay since January 1967.

Maytag has squirreled away money thanks to the premium prices it charges, often 10 percent or more above the competition. With earnings of $45.3 million on sales of $369.1 million last year, Maytag's 12.3 percent return on sales was by far the best in the industry.

The company has spent $60 million in the past five years to expand capacity, boost productivity, and increase product durability. But it can be stingy when it comes to other things. Maytag's annual report usually runs a skimpy 16 pages, eliminating the fluff other companies include.

Maytag plays its finances so close to the vest that it hasn't yet said how much it will pay for Hardwick—or even exactly what it's getting. (Officials at Maytag and Hardwick wouldn't comment on the proposed acquisition, which is subject to the approval of both companies' directors.) Hardwick is a privately held, 100-year-old company in Cleveland, Tenn. It's estimated to have annual sales of $40 million to $50 million.

Hardwick's gas and electric ranges haven't a special niche in the marketplace, as Maytag's products do. Hardwick is said to have so little expertise in microwave technology that its microwave oven was designed

Exhibit 6–2 *(concluded)*

by outsiders. It has hardly made a dent in the rough-and-tumble microwave market. "You never run into them at stores," says the rival executive.

So far, Maytag has said only that Hardwick will operate as a separate
entity, without any changes planned for its products. But analysts agree the
deal makes sense only if Maytag uses its technical know-how to build up
Hardwick's image and at least puts the Maytag name on the microwave
oven. "I'm not sure it's a good move. I remain to be convinced," says
James Magid, an analyst at L. F. Rothschild, Unterberg, Towbin in New
York. "But I have great confidence in their ability."

Retailer hopes

Retailers also are hoping for a Maytag microwave. Sol Polk, who owns
16 appliance stores in the Chicago area and prides himself on carrying a
wide selection, says he doesn't sell Hardwick's table-top microwave model.
But Mr. Polk adds that "I'd take it right away" if it carried the Maytag
name.

A strong brand name on a new product isn't a guarantee of immediate
success, however. Even after 14 years, Maytag's dishwasher isn't as well
known as its laundry equipment, consumer surveys show. Though the
dishwasher has gained a respectable 6 percent market share, that's well
below the 15 percent market share of Maytag's washers and dryers. But
the company's strong dealer network should help it to peddle more
Hardwick stoves than Hardwick does.

These issues mightn't matter much if Maytag can do in the stove business what it does in the laundry business—make a better machine. "The
key so far in laundry has been making things good and simple," Mr. Magid
says. "The real issue is to what degree Maytag will be innovative with
stoves."

evaluated before the acquisition. By 1982 management's plan was clear;
ranges and ovens carried the Maytag name.

A product strategy is deciding how to position each product or combination of products against competition. This involves deciding quality,
price, and features to be offered. The decision establishes key guidelines
for product development and product improvement activities. Referring
to the Maytag illustration in Exhibit 6–2, when management decided to
include the Hardwick line with the Maytag line of washer and dryers,
this decision set some guidelines as to quality, performance, and design
features. It is important to recognize how interrelated product positioning, objectives, branding, and management are in choosing a product

strategy. Also, note how these decisions are interwoven with mission determination, SBU priorities, and target market strategy.

It is important early in the development of product strategy to determine what management expects products to accomplish. For example, if management wants the business to be perceived as the most innovative firm in the product-market, then this objective should be made explicit since it will influence all aspects of product strategy. Product objectives may be used to achieve a variety of purposes for the enterprise or a business unit. Illustrations include market penetration, profit contribution, establishing a reputation for quality, and offering a complete line to distributors. Often, a combination of objectives is used.

Turning now to the next aspect of product strategy, management in a manufacturing firm has several alternatives in choosing a branding strategy. These include:

☐ Using the reputation and support of marketing intermediaries to convey brand reputation (e.g., it's a good brand because Ace Hardware carries it).

☐ Manufacturing products for other firms with their private brands affixed to the products. For example, Whirlpool supplies Sears under the Kenmore label.

☐ Building brand identity by applying the corporate name to the entire mix, a strategy used by Deere and Co., International Harvester, and several other manufacturers.

☐ Establishing brand names for lines of products such as Sears' Kenmore and Craftsman brands.

☐ Using brand names for specific products, such as Chesebrough-Pond's, Vaseline, Ragu, Cutex, and Q-tips brands. Brand names may be used to designate different offerings within a line (e.g., clothing) and for different product categories.[6]

A firm may choose to use more than one of the above branding strategies, such as private branding for others in combination with the firm's own brand.

Finally, the development and implementation of management strategies for new and existing products are essential to guiding product planning and control activities over the life cycle of each product. Included here are new product screening and management procedures, evaluation of the performance of existing products, product modification decisions, and a variety of other decisions. Essential to managing new and existing products is the choice of effective organizational concepts for managing products. One of the greatest dangers is not formalizing product planning activities and not assigning responsibility for planning and control of products. Much of the remainder of the chapter is devoted to developing guidelines for managing products.

Setting priorities

Since all products and product lines are not equally important to the future of a given firm, management should establish priorities as to the importance of each product and/or line. Strategic planning for the enterprise should have made such a determination for each SBU. In instances where multiple products or lines comprise an SBU, strategic priorities should also be indicated for all product categories within the SBU. These priorities are needed to guide product planning activities for the SBU and are useful in showing where to allocate resources for product development and improvement.

Exhibit 6–3 indicates how management of an industrial equipment SBU has positioned each product line (disguised and modified to avoid disclosure) according to business strength (internal) and market (external) factors. The factors that were evaluated to obtain the positioning shown in Exhibit 6–3 included competition, required resources, profit contribution, company strengths, industry potential, and other factors. The positioning represents a composite of these factors. Note the higher resource priorities established for product lines A–E and the strategic guidelines indicated for each product group. While there are various other considerations, Exhibit 6–3 illustrates how management can indicate where resources are to be deployed among various products in the mix. These decisions then guide product planning activities for new and existing products.

Decisions regarding product mix, branding, and positioning establish boundaries to guide new and existing product planning activities. These decisions, along with the priorities management assigns to each product group, line, and specific product, indicate the new product areas of interest to the firm and how resources for product development and improvements will be deployed. First, we shall examine new product planning followed by a discussion of managing existing products.

NEW PRODUCT PLANNING

New products are the center of attention in most companies because of their obvious contribution to the survival and prosperity of the enterprise. Planning for new products is an essential and demanding activity. New products, when matched to customer needs, offer opportunities

Exhibit 6–3
Establishing product line priorities and strategic guides for
an industrial equipment SBU

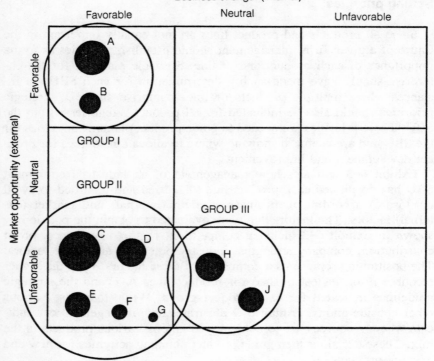

Business strength (internal)

Strategic guides:

Group I: Increase product development/improvement and sales development effort to expand market share.

Group II: Increase profit contribution by reducing costs and selective sales development.

Group III: Reduce assets and reduce costs.

Product Lines A, B, C, D, and E to receive 80 percent of SBU effort.

Note: Diameters of circles indicate relative size of product line based on sales in dollars.

for strengthening position in existing product-markets and a means to move into new product-markets.

Successful new products require a systematic planning program, the major stages of which are shown in Exhibit 6–4. We shall examine each of the new product planning stages to see how they depend upon each other and to demonstrate the importance of a coordinated new product planning program. There are two key considerations related to new product planning:

1. Generating a stream of new product ideas that will satisfy management's requirements for new products.

Exhibit 6–4
New product planning

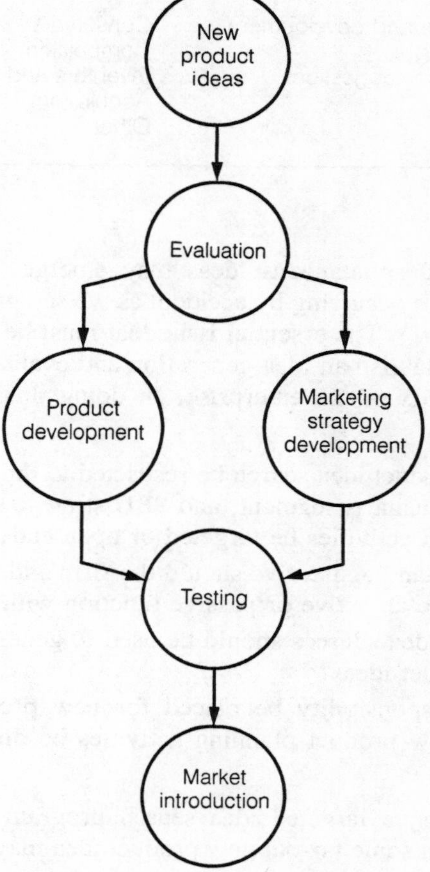

2. Establishing procedures and methods for evaluating new product ideas as they move through the planning stages.

Let's take a closer look at each of these activities.

Finding ideas

Limiting the search for new product ideas to internal research and development activities is far too narrow an approach for most firms. There are many sources of new product ideas as shown in Exhibit 6–5.

Exhibit 6–5
Sources of new product ideas

Internal	*External*
Research and development	Consumers
Marketing	Competition
Employee suggestions	Inventors and patents
Other	Acquisition
	Other

Both solicited and spontaneous ideas may emerge from a variety of sources, sometimes occurring by accident as we saw in the case of Ivory soap (see Chapter 1). The essential issue that must be faced by management is how to establish an idea generation and evaluation program that will meet the needs of the enterprise. In doing this several questions must be answered:

Should new product idea search be restricted to those that correspond to mission, business segment, and SBU strategies—in other words, should search activities be targeted or open ended?

How extensive and aggressive should the firm's idea search activities be? Is it to be an active or passive function within the firm?

What specific idea sources should be used to generate a regular flow of new product ideas?

Where will responsibility be placed for new product idea search? How will new product planning activities be directed and coordinated?

For most firms, a targeted idea search program is recommended. While on occasion some far-out new product idea may change the future of a company, more often an open-ended idea search dissipates resources and misdirects efforts. It is impossible to generalize about the other three questions since they depend upon many situation-specific factors including size and type of firm, the technologies involved, new product needs, resources, management's preferences, and corporate capabilities. The important consideration is that management recognizes these questions and that an idea generation plan is developed that will satisfy the firm's requirements.

There is considerable evidence that many new product ideas originate with customers, particularly for industrial products. In an extensive analysis of the origins of successful new products, one researcher found "strong support for the hypothesis that manufacturers of new products and processes often initiate work in response to explicit customer request for the innovation."[7] Procter & Gamble's use of customer feedback to guide product planning was described in Chapter 1. This and various other applications discussed throughout the book offer several insights into the new product planning stages shown in Exhibit 6–4.

Evaluation

While finding new ideas is important to the survival of a company, evaluating them is even more critical. Assume that a good new product is one that will be a commercial success based upon management's specified criteria for success (e.g., sales, profit contribution, market share). Two kinds of risks are involved. If the risk of rejecting a good product is set too low, then ideas will be developed that will eventually be rejected at some stage in the new product process. The problem, of course, is that by moving too many ideas too far into development and testing, costs become prohibitive. Management must establish a screening and evaluation procedure that will cull out unpromising ideas as soon as possible while keeping the risks of rejecting good ideas at acceptable levels. Since expenditures build up from idea stage to commercialization while the risks of developing a bad new product decline as more and more information is obtained about the product and the market, use of a screening procedure that is not overly tight is indicated. The key is to try to eliminate the least promising ideas before too much is invested in them. The risk occurs at one point in time and can be set by management. The tighter the screening procedure, the higher the risk will be.

Evaluation should occur regularly as an idea moves through the new product planning stages. Rejection may occur at any stage although the objective is to eliminate the poor risks as soon as possible. Various methods and models are useful in evaluating and planning for new products. We shall take a brief look at the array of methods that are available to assist in making new product planning decisions.

A depth discussion of the various tools and methods for product planning is neither feasible nor appropriate here. Several excellent sources are available on the design and marketing of new products.[8] Our objective is to describe the kinds of tools that are available and to show how they fit into the various new product planning stages. Look at Exhibit 6–6 where illustrative methods are placed at the stages where they are used. The information supplied by these and other methods falls into one or more of the following categories: evaluating financial attractiveness, forecasting customer responsiveness, guides to product design, and information for assisting in marketing program development.

Exhibit 6–6
New product planning methods

Product planning stages	Illustrative evaluation and planning methods
Idea generation	Consumer research (e.g., preference mapping), focus group interviews
Screening	Lists of criteria, scoring methods, ranking methods
Comprehensive evaluation	Portfolio analysis, concept tests, Bayesian analysis, financial analysis* (e.g., break even, present value, payback), simulation
Development	Research on positioning, package design, name, advertising, pricing, and other aspects of marketing program design.
Testing	Product use tests, simulated shopping tests, and test marketing (sales and cost analysis, tracking models, and other analytical methods using test market data).
Commercialization	Tracking of market performance, sales and cost analyses

*These techniques are useful for evaluation in subsequent stages.

Organizing for new product planning

How to organize for new product planning has been widely debated for several decades. Various kinds of product management systems have been developed and implemented. All have deficiencies, yet there is common agreement among managers from successful firms that some type of formalized new product planning approach is essential. The objective, of course, is planning and coordination of new product opportunities. The issue is where to place responsibility and how to organize for new products. The prevailing alternatives are:

Executive responsible	*Approach*
Top management	Committee
Marketing	Venture team/task force
R&D	New product/brand manager
New product	New product department

One study of 267 firms found the new product department to be the most popular organizational form, followed by the brand manager with the new product committee in third position.[9] Since there are so many factors at play, it is impossible to generalize about new product organizational structure other than to underscore the need for some formal organization mechanism for new product planning and coordination within the enterprise. Wherever responsibility is placed, there should be close coordination between new product planning, strategic planning, and marketing strategy.

A new product application

An interesting description of the new product planning for Comtrex, the successful new brand entry into the cold remedy market, is provided in Exhibit 6–7. The application illustrates several aspects of new product planning including:

☐ The long time span from concept to market introduction.

☐ The high costs of new product development.

☐ The vital role of consumer research in new product planning.

☐ The interrelated nature of new product planning activities, thus highlighting the importance of close coordination of stages.

This description of new product planning at Bristol-Myers follows closely the planning stages shown in Exhibit 6–4. Many new consumer and industrial products move through all or most of these planning stages.

MANAGING EXISTING PRODUCTS

We turn now to an examination of what is involved in managing existing products. Performing this function requires tracking the performance of the products in the mix as shown in Exhibit 6–8. Management

Exhibit 6–7
Creation of Comtrex: Marketing hit gives Bristol-Myers relief

Anybody who wants a chunk of the $250-million-a-year market for cold remedies must compete with Smith-Kline Corp.'s best-selling Contac—and such well-known rivals as Coricidan, Nyquil, and Dristan.

Ever since the 1960s, Bristol-Myers Co. has tried to compete. First came Durispan, a "long-acting cough tablet," that failed to last long in the test market. Citrisan, a lemon drink served hot for cold sufferers, got a chilly reception, Dayphen never got to test marketing, and Clinicin flopped, too.

But 20 months ago, Bristol-Myers came up with Comtrex. Already a wild success, it has carved out a 10 percent share of the market—largely at Contac's and Dristan's expense—and Bristol-Myers managers think sales may double in two or three years. "Comtrex is a marketing coup," says David Lippman, a securities analyst at Dean Witter Reynolds Inc.

Success demanded a lot more than simply mixing a little of the stuff found in Contac, Coricidan, Nyquil, and Dristan and labeling it Comtrex, though that's just about what Bristol-Myers did. "Comtrex took five years of work, nearly $3 million in research, and 40 percent of my time," says Philip C. Restaino, a Bristol-Myers product manager.

Three prototypes developed

In 1974, Bristol-Myers interviewed 600 consumers to learn what they really wanted in cold remedies—medication easier to swallow, or less soporific, or more effective in dealing with multiple symptoms. Bristol concocted three products to fill the bill: Dayphen, without sleep-inducing antihistamines; Clinicin, an easy-to-swallow lozenge, and Comtrex, to relieve multiple symptoms.

While some Bristol-Myers researchers dreamed up and tested advertising campaigns, others were brainstorming names for the products. For Comtrex, Bristol-Myers came up first with such names as Extran, which they say implies strength; Comtrin, which connotes completeness and aspirin, and finally Comtrex. "It wasn't quite Rx, like a prescription," Mr. Restaino says, "but it implies the state of the art in pharmacology and provides efficacy overtones."

At the same time, package designers took a crack at Comtrex. The stuff now comes in liquid, tablet, and capsule form. (The capsules were introduced last.) For the liquid, Bristol-Myers settled on a molded plastic flask but balked at the cost of making similar flasks for the tablet and the capsule. Instead, Bristol-Myers adopted the same white silo-shaped bottle it used for Bufferin.

Meanwhile, all three new remedies were being used by consumers in household tests. Lacking antihistamine, Dayphen failed to dry the nasal passages of cold sufferers sufficiently. Clinicin was accepted well enough to be sold in test markets—but there it failed to meet test goals, and it was dropped. But Comtrex, test-marketed in Spokane, Washington, and Rockford, Illinois, sold 40 percent above Bristol's projection. Bristol-Myers managers think its box helps; the background printing, a yellow grid, supposedly highlights the long list of cold symptoms for which the labeling

Exhibit 6–7 *(concluded)*

promises relief. The products colors—orange for the liquid, yellow for the tablets, and both for the capsules—also were "warm" and attractive, Bristol-Myers marketers say.

Contac counterattacks

Bristol-Myers' TV commercials directly attacked Bayer Aspirin, Contac, and Dristan for having fewer kinds of cold relief; Contac and Dristan more subtly tried to undercut Comtrex in advertising "because we started taking their business away from them right away," says David Ruckert, division vice president for marketing at Bristol-Myers.

By June 1978, Bristol-Myers was ready to take on the national retail market. Some 400 salespeople made more than 20,000 calls on retail outlets, many of which placed orders; in its first year, sales of Comtrex exceeded the company's projection of $20 million by 25 percent.

Aside from Bristol-Myers' meticulous research and development, credit for Comtrex's success also lies in the nature of the market, says Frank K. Mayers, president of the Bristol-Myers products division and the man who commanded its diversification. Despite the many millions of dollars spent on advertising cold remedies, as late as the early 1970s only 38 percent of cold sufferers took any medication; yet few novel remedies were being introduced. Mr. Restaino, the product manager, quotes O. Henry in accounting for Comtex's success: "Life is made up of sobs, sniffles and smiles, with sniffles predominating."

Source: Gail Bronson, *The Wall Street Journal*, March 10, 1980, p. 37. Reprinted by permission. © Dow Jones & Co., Inc. 1980. All rights reserved.

Exhibit 6–8
Tracking product performance

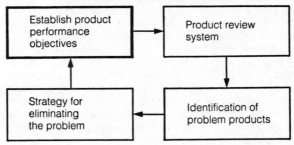

must first establish the criteria and levels of performance for gauging product performance. These may include both financial and nonfinancial factors. Due to the various demand and cost interrelationships among products, establishing how well a particular product is doing requires a good information system and careful analysis by management. The objective of a tracking system is to establish and maintain a product review system that will spot problem products so that management can select a strategy for eliminating the problem. An illustration of tracking product performance and devising a strategy for eliminating a problem in an industrial equipment company is described in Exhibit 6–9.

Exhibit 6–9
One company's battles against losses in market share

A standard product that we sell through distributors started to lose market share. A detailed analysis determined that our prices exceeded those of the competition, and that the benefits to the customer did not warrant the higher price. To correct the situation, we required a complete redesign of the product and a new manufacturing area specifically to mass produce it.

Since the objective of the company was to be the dominant producer in the market, all the corrective steps were taken. Today, we *are* the dominant producer, and we have competitive prices that offer the customer more features than any of our competitors.

In another market area, association statistics again showed we were rapidly losing market share. A more detailed analysis showed that machines based on a different engineering concept than ours were rapidly replacing the type of machine we were building for this market segment.

A plan for corrective action was pulled together. We would have to design a new machine from the ground up, but then the plan was rejected because the cost was high. This market was not considered to be one of major importance to the corporation, and the moneys required for the redesign were needed in other, more important areas.

Our market share continued to slide downward while alternative solutions to the problem were being reviewed. In the meantime, a small manufacturer had entered the field because of technical know-how gained in a different industry. . . . Subsequently it became apparent to him that he had underestimated the cost of entering the market and that this was a drain on the capital he needed to remain dominant in his normal markets. We were able to acquire the rights to his newly engineered product and thus regain our lost market share.

Meanwhile, our competitors continued to improve their machines to match the performance of ours. However, we failed to allocate sufficient engineering and design funds to remain competitive. In time, we started to lose market share, and once again, we had a product in trouble. Analysis showed that we had to improve our product and provide competitive features.

Exhibit 6–9 *(concluded)*

At that point, we had an extreme drain on our engineering groups to provide innovative features and technical steps forward for product lines more important to the well-being of the company. A search was therefore undertaken to locate a foreign manufacturer who did not participate in our market and who had a machine of proven design that would be applicable to our market. A company was found and a licensing agreement made. Initially, foreign machines were imported while our production facilities were being converted to making these machines. Unfortunately, neither the imported machines nor those made at our facilities were able to withstand the operating conditions in our market, and our market share continued to slide.

The remaining alternatives were either to redesign our own machines or to get out of the business. The decision was made to cancel the licensing agreement, and we are now in the process of redesigning our machines to meet the needs of the market.

Marketing services director
An industrial equipment company

Source: David S. Hopkins, *Business Strategies for Problem Products* (New York: The Conference Board, 1977), p. 27.

Strategic options

Once a problem is identified, management has several options for correcting the problem as shown in Exhibit 6–10. Choice of a strategy is primarily influenced by the nature of the problem associated with the product. The most drastic action is to eliminate the product. If a product has outlived its usefulness, it should be dropped.

Product improvement can be handled in several ways. Some firms wait until a problem develops which calls for improving the product. Others schedule improvements each year, every two years, or some other regular interval. Product improvement strategies that anticipate problems and opportunities are, in many instances, more effective than simply responding to problems. And unless there is no competition, product improvement is essential to maintaining and improving market position. Similarly, cost improvement should be a continuing concern of management. Lower costs of producing and distributing products will enable greater profit contributions and/or price reductions.

After the right strategy is selected, it is essential that a specific plan be developed and implemented. Look at the product analysis and planning form used by the Eltra Corporation shown in Exhibit 6–11. It highlights several key aspects of good planning for a problem product. In-

Exhibit 6–10
Strategic options for problem products

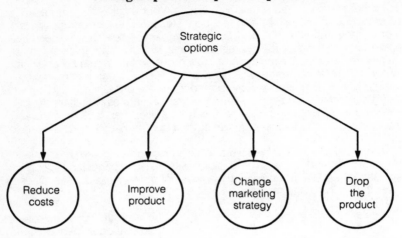

Exhibit 6–11
Product analysis form by the Eltra Corporation

ELTRA
_____DIVISION
LOW PROFIT PRODUCT PROJECT
(000)

Product _____   Market(s) _____

	Actual		Estimated	Plan Year	Forecast		
	19—	19—	19—	19—	19—	19—	19—
Sales							
Gross Profit							
Gross Profit %							

Project schedule

Basic Strategy	Major Steps	Scheduled Completion Date
Prior Increase ☐	_____	_____
Cost Reduction:	_____	_____
Engineering ☐	_____	_____
Manufacturing ☐	_____	_____
Marketing ☐	_____	_____
Volume Increase ☐	_____	_____
	_____	_____

Source: David S. Hopkins, *Business Strategies for Problem Products* (New York: The Conference Board, 1977), p. 24.

cluded are financial analyses and projections, the basic corrective strategy to be used, major activities, and scheduled completion dates.

An interesting application of product planning is described in Exhibit 6–12. Notice how management finally decided that the estimated costs of improving the operating performance of the problem product were so

Exhibit 6–12
How one industrial company decides to eliminate a problem product

Assuming that a product is beginning to show a decline in terms of profitability, we try to determine the causes. It may simply be volume; and if so, this would be reflected by the fact that the product has a variable margin which is good but still inadequate to absorb fixed costs. In such cases, we try to determine why the sales are low and whether something can be done to change the situation.

If the variable margin is bad, we try to see if it cannot be changed by product design, better purchasing, or additional automation to reduce labor costs. In those cases where either the variable margin cannot be improved, or volume cannot be increased to absorb fixed costs, we have no alternative but to abandon the product.

All of these continuing efforts are examined annually when we update our three-year plan. All staff members participate in this effort; and it is not difficult to determine whether a problem product has a solution or whether it should be written off.

A specific example of this is our line of [a component for electric motors]. We began to get information back from the field that our prices were no longer competitive. On the other hand, an examination of costs indicated that if we lowered the price, the line would go from a marginally profitable position to one of significant loss.

We analyzed our manufacturing techniques and compared them with the reasonable knowledge that we had concerning our competition. It became apparent that without an expenditure of approximately $500,000 for new equipment, we would not be able to produce the product for a price that would approach that of our two major competitors.

At the time, we sold about $1 million worth of this product; and we projected that the increased investment in manufacturing would provide a profit of approximately $140,000 before taxes on this volume. We decided that a three-and-one-half-year payout was inadequate and, therefore, phased out the line.

We have benefited from this decision. First, the capital was invested in other product lines, thus increasing their profitability. In addition, by focusing our strengths on fewer products, we were able to increase market penetration on those remaining products so significantly that our total sales today are probably much higher than they would have been had we continued to manufacture the [special component].

President
An electrical equipment company

Source: David H. Hopkins, *Business Strategies for Problem Products* (New York: The Conference Board, 1977), p. 32.

high that forecasted product financial performance would be unsatisfactory. When the decision is made to drop a product, careful planning should be done in advance of the actual drop. Coordination with customers and marketing intermediaries (if involved) is essential in carrying out a product elimination to avoid adverse reaction from customers and other parties involved.

CONCLUDING NOTE

Our look at product/service planning sets the stage for selecting strategies for each of the remaining parts of the marketing program. Product decisions are central to shaping both corporate and marketing strategy and should be made within the guidelines of corporate mission and objectives. Key product decisions include selecting the mix of products to be offered, choice of a branding strategy, and deciding the specifications of each product in the mix. One of management's most important product decisions is establishing priorities for each product to guide product planning.

There are three major product planning decisions that must be made:

1. Should a new product be developed?
2. Should a product be improved (and if so, how)?
3. Should a product be eliminated?

These decisions and the activities necessary to carry them out form the core of product planning in the enterprise. Most successful corporations

Exhibit 6–13
Managers' product planning checklist

☐ Who has responsibility for product/service planning in your organization?

☐ Are product plans coordinated with sales and marketing managers and key executives in other functional areas (e.g., finance, operations)?

☐ Does your company/business unit have an active program for finding new product ideas?

☐ Are your products evaluated as to their performance on a regular basis?

☐ Are improvements needed in your product planning and evaluation activities?

☐ Are sales and marketing plans for new products prepared concurrently with product development?

☐ Do you have any products that should be seriously considered for elimination?

have found that some individual or organizational unit should be assigned responsibility for product planning. Approaches that are used range from a committee to a product planning department. Planning for new products is both exciting and risky but is an essential activity in most firms. New products offer a way to build a strong advantage over competition.

A checklist for reviewing product planning in your organization is shown in Exhibit 6–13. It can be used as a guide to examine your product planning activities.

Product strategy forms the leading edge of a positioning strategy. A product strategy alone is incomplete and must be matched to the right distribution, pricing, and promotion strategies. We shall consider the remaining parts of the positioning mix in the following three chapters.

NOTES

1. Mike Tharp, "Japan's Matsushita, Once a Copycat, Claws Way to Top with Innovative Technology," *The Wall Street Journal,* November 21, 1979, p. 48.
2. "When a New Product Strategy Wasn't Enough," *Business Week,* February 18, 1980, p. 142.
3. *Marketing News,* February 8, 1980, p. 1.
4. "When a New Product Strategy Wasn't Enough," p. 146.
5. Bill Adams, "What Happens If the Product Offers More than Users Need?" *The Wall Street Journal,* September 25, 1980, p. 35.
6. David W. Cravens, Gerald E. Hills, and Robert B. Woodruff, *Marketing Decision Making: Concepts and Strategy,* rev. ed. (Homewood, Ill.: Richard D. Irwin, 1980), pp. 235–36.
7. Eric von Hippel, "Successful Industrial Products from Customer Ideas," *Journal of Marketing,* January 1978, p. 41.
8. See, for example, Glen L. Urban and John R. Hauser, *Design and Marketing of New Products* (Englewood Cliffs, N.J.: Prentice-Hall, 1980).
9. George Benson and Joseph Chasin, *The Structure of New Product Organization* (New York: AMACOM, 1976), p. 21.

7

Distribution planning

Compare the products and markets served by Ethan Allen, Inc. (furniture), Deere and Co. (farm equipment), and Snap-On Tools, Inc. (mechanics' hand tools). There are far more differences than just similarities among these companies. Yet they have one common feature in their marketing strategies. Each has a strong distribution channel which is a major contributing factor to its performance. The Ethan Allen Galleries form a carefully selected network of independent retail dealers that has been instrumental to the success of the manufacturer. The powerful group of over 5,000 U.S. and worldwide farm equipment dealers is envied by all of Deere's competitors. Snap-On Tools' independent dealers in a van are the driving force behind the company's close link with its customers, supplying feedback to guide product improvement, assisting customers in tool selection, and establishing record sales every year.

While some manufacturers distribute directly to end users, many others use marketing intermediaries or agents to make contact with the people or organizations in their target markets. A good distribution strategy requires penetrating analysis of the alternatives so that an effective strategy can be developed. By selecting intermediaries or suppliers in a helter-skelter way, distribution strategy becomes a fragmented series of decisions. Not surprisingly, management often views as customers those firms that purchase its products, be they distributors, dealers, or other manufacturers. Similarly, suppliers become those firms calling upon the company that is buying, regardless of whether the seller is a manufacturer, distributor, or other kind of intermediary. What all this means is that many companies participate in distribution channels that are comprised of various organizations. The way a firm is positioned in

133

the distribution network can either be left to chance or can be viewed as a major strategic decision for the firm. Increasingly, managements are finding out that distribution strategy cannot be left to chance. And even when management recognizes the need for a distribution strategy, selecting the best strategy to fit the firm's opportunities and constraints is rarely an obvious choice. Over time, distribution strategy may need to be altered to take into account changing conditions. For all of these reasons, distribution strategy should command the attention of management on a continuing basis.

There are two key distribution decisions: (1) deciding how to reach end-user target markets, and (2) if the choice is made to use intermediaries instead of going direct, selecting the role (leader or participant) that the firm will play in the channel and the channel network to become a part of. First, we shall look at the role of distribution in marketing strategy, followed by an examination of the alternatives available to management in choosing a distribution strategy. Finally, the considerations that affect the selection of a channel of distribution strategy are discussed.

STRATEGIC ROLE OF DISTRIBUTION

Lenox Inc.'s performance against European and Japanese competition has been impressive. Positioned against names like Wedgewood, Royal Doulton, and Rosenthal, Lenox has the top position in the U.S. fine china market. Its strong marketing capabilities were instrumental in reaching this position. The firm's powerful distribution network plays an important part in Lenox's marketing strategy for its fine china. Other products include wedding and engagement rings and jewelry. Sales should approach $0.3 billion in 1983. Major elements of Lenox's marketing strategy are:

☐ Targeting efforts at college-educated, upper-middle-income women in the 25–44 age group (this age segment will grow by 15 percent from 1980 to 1985).[1]

☐ Offering a high-quality, stylish line of products.

☐ Establishing a strong distribution network of leading department, jewelry, and specialty stores.

☐ Concentrating upon the middle to upper price-quality niche of the market.

☐ Development of a strong brand name through advertising and promotional efforts.

☐ Working with retailers through the company sales force.

By distributing through leading stores and supporting them with national advertising and direct sales contact, Lenox has maintained steady sales and profit growth. Interestingly, the company has concentrated on selling a lifestyle *image* rather than dishes. Management's approach to diversification, masterminded by John Tassie who brought modern marketing to the firm in 1949, has also been quite successful.

> Nearly all the products are premium-priced, prestige items, often given as gifts. The markets involved tended to be fragmented. Tassie's own idea was to find companies in small markets such as these so that Lenox could gain a dominant share using its marketing expertise, its excellent distribution system and—in some cases—its brand name.[2]

Under Tassie's leadership, Lenox moved from a 10 percent share in the U.S. fine china market in 1949 to over 50 percent by 1977. The firm's highly successful distribution network demonstrates how important distribution strategy can be to corporate performance. Note, for example, how Lenox's distribution approach is matched to the target market and is blended with product, pricing, advertising, and personal selling strategies.

Reaching target markets

For the present, we shall consider distribution strategy from a manufacturer's point of view. Although most of the strategic issues apply to firms at any level in the distribution channel (e.g., wholesale, retail), a manufacturer is unique in having the option of going direct to end users rather than serving them through marketing intermediaries. Distribution strategy for organizations at different channel levels will be discussed later in the chapter.

The first question that must be answered is whether the manufacturer will go direct to end users or instead serve them through marketing intermediaries. Several factors that bear upon this decision are shown in Exhibit 7–1. The alternatives fall into three categories: (1) direct distribution; (2) use of intermediaries; or (3) either may be a feasible alternative. It is necessary to evaluate the factors shown in Exhibit 7–1 in order to determine which option prevails in a given situation. Let's examine them.

End-user considerations. Target market customers have a lot to do with deciding whether or not to use a direct distribution approach. Study of customer characteristics will often indicate whether it is feasible for a manufacturer to go direct to end users. The amount and frequency of purchase must be considered as should available margins over manufac-

Exhibit 7-1
Factors affecting distribution strategy

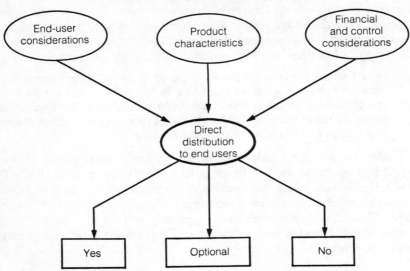

turing costs that will be available to pay for direct selling costs. Customer geographical locations are also important in evaluating the economics of direct selling. The customer's needs regarding product information and applications assistance must be appraised and a determination made of whether the manufacturer or marketing intermediary best satisfies these needs in terms of the expertise required and the costs of providing assistance and service. For example, Caterpillar Tractor Co., in Peoria, Illinois, the world's largest producer of earth-moving equipment, has found independent dealers to be a key factor in the firm's successful business strategy. On-the-spot service is critical in construction work, and contractors are willing to pay premium prices for Caterpillar products due to their performance and because of a dependable dealer network that is the envy of Cat's competitors:

Caterpillar spent $169 million for research and development last year, and about $1 billion in the past 10 years. The results have been steady, with at least three or four models or products coming out annually.

Probably of equal importance to Caterpillar is its dealer organization; indeed, some observers say the dealers have made the company. Competitors privately concede that their own dealer networks can't approach Caterpillar's in size or service. The company has 122 dealers in the United States and 148 abroad, operating out of 900 places of business. The average dealership's net worth is around $8 million, and some dealers have sales of more than $100 million a year.

One such dealership is the John Fabick Tractor Co. of Fenton, Missouri, near St. Louis. Fabick has more than 400 employees operating out of Fenton and four branches in Missouri and Illinois. Besides large facilities for repairing machines, the dealer also maintains a fleet of 100 trucks, on 24-hour call, to minister to ailing equipment. Each truck, specially equipped, costs about $50,000. Chairman John Fabick explains:

"Service is the key to this business; to sell, you have to service. Downtime is the worst enemy of a contractor. When something goes wrong with his equipment, you can't provide service fast enough for him."

Fabick also has an airplane based at a nearby airport to speed deliveries of parts.

Because most Caterpillar dealers are larger and better capitalized than competitors, they're able to offer customers a better supply of parts and a wider selection of equipment. Caterpillar dealers also are responsible for all equipment operating in their territory whether or not it was purchased from them, an arrangement that few competitors have with their dealers.

John C. Deagon, equipment vice president for Morrison-Knudsen Co., the big construction concern based in Boise, Idaho, praises the performance of Caterpillar dealers. "Only with Cat do we seem to get consistently good service around the world," he says.

Caterpillar has many competitors, with some smaller companies selling only one or two lines of equipment. The major competitors are well-known and strong in some lines. The big ones include International Harvester Co., Deere & Co., Clark Equipment Co., Terex division of General Motors, J. I. Case division of Tenneco Inc., Fiat-Allis (a joint venture of Allis-Chalmers Corp. and Fiat S.p.A. of Italy) and Komatsu Ltd. of Tokyo.[3]

The Caterpillar illustration suggests that channel strategy may only be a concern of large corporations rather than small firms with limited resources. This is not the case. Rather, the decision rests upon finding the best means of meeting customer needs considering the functions that are to be provided and the costs of doing so.

Product characteristics. Complex products and services often require close contact between customer and the producer who may be required to provide application assistance, service, and other supporting activities. Chemical processing equipment, large computer systems, pollution control equipment, and engineering design services are illustrative products and services that manufacturers often market direct to end users via their sales forces. Another factor is the mix of products offered by the manufacturer. A full line may make direct contact economically feasible whereas the costs of direct sales with a single product may be prohibitive unless the item represents a major purchase. Companies whose products are improved frequently due to rapidly changing technology often adopt direct sales approaches. And qualified marketing intermediaries may not be available, given the characteristics of the product and the requirements of the customer. Direct contact with end users often provides feedback to the manufacturer as to new product needs, problem areas, and other information. Thus, the characteristics of the product must be considered in deciding whether to use a direct or distribution channel strategy. In some instances the decision is clear, whereas in others either alternative may be feasible.

Financial and control considerations. Some firms do not have the financial resources to serve their end users. Others are unwilling to make large investments in field sales and service facilities. Recall our earlier discussion of Caterpillar's nearly 300 worldwide dealerships and the large investment required by each dealer. Management must decide if the necessary resources are available and, if they are, whether direct sale to end users represents the best use of the resource. Costs and benefits must be estimated. Direct distribution will give more control over distribution to the manufacturer, since independent organizations cannot be managed in the same manner as can employees.

After taking into account the various factors we have been discussing, the choice of direct or indirect distribution must be made. While the decision is situation-specific, an illustrative comparison between consumer and industrial products is shown in Exhibit 7–2. Due to end-user considerations, product characteristics, and financial and control considerations, producers of industrial products are more likely than producers

Exhibit 7–2
**Comparison of distribution approaches for consumer
and industrial products**

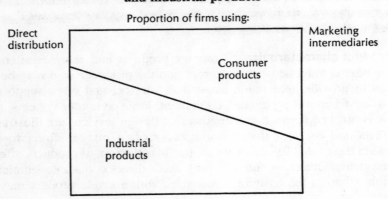

of consumer products to utilize direct distribution to end users. During the rest of the chapter, we shall assume that management plans to use one or more distribution channels to reach end users.

Distribution functions

Several functions take place in a marketing channel in moving the product from the producer to end users. Let's briefly review the activities that often occur in a distribution channel. Transactions and other communications between buyers and sellers and other channel organizations (e.g., advertising agencies) trigger a number of activities. These include information flows, processing and storage, transportation, financial flows, and the transfer of ownership and risk. These functions are necessary in meeting customer needs and wants so the real issue is deciding which organizations shall be responsible for each activity and the level of service to be provided. Intermediaries offer substantial transactional efficiencies when distribution functions are allocated to appropriate specialists. Consider, for example, the inefficiencies that would occur if an automobile parts manufacturer attempted to provide a direct source of supply to automobile repair shops. Xerox, seeking transactional advantages in serving small businesses, opened retail stores in 1980 due to the prohibitive costs of direct contact of small firms with the Xerox sales force.

Once the channel of distribution design is complete and responsibilities for the various marketing functions are assigned, channel strategy decisions establish guidelines for pricing, advertising, and personal selling. For example, pricing decisions must take into account the requirements and functions of intermediaries as well as prevailing practices in the channel. Likewise promotional efforts must be matched to the various channel participants' requirements and capabilities. Consumer products manufacturers often direct advertising to buyers to help pull products through distribution channels. Intermediaries may also need help in planning their marketing efforts and other supporting activities.

STRATEGIC ALTERNATIVES

Let's turn now to the distribution strategy alternatives that must be considered by management in selecting a distribution scheme. Three decisions establish key channel strategy guidelines for a company. As shown in Exhibit 7–3 these include the type of channel arrangement to be used, the desired intensity of distribution, and the selection of a chan-

Exhibit 7–3
Channel of distribution strategy

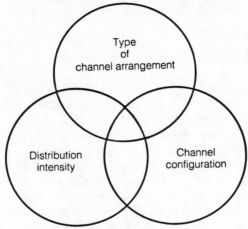

nel configuration. We shall examine each of these decisions to gain an understanding of how together they determine the distribution approach that is adopted by a firm.

Type of channel arrangement

There are two major types of distribution channels: conventional and vertically coordinated channels. The conventional channel is a group of independent organizations, each trying to look out for itself, with little concern for the total performance of the channel. Not surprisingly, managers in an increasing number of firms have seen the potential advantages to be realized in managing the channel as a coordinated or programmed system of participating organizations. These vertical marketing systems dominate the retailing sector today and are also significant factors in the industrial products sector.

Perhaps the best way to identify a channel arrangement is by determining if it possesses the characteristics necessary to be a vertically coordinated channel. Otherwise, it is a conventional channel. Characteristics of vertical marketing systems typically include:

☐ Management (or coordination) of the entire channel by a particular firm.
☐ Programming and coordination of channel activities and functions.

VORSICHT

Bei Verwendung von Löse- und Reinigungsmittel auf der Basis halogenierter Kohlenwasserstoffe wie z. B.

1, 1, 1 - Trichloräthan und
Methylen-Chlorid (Dichlormethane)

können am Aluminiumbecher, Pistole sowie an galvanisierten Teilen chemische Reaktionen auftreten (1, 1, 1-Trichloräthan mit geringen Mengen Wasser ergibt Salzsäure).

Die Teile können dadurch oxydieren, im extremen Fall kann die Reaktion explosionsartig erfolgen.

Verwenden Sie darum für Ihre Farbspritzgeräte nur Löse- und Reinigungsmittel, die die obengenannten Bestandteile nicht enthalten. Zur Reinigung auf keinen Fall Säure verwenden.

SATA-Farbspritztechnik GmbH
Wernerstraße 47 · 7140 Ludwigsburg · Telefon 071 41/2 68 51-5

ATTENTION

The solvents

1, 1, 1 - Trichloroethane and
Methylene Chloride (Dichlormethane)

(sometimes called methyl chloride) can chemically react with the aluminium used in most spray equipment, and these cups, to produce an explosion hazard.

Read the label or data sheet for the material you intend to spray. Do not use any type of spray coating material containing these solvents.

Do not use these solvents for equipment cleaning or flushing. If in doubt as to whether a material is compatible — contact your material supplier.

SATA-Farbspritztechnik GmbH
Wernerstraße 47 · 7140 Ludwigsburg · Telefon 071 41/2 68 51-5

- [ ] Participating organizations linked together through ownership, contractual arrangement, or an administrative relationship.
- [ ] Prescribed rules and operating guidelines for all members concerning the functions and responsibilities of each participant.
- [ ] Management assistance and services given to participants by the firm that is the channel leader.

Several illustrations of firms utilizing vertical marketing systems are shown in Exhibit 7–4. Note that the firm managing the channel is not always a manufacturer. Also, a company may utilize a combination arrangement (e.g., ownership and contractual). The distinction between an administered and conventional channel is more difficult than for the other kinds of vertical systems since there is often no formal way to identify the administered relationship. The difference is more one of degree than of kind.

By forming (or joining) a vertically coordinated channel, the presumption is that performance of the total system as well as each participant will be greater than in a conventional channel arrangement. This is probably a correct assumption for the managing firm, although it is less clear that each participating firm will also be as well off. The economic returns in vertical marketing systems should be higher than conventional channels if the system is properly designed and managed. Yet a coordinated approach forces certain concessions on the part of the firms in the

Exhibit 7–4
Illustrative vertical marketing systems*

	Product/Service	
	Consumer	Industrial
Ownership	Fotomat (film processing)	W. W. Grainger, Inc. (electric motors and equipment)
	Sears, Roebuck and Co. (retailing)	Xerox Corporation (retail office equipment stores)
Contractual	Ethan Allen, Inc. (furniture)	Snap-On Tools, Inc. (mechanics' tools)
	Wendy's International, Inc. (fast foods)	Deere & Company (farm equipment)
Administered	Lenox Inc. (fine china)	Butler Manufacturing Co. (metal building)
	General Electric (appliances)	

*Several of the companies fall into more than one of the categories below.

channel. There are rules to be followed, control is exercised in various ways, and generally there is less flexibility. Also, some of the requirements of the total system may not be in the best interests of particular participants. On the other hand, consider entering a conventional distribution channel with your own hamburger store. Without some special advantage, the competition would be fierce, and your financial performance would no doubt fall far short of what it would be if you were a McDonald's franchisee. We shall return to the channel strategy decision after completing our examination of the alternatives.

Distribution intensity

Distribution intensity can best be visualized in reference to a geographical area, such as a trading area. If we choose to distribute our product in all or most of the retail outlets in a trading area that might normally carry such a product, we are using an intensive distribution approach. In contrast, if only one dealer in the trading area is selected to distribute the product, we are using an exclusive distribution strategy. Thus, there is a range of distribution intensities that can be selected. The two extremes and a middle position distribution intensity are shown in Exhibit 7–5, along with illustrations.

Distribution intensity depends upon several factors; some are subject to management's preferences while others are determined by uncontrollable influences. The major steps in making this decision consist of:

☐ Identifying the range of feasible distribution intensities taking into account the size and characteristics of the target market, the product, and the requirements likely to be imposed by prospective intermediaries.

☐ Selection of the alternatives that correspond with the proposed target market and marketing program positioning strategy.

☐ Choice of the alternative that: (1) provides the best strategic fit; (2) meets management's financial performance expectations; and (3) will be sufficiently attractive to intermediaries so that they will properly perform assigned functions.

The type of product and the target market to be served often will establish a feasible range for distribution intensity. For example, expensive products, such as a Mercedes automobile, do not require intensive distribution to make contact with the people that are able and willing to buy such a product. Moreover, it is unlikely that several dealers in a trading area could survive due to the sales potential for this expensive automobile. In many situations, factors such as these identify the distribution intensity alternatives that are appropriate for consideration by

Exhibit 7–5
Distribution intensity illustrations

Trading area

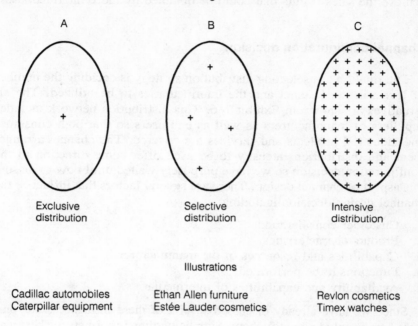

A	B	C
Exclusive distribution	Selective distribution	Intensive distribution

Illustrations

| Cadillac automobiles | Ethan Allen furniture | Revlon cosmetics |
| Caterpillar equipment | Estée Lauder cosmetics | Timex watches |

management. For example, once a target market is specified, considerable direction is provided in making the intensity decision. Ethan Allen's management, in choosing to serve the middle to upper price-quality niche of the market with American traditional furniture, essentially pre-empted consideration of an intensive distribution strategy.

The distribution intensity adopted should be matched with the marketing strategy selected by management. For example, Estée Lauder distributes cosmetics through selected department stores that carry quality products. The firm's management decided not to meet Revlon head-on in the marketplace, instead concentrating efforts on a small number of retail outlets. Thus, Estée Lauder avoids huge national advertising expenditures and uses a promotional pricing scheme to help attract customers to retail outlets.

Strategic requirements, preferences, and constraining factors must be evaluated to determine which intensity provides the best strategic fit and performance potential. The requirements of intermediaries must also be considered along with management's desires in controlling and motivating them. For example, exclusive distribution offers a powerful incentive to intermediaries and also simplifies management and control for the channel leader. But if the exclusive agent is unable (or unwilling) to fully serve the needs of target customers, then the manufacturer will not achieve the sales results that could be obtained by more intermediaries.

Channel configuration decision

The final link in selecting distribution strategy is deciding the number of levels in the channel and the intermediaries to be utilized. The alternatives are shown in Exhibit 7–6. This distribution network includes suppliers of manufacturers as well as end users so that both consumer and industrial products and services are covered. The channel arrangement and distribution intensity to be used offer some direction to the configuration decision so we have purposely waited until now to discuss this aspect of channel design. There are several factors that influence the channel design decision including:

1. Customer considerations.
2. Product characteristics.
3. Capabilities and resources of the manufacturer.
4. Functions to be performed.
5. Availability and capabilities of intermediaries.

Since we have already discussed several of these influences, our purpose here is only to identify them. Simplicity often represents the best way to design something, and the channel of distribution is no exception. A channel with only one level between the producer and end user simplifies coordination and management. The more complex the channel network, the more challenging is accomplishing the various distribution functions. Nevertheless, the allocation of functions to various channel specialists (e.g., brokers, wholesalers, dealers, financial institutions, transporters) may offer substantial economies. Thus, as we shall see in the next section, the final choice of a channel design ultimately rests upon evaluating several important trade-offs that management must resolve.

SELECTING A CHANNEL STRATEGY

Decisions to be made include management's choice of the channel arrangement to be used, desired intensity of distribution, and the channel configuration decision. One of the first issues in selecting a channel strategy is deciding whether to attempt to manage the channel or to assume a participant role. This choice often depends upon how much influence and power a company has. This really amounts to how much

Exhibit 7–6
Distribution network from a
manufacturer's point of view

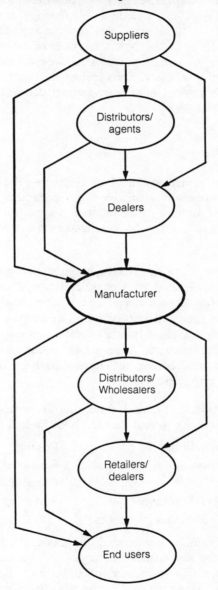

bargaining power management can bring to bear in negotiating with other organizations in the channel system. Power may be due to a firm's financial resources, expertise, market position, and other business strengths. Management may decide to (1) manage or coordinate operations in the channel of distribution, (2) become a member of a vertically coordinated channel, or (3) become a member of a conventional channel system. Regardless of which position is chosen, management should have an understanding of the various factors that affect the channel strategy decision. Let's look at how management can analyze and evaluate strategic alternatives.

Strategic analysis

Selecting a channel strategy involves evaluating those alternatives that are feasible and potentially attractive for a particular firm. Analysis is admittedly complex and very much situation-specific. We shall examine the key factors that affect the channel strategy decision, illustrating how they are used in analysis.

Access to target market. Management's choice of a target market must be closely coordinated with channel strategy since the channel is the link between suppliers and end users. The target market decision cannot actually be finalized until channel strategy is also established, again demonstrating the close link between target market and marketing program positioning strategy. Information about customers will often guide management in screening out channel strategy alternatives that are not suitable for serving end users.

Channel functions. Several functions are performed in moving products from producers to end users. These include:

Buying and selling	Pricing
Transportation	Risk-bearing
Financing	Communications
Processing and storage	Servicing and repair
Advertising and sales promotion	

Deciding which functions are needed and designating the organizations to be responsible for each function are major influences upon the channel strategy decision. As described in Exhibit 7–7, the choice by Entenmann's owners to deliver bakery products directly to the shelves of supermarkets and Mom and Pop groceries required Entenmann's to assume several of the functions normally provided in the food industry by brokers, wholesalers, and other intermediaries.

Exhibit 7–7
How Warner-Lambert's recipe helps Entenmann's go national

When Warner-Lambert spent $242.7 million to buy Entenmann's Inc. two years ago, the price and the risk were high. Was a bakery that was almost unknown outside of New York, a few other parts of the Northeast, and Florida worth 22 times annual earnings? Wall Street and the food industry wondered whether Entenmann's formula for selling unadvertised, high-priced bakery goods could be duplicated elsewhere.

Those doubts have been stilled. The acquisition has turned into a model of how a regional success can become a national one with the help of a well-heeled parent that can resist needless tampering with a winning method.

The evidence: Six cities have been added to Entenmann's marketing area without major problems. Entenmann's sales this year will top $280 million, up at least 67 percent from 1978, the year the company was acquired. Profits also have advanced, helping to offset softness in Warner-Lambert's consumer products division, which markets Trident, Certs, and other gums and candies. By 1984, Warner-Lambert predicts, Entenmann's sales will reach $600 million.

As with most successes, though, Entenmann's has begun to attract competition that could slow its growth. Followers include Campbell-Taggart, Campbell Soup's Pepperidge Farm unit, and Squibb's Table Talk division. "We see a trend, and we're following it," says a spokesman for Campbell-Taggart, a leading baker. "What we don't have is Entenmann's great name."

Lack of capital led Entenmann's to search for a buyer. It already had strong management (the company is run by three grandsons of William Entenmann, Sr., who founded it in 1898), quality products, and a well-recognized brand name in the areas where its goods were sold.

Without Warner-Lambert, "it would have taken us at least twice as long to expand into the new markets," says Robert Entenmann, chairman. With Warner-Lambert's money, adds his brother William, president, "our potential is unlimited."

Entenmann's chief strength was its so-called store-door delivery system. Rather than following the food industry practice of distributing its products through brokers, wholesalers, or other middlemen, Entenmann's used its own trucks and drivers to sell and deliver its fresh-baked products directly to special Entenmann's racks in supermarkets and Mom-and-Pop groceries. Drivers, whose commissions sometimes totaled $50,000 yearly, replenished store inventories daily. Store-door delivery, which is also common to the snack chips and soft-drink industries, is more expensive than other distribution methods but gives manufacturers tighter control of the way their products are merchandised.

But the ingredients that made Entenmann's work as a regional operation made its expansion difficult. Selling to a new market would require the costly addition of trucks, warehouses, and production facilities.

Enter Warner-Lambert. Within months of the acquisition, Warner-Lambert bought a Chicago bakery from Beatrice Foods and then introduced Entenmann's products to Chicago and, later, to St. Louis, Cleveland, and Pittsburgh. A Florida bakery was expanded to service Atlanta. This week

Exhibit 7-7 *(concluded)*

Entenmann's opened a warehouse and distribution center in Albany, N.Y., for customers upstate.

Surprisingly, going into markets where Entenmann's name wasn't familiar was relatively easy. In addition to offering products with high margins, rapid turnover, and low handling costs, Entenmann's convinced grocers that its baked goods built store traffic. "It brings in shoppers you might not ordinarily get," says an executive of the Pathmark chain in the New York area.

Even chains with their own bakery departments accepted Entenmann's. "If we didn't carry Entenmann's, our competition would," says the bakery manager of a Midwest supermarket chain. Since adding Entenmann's, sales of the chain's own bakery department are down 15 percent, but total store volume of baked goods is up 2 percent.

Although sale of the family business meant that the three Entenmann brothers who ran the company no longer had to work for a living, they stayed on. Still, Warner-Lambert hasn't been a completely silent partner. After all, the company had learned a few things from marketing Listerine, Rolaids, Schick razors, among other products.

Advertising is a marketing skill that Warner-Lambert, as the nation's eighth largest advertiser, knew a lot about. Entenmann's television commercials began in Cleveland this summer. Although sales there are up slightly, company officials say its too soon to judge the value of expensive commercials. Newspaper and billboard ads have been used to introduce products in new markets. (Entenmann's also has turned to advertising recently to quiet rumors that its true owner is the Unification Church.)

Other Warner-Lambert influences: New products, including fudge, doughnuts, and cream-filled cupcakes, have been added; chocolate candies will be tried soon. Entenmann's also has begun detailed market research. And to entice new customers, the company hands out free samples extensively. For its debut in St. Louis, Entenmann's distributed slices of a 600-pound cake replica of a Mississippi River steamboat.

The only apparent cloud on Entenmann's horizon is competition, as other companies are attracted to the $6.4 billion market for sweet baked goods. Campbell-Taggart, for example, has beaten Entenmann's to Cincinnati. In its Pittsburgh test market, Pepperidge Farm bumped Entenmann's from the shelves of Giant Eagle supermarkets.

"We are a very visible target," says David Johnson, a Warner-Lambert veteran who became Entenmann's executive vice president after the acquisition. The company's response to new competitors, says Mr. Johnson, is to be "very careful not to expand too quickly and not to get too carried away with its recent and quick successes."

Source: Michael Waldholz, *The Wall Street Journal,* October 23, 1980, p. 37.
Reprinted by permission. © Dow Jones & Co., Inc. 1980. All rights reserved.

Financial considerations. Two financial questions bear upon channel strategy. First, are resources available for launching management's preferred strategy? Recall the Entenmann's illustration (Exhibit 7–7). In order to grow at a rate desired by management and to use the channel strategy which had been so successful in the past, it was necessary to sell the company to Warner-Lambert to finance the rapid expansion that management wanted.

Second, the revenue-cost impact of alternative channel strategies must be estimated. This task grows more complex as the channel network is expanded to include several levels and types of organizations. The impact of channel strategy alternatives upon financial performance of the firm should be estimated. Typical analyses include cash flow, income, return on investment, and operating capital requirements.

Other considerations. Additional factors may influence the channel strategy decision including management's desire for flexibility (e.g., ease of change) in channel design and the extent of control preferred over other channel participants. To some extent, greater control reduces flexibility. For example, a conventional channel provides little opportunity for control by a particular firm, yet there is considerable flexibility in channel relationships. Legal and regulatory constraints also may affect channel strategies. Areas affected include pricing, exclusive dealing, division of markets, and other aspects of channel relationships.[4]

Strategy at different channel levels

Until now we have looked at the channel largely from the producer's viewpoint. Distributors are also concerned with channel strategies, and in some instances they may exercise primary control over channel operations. Sears, for example, is a powerful force in the channels of which it is a part. Large food wholesalers like Malone & Hyde are major factors in their channels of distribution. Moreover, decisions by wholesalers, distributors, brokers, retailers, and other intermediaries about what manufacturers' products to carry often have a major influence upon the performance of all channel participants.

Channel strategy can be examined from any level in the distribution network. All of the factors we have discussed can be used to guide evaluation of channel alternatives at any level. The major distinction lies in the point of view used in strategy development. Intermediaries may have fewer alternatives to consider than producers and thus less flexibility in channel strategy. Nevertheless, they should look at channel strategy on an active rather than a passive basis.

CONCLUDING NOTE

The changes that occurred during the last decade in marketing practices establish beyond any question the type of business arena that will prevail in the future. Both institutions and patterns of distribution are experiencing shorter and shorter life cycles. The fast-food industry reached maturity in less than a decade. Management must appraise channel strategy on a regular basis to maintain desired performance levels and to avoid problems caused by changing external conditions. Innovation, competition, and modified needs and wants all can alter the situation that influenced the initial design of channel strategy.

The choice of channel type, distribution intensity, and channel configuration set the stage for the various specific channel design and management activities. Management must determine early in its formulations whether the firm will manage or instead become a member of a channel network. In this chapter we saw how distribution strategy represents a crucial step in deciding how to reach target markets. This strategy is guided by end-user needs and characteristics, product characteristics, and financial and control considerations. The strategic choices depend upon whether a conventional or vertically coordinated channel is used, the distribution intensity (intensive, selective, or exclusive) selected, and the channel configuration that is adopted. We discussed the analysis of channel strategy alternatives, indicating how market target, financial

Exhibit 7–8
Managers' distribution planning checklist

☐ Is your company/business unit marketing direct to end users, or are you part of a distribution channel?

☐ During the last few years has your company evaluated the distribution approach used to reach target market(s)?

☐ Are there indications of problems in your distribution system (e.g., customer complaints, stockouts, distributors dropping your products, etc.)?

☐ Are there actions that can be taken to strengthen channel relationships and improve performance?

☐ Should changes in channel design be considered to improve performance or adjust to new market/competitive conditions?

☐ Should the addition or deletion of channel participants (e.g., manufacturers, representatives) be considered?

☐ Have you considered using multiple distribution channels to gain better access to target markets?

☐ Are you studying industry trends to help identify changes in distribution approaches and practices?

considerations, and other factors must be examined in deciding the channel strategy to adopt. Channel strategy establishes several guidelines for price and promotion strategies, to which we shall turn our attention in the next two chapters.

A checklist for distributing planning is shown in Exhibit 7–8. Of course if you do not use distribution channels the guide is not relevant to your business. Nevertheless, if use of distribution channels is a possible option, you may find it helpful to evaluate the pros and cons of going direct to end users versus distribution through channels.

NOTES

1. *The Value Line Investment Survey, Ratings and Reports,* September 5, 1980, p. 1529.
2. "Rings on Her Fingers, China on Her Table," *Forbes,* February 20, 1978, p. 81.
3. Harlan S. Byrne, "What Recession? A Leaping Caterpillar Is a Wondrous Thing, Even Its Rivals Agree," *The Wall Street Journal,* April 19, 1976, p. 12.
4. See chap. 8 of Louis W. Stern and Adell I. El-Ansary, *Marketing Channels* (Englewood Cliffs, N.J.: Prentice-Hall, 1977).

8

Price planning

Price planning has many characteristics in common with a bomb! The consequences of pricing decisions can be explosive and far reaching, and it may be difficult to alter a strategy once it has been implemented, particularly if the change calls for significant price increases. And, if used improperly, pricing actions can land you in jail. Price has many possible uses in corporate and marketing strategy. During the turbulent 70s price gained a far more active role in strategy than in the past. This revolution in pricing practices has led to building much greater flexibility into price strategies and tactics in many firms.

The implications of the contemporary pricing environment are significant for management and require price strategies that correspond to the times. Pricing policies and structure must be developed to properly establish price's role in marketing strategy while retaining enough flexibility to respond to changing conditions.

First, we shall examine the role of price in marketing program positioning strategy and discuss several key influences upon price strategy. An approach to analysis for pricing decisions is presented and applications are provided to illustrate the nature and scope of analysis activities. Next, the selection of a price strategy is considered. Finally, guidelines for establishing pricing policies and structure are considered.

GUIDE TO PRICE PLANNING

Price is gaining far more attention from management than in the past as described in the following illustration:

Ralston Purina turned to a simple attention-getter earlier this year when it wanted to hype its sales of canned cat food. The company lowered the wholesale price by about four cents a can.

That sort of action has been almost unheard of among packaged-goods marketers until recently. Their typical sales blandishments are cents-off coupons, bigger ad budgets, sweepstakes, refunds, temporary price discounts, or minor product changes resulting in claims that brands are "new and improved."

"We're paying a lot more attention to price now," says Blair Gensamer, marketing director for Ralston's grocery products division, which also has lowered prices of its Mainstay and Moist & Chunky dog foods. "It's a tool that's being neglected."

That view apparently is shared by such leading consumer-products marketers as Procter & Gamble, Kellogg, Coca-Cola, Scott Paper, Mobil, Union Carbide, and Lever Brothers. For various reasons, all recently have cut their prices on certain brands. Some of the companies are fighting private-label and generic products, while others want to reduce temporary discounts known as "trade deals" or to revive lagging products.[1]

Of course, recognizing the importance of price should not imply that lowering prices is the correct strategy. The important consideration is to develop a plan as to how price will be used in the marketing program.

We define a price strategy as:

☐ Deciding how to position price within the range of feasible prices.
☐ Establishing whether price shall be used as an active or passive element in the marketing program.
☐ Setting the specific objectives to be accomplished by price.
☐ Establishing policies and structure for guiding pricing decisions.

These decisions are part of several price planning activities as shown in Exhibit 8–1. Identifying price alternatives is facilitated by examining the requirements and constraints imposed by product and distribution strategies. The next step in price planning is the analysis of the product-market, costs, competition, and legal and ethical factors which together provide a basis for estimating how much flexibility exists in price strategy. These steps then lead to identifying and evaluating alternative price positions. The selection of a price positioning strategy leads next to choosing how active (or passive) price will be in the marketing program. This is followed by setting price objectives and developing the policies and the structure for setting specific prices for the products in the mix. Once made, these plans must be implemented and the price strategy managed to deliver the results expected from the price function. We shall examine each of the steps shown in Exhibit 8–1 in the remainder of the chapter.

Designating responsibility for price strategy is often situation-specific

Exhibit 8–1
Guide to price planning

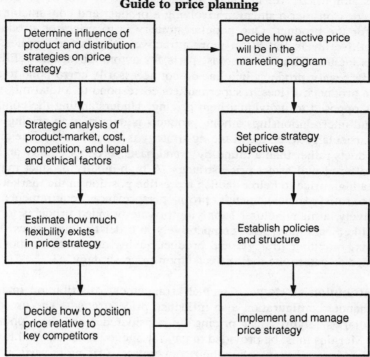

and may not be assigned to the chief marketing executive. There will be some danger of fragmentation of marketing strategy if pricing is not included in the chief marketing executive's responsibilities since price decisions must be coordinated with other marketing program decisions. Operations, financial, and other executives should, of course, participate in strategic pricing decisions regardless of where responsibility is assigned.

Product and distribution strategies

Factors such as product quality and features, type of channel of distribution, margin requirements of intermediaries, end users served, and designated functions of intermediaries all help to establish a price range that is appropriate in a given situation. Of course, if direct distribution is used, then the channel distribution considerations are not an issue in pricing strategy.

Product strategy. When a single product is involved, the price decision is simplified. Yet in many instances a line or mix of products is involved. Consider a situation involving a product and consumable supplies for the product. One popular strategy is to price the product at competitive levels and to set more attractive margins for supplies. Examples include film for cameras, parts for automobiles, and refills for pens. Prices for products in a line do not necessarily correspond to costs for the products. Prices in supermarkets correspond to a total mix strategy as opposed to individual item pricing. Understanding the composition and interrelationships among products is important to pricing strategy, particularly when the branding strategy is built around a line or mix of products rather than a brand-by-brand basis. Product quality and features offered will affect price strategy. A high-quality product may require a high price to help establish a prestige position in the marketplace and to satisfy management's profit performance requirements. Alternatively, a manufacturer supplying private branded products to a retailer like Sears must price competitively in order to obtain sales. Product mix, branding strategy, and product quality and features should be analyzed to determine their effects upon price strategy.

Distribution strategy. Channel arrangement, distribution intensity, and channel configuration also influence price strategy. The use of intermediaries requires that pricing be considered from their points of view. Margins must be provided to pay for agents' functions and to offer sufficient incentives to obtain their cooperation. Pricing in vertically coordinated channels will reflect total channel considerations more so than is the case in conventional channels. Intensive distribution is likely to call for more competitive pricing than with selective or exclusive distribution. These illustrations suggest the importance of analysis of pricing strategy from a channel of distribution perspective.

PRICE ANALYSIS

Moving now to the second step in price planning, analysis of price is necessary in several different situations. The need is obvious in the case of a new product or new venture. Pricing questions are important in evaluating new product ideas, in test marketing, and in selecting a national introduction strategy. Analysis also is necessary for existing products or brands due to changes in the market and competitive environment, unsatisfactory performance of products, and modifications in marketing strategy over the life cycle of the product. Regular surveillance of the performance of price strategy is essential. Let's examine the major areas where analysis should be accomplished.

Product-market analysis

Product-market analysis with respect to price should yield the following information:

1. How large is the product-market in terms of buying potential? Is it a $1 million market or a $10 million market, or what?
2. What target market strategy is to be used?
3. How elastic (sensitive) is demand to changes in price? How much effect will price changes have upon quantities demanded by buyers?
4. How important are nonprice factors in the buyer's decision to purchase a product or service?
5. What are the forecasts of sales for the price alternatives under consideration?

Since estimation of product-market size and target market strategy were discussed in Chapters 3 and 4 we shall concentrate upon questions 3 through 5.

Price elasticity.   Price elasticity is defined as the percentage change in the quantity demanded divided by the percentage change in price. Note that elasticity corresponds to changes in price from some reference price level and is not necessarily constant over the range of prices under consideration. And, for some products, research indicates that people will demand more quantities at higher prices, thus following a price-quantity relationship that slopes upward to the right. In these instances buyers seem to be using price as a measure of quality. Estimating the exact shape of the demand curve (price-quantity relationship) is probably impossible in most instances. Even so, there are ways that we can estimate how sensitive sales are to price. Test marketing is sometimes used for this purpose. Analysis of historical price and quantity data may be helpful. End-user research studies, such as consumer evaluations of price, are also used. These approaches, coupled with management judgment, can provide an estimate of the sensitivity of sales to price. We must estimate how responsive buyers will be to changes in price that are within the range of prices under consideration.

Nonprice factors.   The influence of nonprice factors may be important in some buying situations. Buyers may be willing to pay a premium price in order to gain other advantages or to forego certain advantages for lower prices. Irwin Gross, manager, marketing research division, E. I. du Pont de Nemours & Company, comments upon this point:

> Research into the marketing process has suggested that it is the buyer's perception of the total relative value of the offerings that will result in a

willingness to pay a premium price for one offering as compared with another, or consistently to choose one offering over another at the same price. . . . In the face of a perceived need, the buyer is aware of, or acquires awareness of, alternative means of satisfying that need. Prior knowledge, combined with communications from sellers and others, results in perceptions of the attributes of the sellers' offerings.[2]

According to Gross the price of a product with in-kind competition can be separated into two components: (1) the commodity price which fluctuates with the ebbs and flows of supply and demand; and (2) the premium price differential which one or more firms may achieve due to customers' perceived values. An illustration of this advantage for one of Du Pont's products is shown.

	Du Pont advantage
Quality	$1.70
Innovation	2.00
System	0.80
Service	0.25
Delivery	0.15
Retraining	0.40
Total	$5.30
Base price: $100	

Source: Irwin Gross, "Insights from Pricing Research," in *Pricing Practices and Strategies,* ed. Earl L. Bailey (New York: The Conference Board, 1978), p. 39.

Forecasts. The final step in product-market analysis for pricing decisions is to forecast sales for the range of prices that management wishes to consider given the results of demand analysis. These forecasts, when combined with cost estimates, will enable management to examine the financial impact of different price strategies. We are interested in estimating sales in units for each product (or brand) at the prices under consideration. Assuming that all other marketing program variables remain at a constant level, elasticity estimates can be used to develop sales projections for review by management.

Cost analysis

An understanding of product costs is an essential input to the selection of a price strategy. A recommended approach to cost analysis is shown in Exhibit 8–2. First, the structure of the cost of producing and distributing each product under consideration should be determined. This involves determining fixed and variable components of cost. We also need to know what portion of product cost is accounted for by purchases from suppliers. For intermediaries this will be a large part of the total cost. Separation of cost components into labor, materials, and capital categories is useful in studying cost structure.

Once the basic cost structure is established, cost and volume relationships should be examined next. How are costs expected to vary at different levels of production or quantities purchased? To what extent can economies of scale be gained over the volume range that is under consideration, given the target market and intended program positioning strategy? At what volumes are significant cost reductions possible? The main issue in this part of the analysis is to determine the extent to which

Exhibit 8–2
How to analyze product costs

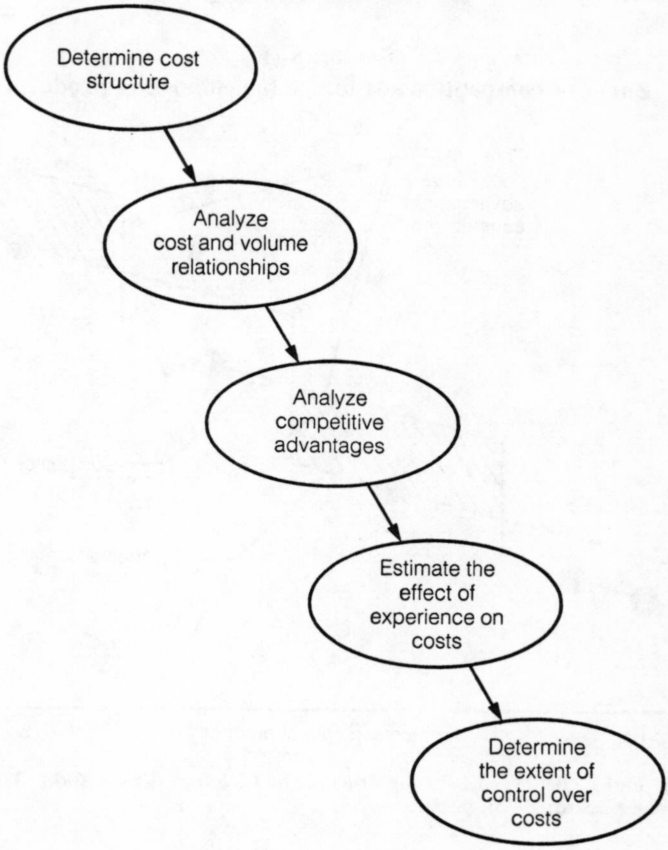

the volume produced (or distributed) should be taken into account in selecting a price strategy.

How our costs compare to key competitors is often an important influence upon price strategy. Are they higher, lower, or about the same? Gaining this information is sometimes difficult, although it is surprising how much insight experienced managers and analysts have concerning the costs of competitors. The important consideration is placing key competitors into relative product cost categories. In some situations competitive cost information can be estimated from a knowledge of wage rates, materials costs, production facilities, and related information. An interesting illustration of competitive cost advantage is shown in Exhibit 8–3. The basis of comparison is the power output of the product, a commercial equipment item. Notice how competitive advantage changes at different power outputs for companies X and Y. Company X, which is smaller than Y, the industry leader, has some important cost advantages over Y as power output increases due to technical differences in their products.

The next aspect of cost analysis, referring back to Exhibit 8–2, is

Exhibit 8–3
Zones of competitive advantage for competing products

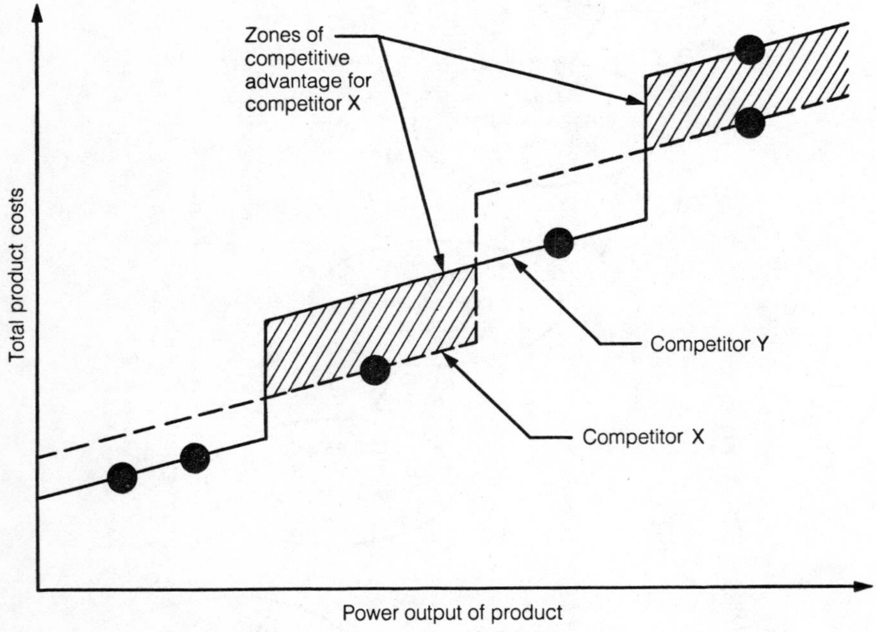

Source: Earl L. Bailey, ed., *Pricing Practices and Strategies* (New York: The Conference Board, 1978), p. 52.

estimating the effect of experience upon costs. Experience or learning curve analysis (using historical data) indicates that costs (and prices) for many products decline by a given amount each time the number of units doubles. Price declines may be uneven due to competitive influences. When plots are made of unit cost (vertical axis) against total accumulated volume (horizontal axis), costs decline with volume. The underlying logic supporting these studies is that experience increases the efficiency of production operations. Experience curve analysis is a central part of the Boston Consulting Group approach to strategic planning. The extent of the experience curve effect should be examined on an industry and company basis since the effect is not the same across all product categories.

Finally, management should determine how much influence or control the firm may have over costs in the future. To what extent can research and development, bargaining power with suppliers, innovation, and other factors be expected to reduce costs over the planning horizon. These considerations are interrelated with experience curve analysis yet may operate over a shorter time range. Bargaining power, for example, in channels of distribution can have a major effect upon costs, and the effects can be immediate.

Competitor analysis

Moving now to the third area of price analysis, in addition to studying competitor's product costs, management should evaluate each competitor's price strategy to determine:

☐ How competing firms are strategically positioned on a relative price basis and the extent to which price is used as an active part of marketing strategy.

☐ Which firms represent the most direct competition (actual and potential) for the target market under consideration.

☐ How successful each firm's price strategy has been.

☐ What are key competitors' probable responses to the alternative price strategies being considered?

The most difficult of these is predicting what key competitors will do in response to the alternative strategies under consideration. No changes are likely unless one firm's price strategy is viewed as threatening (low) or greedy (high). Competitive pressures, actual and potential, often narrow the range of feasible price strategies and rule out the use of extremely high or low prices relative to competition. In new product-markets, competitive factors may be insignificant other than the fact that very high prices may attract potential competitors. For example, Tylenol's high profit margin was a major reason for Datril's entry into the nonaspirin market in the mid-1970s.

Legal and ethical considerations

Last in our consideration of strategic analysis activities is the identification of legal and ethical factors that may bear upon the choice of a price strategy. Consider the following description of what happened when several companies in the paper industry were involved in price-fixing cases:

> Fines and damages paid by various paper companies in a barrage of anti-trust actions now add up to more than $500 million. Several executives have also spent a little time in jail. Not since the electrical equipment cases of the 1960s has an industry been so heavily punished. . . . That there was price-fixing in various paper products on a large scale is beyond dispute. But unresolved, despite all the ferment, are critical questions about the intent and consequences of these illegal actions.[3]

Countless examples exist of companies running into alleged violations of U.S. antitrust policy, thus highlighting the importance of establishing and implementing price strategies to avoid potential legal conflicts. Those pricing practices that have received the most attention by government are:

☐ *Price fixing*—price collusion between competitors, such as the paper industry illustration. Situations involving narrow profit margins are more likely to lead to price fixing.

☐ *Price discrimination*—charging different customers different prices without an underlying cost basis for discrimination.

☐ *Price fixing in channels of distribution*—specifying the prices of distributors.

☐ *Price information*—requirements concerning the form and the availability of price information for consumers. Unit pricing and consumer credit requirements are examples.[4]

Turning now to ethical issues in pricing, the guidelines that exist here are far more subjective and dependent upon a firm's point of view versus the other firms and individuals that may be affected by a pricing strategy that could be considered unethical. As an illustration, let's examine the price strategy used by the American Telephone & Telegraph Co. (AT&T) for its Picturephone.[5] Satellite Business Systems (SBS) argued that AT&T had kept rates artificially low, subsidized, in effect, by AT&T's monopoly telephone services. To some observers this claim may seem surprising since the rates for Picturephone use ranged from $150 to $395 an hour! Yet there seemed to be a developing market for Picturephone for use in holding remote video business meetings to counter high travel and lodging costs. Anticipating this opportunity in teleconferencing services, SBS could not compete at AT&T's current rates. AT&T argued that while the rates were not "cost justified," they were not harmful to competition. This illustration points out the difficulty in determining what is unethical. A firm will typically adopt a price strategy that is in its best interests.

How much flexibility exists?

One of the major outcomes of the strategic analysis activities we have examined is establishing how much flexibility there is in the choice of a price strategy. The various aspects of analysis are combined in Exhibit 8–4 to illustrate how they determine the extent of flexibility. This feasibility range for price may be narrow or wide in a given situation. If the gap is narrow, then management will be constrained as to possible price strategies, thus simplifying the decision. A wide gap suggests a greater range of feasible strategies.

Exhibit 8–4
How much flexibility in price strategy?

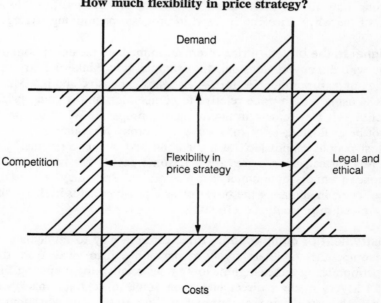

PRICE STRATEGY DETERMINATION

We have now reached the stage in price planning where a price strategy can be selected. Product and distribution strategies, in combination with analyses of factors affecting price, may indicate a particular price strategy as the one to be used. Referring back to Exhibit 8–1, if alternative strategies are feasible, they will be the result of deciding how to position price and choosing how active price will be in the marketing program. We shall examine these questions followed by a discussion of price objectives.

Price as an instrument of strategy

How a firm's prices are positioned relative to other firms in a product-market and whether management chooses to use price as an active or passive instrument of strategy establish the arena for price strategy. Under pure competition a single firm has no control over the situation, whereas a monopolist or a cartel has a substantial influence on prices, particularly when there is no government regulation as in some international commodity situations (e.g., oil and diamonds). When pricing a mix of products and specific products within each line, establishing pricing structure becomes even more challenging than for an individual item, as we shall see later in the chapter. The key question, of course, is deciding how to use price as an instrument of strategy. Let's look at some of the ways price can be used in program positioning strategy.

Signal to the buyer. Price offers an immediate means of communicating with the buyer. Consider, for example, how Maker's Mark refers to price in its promotional efforts—"it tastes expensive and is." Maker's Mark is using a high price relative to competition and is using price as an active, visible element in the marketing program. When the product cannot be evaluated, price may serve as a proxy for value.

Most people cannot look at a diamond and evaluate its quality and may rely instead upon price. In fact, some people are hesitant to buy diamonds from discount outlets because of this. Price may be used as an active factor in signaling the buyer or as a passive factor in that price is not stressed in promotional efforts.

Instrument of competition. Price offers a way to immediately attack competitors or alternatively to position a firm away from direct competition using either high or low prices relative to competing firms. Bristol-Myers made a direct attack on Johnson & Johnson's Tylenol brand with Datril using a cutthroat pricing strategy in an attempt to penetrate the acetaminophen product-market that had been dominated by Tylenol. The strategy backfired when J&J countered by lowering Tylenol prices to competitive levels. In contrast, catalog showroom retailers, such as Service Merchandise, have successfully used a low-price strategy against discount chains and other retailers.

Achieving financial performance. Price, along with costs, determines financial performance. Price strategies should be assessed as to their estimated impact on the firm's financial statements, both in the short and long run. Historically, financial considerations have been major factors in the pricing strategies of large firms in mature industries, such as oil, steel, rubber, automobiles, and chemicals. In all firms, pricing strategies are typically evaluated as to estimated financial consequences. In fact, these industries have historically used target return methods for pricing; that is, setting a desired profit return and then computing the price necesary to achieve this return. International competition in the late 70s has forced a growing number of firms to consider pricing approaches that are more demand oriented. Financial objectives may include pricing for short-term recovery of investment, long-term profitability, or market penetration on a break-even basis. The issue is the nature and extent to which financial considerations will be used to establish the role of price in a given firm.

Marketing mix considerations. Price is a substitute for selling effort, advertising, and product quality. Alternatively, price may be used to reinforce other marketing program activities. The role of price may often depend upon how other marketing mix variables are used. For example, price can be used as an incentive to intermediaries and company salespeople, as the focus of promotional strategy, and as a signal of value. Determining the role of price in marketing strategy requires that management evaluate its importance to customers, competitive positioning, financial requirements, and marketing mix interrelationships.

Selecting a strategy

The choice of a price strategy depends upon how management decides to position price relative to competition and upon whether price will be assigned an active or passive role in the marketing program. Four illustrations of different strategies are shown in Exhibit 8–5. We shall examine each to demonstrate the range of price strategies that can be used by companies. As we do this, keep in mind that there are various strategic price positions that a firm might choose within the arena shown in Exhibit 8–5. Moreover, there are many firms that choose to

Exhibit 8–5
Price's strategic arena

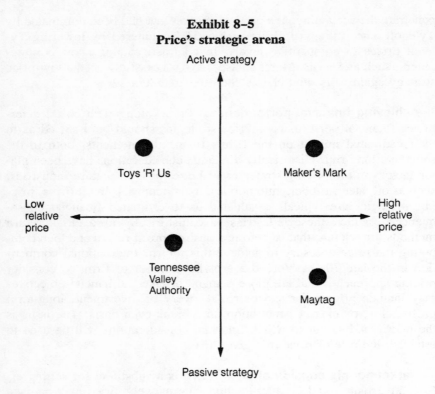

price at or near the prices of key competitors, and instead they emphasize the nonprice factors in their marketing strategies.

It should be clear as to our intended meaning of the relative price
dimenison of Exhibit 8–5. The use of price as an active versus passive
factor refers to how actively price is used in advertising, personal selling, and other promotional efforts. Does price stay in the background,
or is it used as an active factor in the marketing program?

High-active strategy. Although not widely used, there are several
possible conditions where this strategy may be appropriate. When the
buyer cannot easily evaluate the quality of a product, price can serve as
a signal of value. This helps to explain the active use of price in promoting Maker's Mark whiskey. High prices may be essential to gain the
margins necessary to serve small target markets, produce high-quality
products, or to pay for new product development. While high prices are
more frequently used as a passive factor in a marketing program, making price visible and active can appeal to buyers' perceptions of quality,
image, and dependability of products and services. Use of a high-price
strategy is also less subject to retaliation by competitors, if product dif-
ferentiation exists.

High-passive strategy. Management may choose to concentrate upon nonprice factors in attempting to convince buyers to purchase a product. Product features and performance can be stressed when the people in the target market are concerned with product quality and performance. The Maytag Co. has used high prices relative to competition to achieve strong financial performance, while assigning price a passive role in marketing strategy. Maytag has consistently outperformed other appliance manufacturers on the basis of net profits to sales. Interestingly, the company has no debt and is able to use cash flow to meet capital needs.

Low-active strategy. There are many examples of companies that use this strategy including Kroger (supermarkets), Dollar General Stores (retail apparel), Toys 'R' Us (retail toys), and Pic N Pay Shoe Stores (family shoes). We shall examine Toys 'R' Us' price strategy later in the chapter. When price is an important factor in the buyer's decision, a low-active price strategy can be very effective. Offering price-conscious consumers acceptable quality at low prices has been an effective strategy for many firms. One possible disadvantage of this strategy is starting a price war, so it is a more attractive strategy when the competition for the target market is not heavy or when a company has a strong position in its product-markets and has cost advantages.

Low-passive strategy. This is not a widely adopted strategy although it is used by some firms with lower quality products than their key competitors. By not emphasizing low price there is less danger that potential buyers will link price with quality. Some firms participating in conventional channels may not spend much on marketing their products and thus may use low prices because of lower costs. Not-for-profit government organizations, such as the Tennessee Valley Authority, price at cost and yet do not aggressively market their services.

The marketing objectives that are assigned to price have a direct bearing upon the choice of how price will be positioned against competition and how active price will be in the marketing program. Because of this, consideration of objectives must enter into the choice of a price strategy. We turn now to a look at the kinds of objectives to which price strategy may be expected to contribute.

Pricing objectives

Companies establish various objectives to be accomplished by their price strategies. These may include pricing for results (sales, market share, profit), for market penetration or position, for doing certain functions (e.g., promotional pricing), or to avoid government intervention in a firm's pricing affairs. Normally, more than one objective will be involved, and some objectives may conflict with each other. If so, limits may need to be imposed on one of the conflicting objectives. For example, if a pricing objective is to increase market share by 20 percent while another is to price to break even on sales, management should determine if both objectives are feasible. If not, one must be adjusted. Objectives establish essential guidelines for pricing policies and structure, which is the final step in price strategy.

ESTABLISHING POLICIES AND STRUCTURE

An illustration will be helpful in showing the interrelationships of the decisions that comprise a price strategy. Toys 'R' Us is an exciting example of the success of specialty retailing in the 1970s. The largest retailer of toys in the United States, company sales should reach $1 billion in 1982. With nearly 150 outlets and more scheduled to open in 1983, rapid growth will continue in the 1980s. Toys 'R' Us is unique in that its stores handle only toys, in barnlike outlets averaging a large 43,000 square feet.[6] Here are the major elements of the company's strategy:

☐ Low-low prices are the keystone of the firm's corporate and marketing strategies, with additional volume generated by aggressive expansion of stores.

☐ A tight rein is kept on inventories using a computer control system.

☐ Management prides itself on never running a sale and, to keep customers coming back, prices its goods accordingly.

☐ People are being added in stores to provide fast service and keep customers happy.

Price forms the cutting edge of this firm's marketing strategy. Growth and financial performance of the firm have been impressive. Notice how the price strategy is clearly established and how objectives (e.g., profit performance) depend significantly upon the success of the strategy. When you think about the range of prices, from $1 items to well over $100, and the variety of playthings, from dolls to electronic games, the need for pricing policies and structure is clear. It is necessary to understand relationships among products, establish price structure, and then determine specific prices. Our final task in this chapter is to overview some of the more important policy and structure issues. Since to a large extent these activities are specific to a particular firm, we must be somewhat general in our treatment of the area. Moreover, our primary objective is to link these operational and tactical activities to the strategic aspects of price, rather than to discuss specific pricing techniques.

Product relationships and price structure

Any time more than a single product is involved, product mix and line interrelationships must be determined in order to establish price structure. For example, Toys 'R' Us' strategy of low-low prices does not automatically provide management with specific prices for each item offered by the firm. And when more than one target market is involved, what relationships exist between the products offered in each target market? Assuming differences in products, should price be based upon costs, demand, competition, or what?

Price structure is concerned with how to price individual items in the line relative to each other. The items may be aimed at the same target market or different end-user groups; for example, the offering of economy and premium product categories by department stores. In the case of a single product-market, price differences among products are typically not due only to variations in costs. For example, large supermarket chains price for total profitability of the product offering rather than for performance of individual items. Some of these firms have developed computer analysis and pricing procedures to achieve certain objectives, such as sales, market share, and profit contribution.

Once product relationships are established, some basis of determining price structure must be selected. In a great many instances price structure is based upon market and competitive factors as well as differences in the costs of producing each item. Some firms use multiple criteria for price structure determination and have sophisticated computer models to examine alternate pricing schemes. Others use rules of thumb developed from experience. Kent Monroe suggests the following guidelines for the correct pricing of a product line:

1. Price each product in relation to all others; perceptibly noticeable differences in products should be equivalent to perceived value differences.
2. The top and bottom prices in the line should be priced so as to facilitate desired buyer perceptions.
3. Price differences between products should become larger as price increases over the line.[7]

Most approaches include not only cost, but also demand and competitive considerations in their establishment of price relationships among their products. For example, industrial equipment manufacturers sometimes price certain products at or close to cost and depend upon sales of high margin supplies, parts, and replacement items to generate profits. The important consideration in any firm is to price the entire mix and line of products so that strategic price objectives will be accomplished.

Special considerations

Beyond product relationships and price structure there are several other price considerations that often require the special attention of management. We shall briefly examine three that are often encountered. The first concerns new product pricing. How shall a new product be priced? A range of possibilities exists from charging a relatively low entry price with the objective of building volume and market position to use of a high price intended to generate a smaller market response than with the low entry price. Cost, competitive, and product-market factors are typically important in making these decisions.

Another policy consideration is deciding how flexible prices will be. Will prices be set and held firm, or are they intended to be negotiated between buyer and seller? Recall, for example, Toys 'R' Us' use of low yet firm prices and the avoidance of special sales to attract customers. Perhaps the most important issue is making this a policy decision rather than being forced into price flexibility as a tactical response. You, no doubt, can think of companies whose price lists are very rigid and others whose list prices give no indication of actual selling prices.

The third policy consideration concerns life-cycle pricing. Some firms have developed policies for guiding pricing decisions over the life cycle of the product. Depending upon the stage in the product life cycle, pricing of a particular product or an entire line may be based on building market share, profitability, cash flow, or other objectives. Because of life-cycle considerations, different objectives and policies may apply to particular products within a mix or line. For many products, price becomes a more active element of strategy as a product moves through its life cycle. Certainly the opportunity for this to happen is much greater as competive pressures build, costs decline, and volume increases. Life-cycle pricing should correspond to the overall marketing program positioning strategy that is used.

Determining specific prices

Finally, the point is reached in price planning where it is necessary to either assign a specific price to each product item or to provide a method for computing price for a particular buyer-seller transaction. Many methods and techniques are available for calculating price. Several of the sources of variability in the choice of specific prices should have been eliminated or at least reduced after selecting price position, deciding how active price will be, setting objectives, and establishing product relationships and price structure. After analyzing how these decisions affect specific price determination, actual prices can be calculated.

CONCLUDING NOTE

Price strategy gains considerable direction from the decisions management makes about the product mix, branding strategy, and product quality. Distribution strategy also influences the choice of how price will work in combination with advertising and sales force strategies. Price, like other marketing program components, is a means of generating market response. Looking ahead in the 1980s, two important trends are apparent in the use of price as a strategic variable. First, companies are designing far more flexibility into their strategies to enable coping with the rapid changes and uncertainties in the strategic environment. Second, price is more often used as an active rather than passive element of corporate and marketing strategies. This trend is particularly apparent in the retail sector where aggressive low-price strategies are used by firms such as Toys 'R' Us, Dollar General Stores, and many others. Recall that assigning an active role to price does not necessarily lead to low prices relative to competition. Companies may use relatively high prices in assigning price an active role in their marketing strategies.

Our look at the strategic importance of price demonstrated how product, distribution, price, and promotion strategies must fit together into an integrated program positioning strategy. A guide to strategic price planning was developed showing the major stages that lead to selection of a price strategy (Exhibit 8–1). This planning guide can be used in any firm to develop a price strategy for a mix or line of products. It can also be used in selecting a price strategy for a new product or brand.

Underlying strategy formulation are several important strategic activities including analysis of the product-market, cost, competition, and legal and ethical considerations. These analyses indicate the amount of

Exhibit 8–6
Manager's checklist for price planning

☐ How responsive are the people/organizations in your target market to changes in price?

☐ How is price used in your marketing program?

☐ Who makes price decisions in your company or business unit?

☐ How much flexibility exists in your price strategy?

☐ How should your company's prices be positioned relative to key competitors?

☐ Should price play an active or passive role in your marketing program?

☐ Are there any indications that changes need to be made in your price strategy?

price flexibility that exists. Next, we examined price positioning alternatives and the extent to which price may be used as an active element in the marketing program. This was followed by a consideration of setting price objectives. Finally, price policies and price structures were discussed. These policy guidelines and price relationships establish the basis for implementing and managing price strategy.

A checklist for price planning is shown in Exhibit 8–6. It is built around the planning guide outlined in Exhibit 8–1.

NOTES

1. Bill Abrams, "Consumer-Goods Firms Turn To Price Cuts to Increase Sales," *The Wall Street Journal,* May 13, 1982, p. 37.
2. Irwin Gross, "Insights from Pricing Research," in *Pricing Practices and Strategies,* ed. E. L. Bailey (New York: The Conference Board, 1978), p. 35.
3. Jean A. Briggs, "For Whom Does the Bell Toll?" *Forbes,* June 25, 1979, pp. 34–35.
4. These and other aspects of marketing and the law are discussed in David W. Cravens, Gerald E. Hills, and Robert B. Woodruff, *Marketing Decision Making: Concepts and Strategy* (Homewood, Ill.: Richard D. Irwin, 1980), chap. 21.
5. Jeffrey A. Tannenbaum, "Picturephone Pricing Riles AT&T Rival," *The Wall Street Journal,* August 28, 1980, p. 21.
6. The following account is drawn up from "Up and Down Wall Street," *Barron's,* October 27, 1980, pp. 1, 35.
7. For an excellent examination of product line pricing, see Kent B. Monroe, *Pricing: Making Profitable Decisions* (New York: McGraw-Hill, 1979), pp. 115–19.

9

Advertising and sales planning

Promotion consists of communications to inform and persuade people in a firm's market targets, channel organizations, and the public at large. These communications consist of advertising, personal selling, sales promotion, and public relations activities. Increasingly, marketing management is finding it profitable to combine advertising, personal selling, packaging, point of purchase, direct mail, product sampling, publicity, and public relations decisions into an integrated promotion strategy for communicating with buyers and others involved in purchasing decisions. Since each promotion component has certain strengths and shortcomings, the strategy adopted should capitalize upon the advantages of every component in shaping a cost-effective communications mix. In this chapter we shall concentrate upon advertising and sales force strategies, although the approach used can be applied to select strategies for any combination of communications activities.

An example will demonstrate the critical role of promotion strategy in the overall success of a marketing strategy. Shopsmith, Inc., manufactures a multipurpose woodworking power tool. It is a combination boring machine, table saw, drill press, lathe, and disk sander. The tool was first introduced after World War II, and production was discontinued in the 1960s. In 1971, John Folkerth, a stockbroker, discovered that the tool was no longer available. Convinced of its merits, he decided to try to bring the product back into the market, and the venture offered him an opportunity to launch his own business.[1] The product was an excellent and economical tool system, but as Folkerth discovered, convincing buyers of this fact was difficult and required an effective communications and distribution strategy. Initially distributing through hardware stores, he found that buyers were not attracted to the retail

173

stores because there was no large national advertising program. Those who came into the stores for other purchases were not aware of the product, and dealers were not aggressively promoting it. Folkerth finally learned how crucial a demonstration of the tool was in convincing the potential buyer of its merits. Building his promotional strategy around this communications need, today the product is marketed using shopping mall demonstrations, by holding power tool seminars and factory demonstrations in motels, and in exhibits at home products shows. Shopsmith also has a direct-mail promotional program, and the company publishes a bimonthly magazine, *Hands-On.* By 1980, 52 percent of the company's sales came from mall demonstrations and another 33 percent from a closely related direct-mail program.[2] For the past five years sales and earnings have expanded rapidly with sales approaching $25 million in 1980 (representing about 10 percent of the market for bench power tools).

In this chapter we shall first examine the selection of a promotion strategy. Next, the major decisions that are made in choosing advertising and personal selling strategies are discussed and the factors affecting these decisions are considered. Finally, several determinants are identified that should be taken into account in deciding upon a promotional mix and adjusting it over time.

DEVELOPING A PROMOTION STRATEGY

Promotion strategy is deciding what objectives promotion will be responsible for in the marketing program positioning strategy; establishing the mix of communications; and selecting specific strategies for advertising, sales force, and sales promotion. These major steps to developing a promotion strategy are shown in Exhibit 9–1 in the sequence they should be accomplished.

Market targets and marketing mix decisions set important guidelines for promotion strategy as shown in Exhibit 9–2. These guidelines help to establish:

1. The role of promotion strategy in the marketing program.
2. The specific communications tasks to be accomplished by promotion activities.

One important question is deciding whether promotion will play a primary or supporting role in marketing strategy. Typically, advertising, personal selling, or some combination of the two is a major part of a firm's marketing strategy. When promotion is not an important part of the marketing program, this usually means that promotion of the product or service is handled by other firms in the distribution channel. For ex-

Exhibit 9–1
Steps to developing a promotion strategy

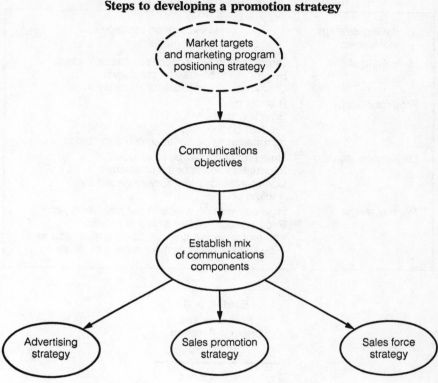

ample, producers of private label brands normally depend upon retailers for promotion activities.

Communications objectives

An essential guide to forming a promotional mix is deciding what you want the promotion to accomplish. Setting communications objectives provides the basis for selecting how advertising, personal selling, and sales promotion will be used in the marketing program. The stages of a buyer's decision process shown in Exhibit 9–3 are useful to indicate the range of communications objectives that may be selected by a firm. The arrows show the general stages through which a buyer moves from the initial recognition of a need to the point of purchase and then usage of the product or service. Let's examine each stage.

Exhibit 9–2
Illustrative guidelines for promotion strategy

Marketing strategy component	Promotion strategy guidelines
Market target	Target customers' descriptive characteristics. Buyers' decison-making processes. Customers' and prospects' information needs.
Product strategy	Product mix. Branding strategy. Product positioning. Information to be communicated to customers.
Distribution strategy	How end users will be reached. Information needs of intermediaries. Communications functions provided by intermediaries.
Price strategy	How active price will be in the marketing program. Price position relative to key competitors. Information about price to be communicated to customers and intermediaries.

Exhibit 9–3
Stages in the buyer's decision process

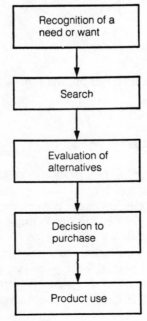

Need recognition.   One communications objective may be to trigger a need or want. New product introductions typically include promotional efforts aimed at need recognition. Promotion of word processing equipment is currently focusing on this objective. Existing products also are often promoted to encourage potential buyers to recognize a need or want. This is particularly apparent in the case of products and services for which the buyer can postpone or choose not to purchase. Consider, for example, the advertising efforts of life insurance companies. Several emphasize the consequences of not being insured in the event one should die. Personal selling as well as advertising can be used to encourage the buyer to recognize a need or want.

Gathering information.   A buyer's search for information can be aided by a firm's promotional efforts. Often one of the objectives of new product promotional activities is to assist buyers in learning about the product. Much of the initial promotional efforts used in the launching of General Motors new line of J cars in 1981 was aimed at informing potential buyers about the features of the automobiles. Aiding information search activities is a function where advertising may be more cost effective than personal selling, particularly when the information can be supplied via electronic or printed media. For example, television advertising can expose 1,000 viewers to a message for less than $10 whereas the average cost of an industrial sales call on one customer is over $100.

Evaluation of alternatives.   At this stage of the buyer's decision process, promotional communications can be used to help the buyer choose among alternative products or brands. Comparative advertising is sometimes used for this purpose. Personal selling can also be effective in demonstrating a brand's strengths over competing brands. For example, in late 1980 the Drackett Co., the maker of Vanish toilet bowl cleaners, was preparing to launch a multimillion dollar campaign against some of its competitors, alleging that their products may be unsafe.[3] Drackett, a business unit of the Bristol-Myers Co., was attacking the automatic toilet cleaners that used the chemical, hypochlorate, arguing that these cleaners could destroy plastic, rubber, and even metal plumbing fixtures if toilets were not flushed regularly. Critics argued that Drackett's promotional strategy was aimed at regaining lost market share.

Decision to purchase.   The primary objective of door-to-door selling organizations, such as Avon, is to close sales. These highly programmed approaches to personal selling are aimed at encouraging the buyer to decide to purchase the product. Point-of-purchase advertising, such as displays in retail stores, are also intended to encourage the purchase decision. One of the advantages of personal selling over advertising is its flexibility in responding to the buyer's objectives and questions.

Product use. Increasingly, companies are finding that communications with buyers after purchase are important promotional activities. Follow-up by salespeople with their customers, advertisements stressing a firm's service capabilities, and 800 numbers placed on packages to encourage users to report problems are illustrative of postpurchase communications.

As you can see by our brief discussion of the different objectives that promotional effort may be directed toward, there are many uses of promotion in a marketing program positioning strategy. These uses will vary according to the stage of the buyer's decision process that marketing management wants to influence, the maturity of the product-market, the role of promotion in the marketing program, and various other influences.

Mix of communications components

Referring to Exhibit 9–1, the mix of advertising, sales promotion, and sales force strategies represents the choice of how resources will be allocated among these areas. Management must select the size of the promotion budget and decide how much to allocate to each communications component. An illustrative comparison of the unique strengths of advertising and personal selling is shown in Exhibit 9–4. While they share several common characteristics, each has some unique advantages. Perhaps the greatest distinction between the two is the *mass* orientation of advertising versus the *one-on-one* nature of personal selling.

An example will demonstrate how the communications mix is determined for a particular business situation. The choice of a promotion mix in a small firm is particularly challenging due to the firm's resource limitations. Consider, for example, Mercury Savings and Loan Association located in southern California.[4] Founded in 1964 by Leonard Shane, Mercury's assets had grown to $850 million by 1981. By industry standards, Shane developed an unusual promotional mix. Let's examine his strategy:

☐ The target market consisted of suburban households, thus concentrating Mercury's operations away from major financial centers where the large and strong financial institutions were heavily concentrated.
☐ Shane decided to use door-to-door contact as the firm's major promotion component, a rare practice in an industry where advertising accounts for a major part of the marketing budget.

Exhibit 9–4
Illustrative comparison of advertising and personal selling strengths

Unique strengths of advertising	Common features	Unique strengths of personal selling
Low cost per exposure when there is a good match between target audience and media.	Create awareness of the product or service.	Interact with the buyer to answer questions and overcome objections.
Opportunity for creative design of message.	Transmit information.	Locate and concentrate upon individual buyers or very small target groups.
Content of communications is consistent across target audience.	Persuade.	Cannot be rapidly copied by competition.
Easily adjustable to new communications objectives.	Resource requirements are often substantial.	Capacity to accumulate market knowledge and provide feedback.

☐ Part-time school teachers were trained to call on households in each branch trading area, informing people about the association and inviting them to come by the branch for their free personalized memo sheets.

☐ Savings counselors were carefully trained to provide prompt and friendly services to customers and prospects.

☐ Mercury also encouraged community groups to use its meeting room for luncheon meetings hosted by the association. The only promotional effort by Mercury consisted of the offer to make memo sheets for everyone.

While there are many other specific features of Mercury's marketing and promotion strategy, from this brief description you can easily see the main components of the communications mix. Perhaps the best statement of the strategy is in Shane's own words: "We will not meet the giants on their battlefield using their weapons; rather we will seek our own arena and fashion our own tools."[5] This statement is the essence of a sound marketing program positioning strategy. Mercury's management developed an effective way to communicate with its target customers. We should emphasize that Mercury's choice of direct contact rather than heavy use of advertising media is not a promotion strategy appropriate for all firms. Rather, the example highlights the importance of selecting the proper promotion mix for a given situation. We shall return to a discussion of the factors that affect the choice of a promotion mix later in the chapter after examining advertising and selling strategies.

ADVERTISING AND SALES PROMOTION STRATEGY

Beginning with the definition of the target audience, the steps in developing an advertising strategy are shown in Exhibit 9–5. The role and scope of advertising should be established including an approximate range as to how much can be budgeted for advertising. Specific objectives should be set for advertising to accomplish. The creative strategy represents the way the objectives will be accomplished, while the media and programming schedule are used to implement the creative strategy. Finally, the advertising program must be implemented and adjusted over time. Let's examine each of the steps in developing an advertising strategy.

Exhibit 9–5
Steps in developing an advertsing strategy

1. Describe and analyze the target audience.
2. Determine the role of advertising in the promotional mix.
3. Indicate advertising objectives and size the advertising budget.
4. Select the creative strategy to be used.
5. Determine media and programming schedule.
6. Implement and manage the advertising program.

Since we considered the target market in Chapter 4, we shall comment only briefly upon it here. One of the most important considerations is that the end user does not always represent the audience toward which advertising is directed. For example, Johnson & Johnson, the maker of Tylenol, did not advertise to consumers until forced to do so in the mid-1970s when Datril entered the market. For several years, Tylenol had been promoted using printed media that reached physicians and dentists. Thus, it is essential in designing an advertising strategy to identify the individuals and organizations that may influence sales to end users. Communications to these points of influence may represent essential parts of the promotional program.

Role, objectives, and budget for advertising

Determining what effect advertising will have on market response is one of management's most demanding tasks. Estimating advertising's impact on buyers is the basis for deciding the role and scope of advertising in the marketing program and for choosing the specific objectives for which advertising will be responsible. Management's perceptions about what advertising can do also weigh heavily upon the decision as to how large the advertising budget will be.

Advertising's role in marketing strategy. We saw in Exhibit 9–4 several of advertising's unique strengths. There is a tendency among marketing professionals to argue that firms with industrial products concentrate budgets more heavily upon personal selling than advertising, whereas just the opposite occurs in consumer products firms. Many exceptions can be found in this pattern, which suggests that more basic determinants may affect the role of advertising in a particular firm. A study that utilized the PIMS (profit impact of marketing strategy) data bank may be useful in locating some of the factors that underly advertising's role in marketing strategy. Using a sample of 789 businesses that spent at least 0.01 percent of sales on advertising and promotion, Farris and Buzzell found the following factors present in firms with higher advertising and promotion to sales ratios compared to other firms in the sample with lower ratios.

☐ Standardized products.
☐ Many end users.
☐ Typical purchase amount is small.
☐ Auxilliary services important.
☐ Sales through channel organizations.
☐ Premium-priced product.
☐ Manufacturer's contribution margin is high.
☐ Relatively small market share and/or surplus production capacity.
☐ High proportion of sales from new products.[6]

Although the analysis, using multiple regression, describes existing relationships rather than indicating what they should be, it represents a large cross section of firms. The factors found linked to high advertising and promotion expenditures appear to offer useful guides to examining the role and scope of advertising in contrast to the consumer and industrial products distinction that is often recommended.

Advertising objectives. Alternative levels for setting advertising objectives are shown in Exhibit 9–6. Moving from the lowest level (exposure) toward the highest level (profit contribution) represents objectives that are increasingly closer to the purchase decision. For example, knowing that advertising has caused a measurable increase in sales is much more useful to the decision maker than saying that advertising exposed a specific number of people to an advertising message. The important question, of course, is the extent to which the lower levels shown in Exhibit 9–6 are linked to purchase behavior. For example, will people that are more aware of a brand be more likely to purchase it? In contrast, achievement of lower and midlevel objectives often can be measured whereas those at the top of Exhibit 9–6 often cannot be measured.

Exhibit 9–6
Alternative levels for setting
advertising objectives

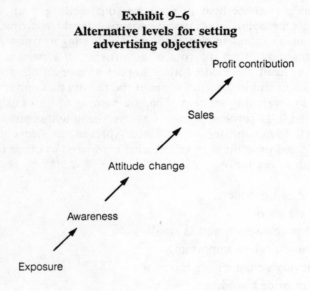

Let's look for a moment at the *awareness* level. There is research evidence that brand awareness does lead to increased market share and in turn to greater profits. The results of a study conducted by the Strategic Planning Institute involving 73 industrial-products businesses supports the linkage between brand awareness, sales, and profits.[7] There is also some support for the linkage of attitude change to sales and profits. Exposure measures of advertising effectiveness are much more subject to debate and are more useful in guiding media allocation decisions than in gauging the value of advertising to a firm.

Budget determination. There are several methods that are used to determine how much to spend on advertising. An overview of the major approaches to budget determination is provided in Exhibit 9–7. Since the essential characteristics of all of the approaches except models should be easily understood, we shall concentrate our attention upon budgeting models. A brief look at one promising budgeting model will show the potential of models for use in budgeting. Adviser 2, a comprehensive marketing mix budgeting model developed for industrial products, can be used to set a marketing budget and then split it into budgets for personal and impersonal (e.g., advertising) communications.[8] Adviser is a multiple regression-type model which incorporates several predictor variables including number of users, customer concentration, fraction of sales made to order, attitude difference, proportion of direct sales, life-cycle stage, product plans, and product complexity. The model is similar in concept and approach to the PIMS model, although Adviser concentrates upon the marketing budget and its components, rather than offering complete strategies for business units or products.

Exhibit 9–7
Approaches to advertising budget determination

Method	Features	Limitations
Percent of sales	Budget is determined by using fixed percent of sales, often based on past expenditure patterns.	The method is very arbitrary and may yield a budget that is too high when sales are high and too low when sales are low.
Comparative parity	Budget is based largely upon what competition is doing.	There may be other differences in marketing strategy that require different budget levels.
Objective and task	Set objectives and then determine tasks (and costs) necessary to meet the objectives.	The major issue in using this method is deciding the right objectives, so measurement of results is important.
Budgeting models	Budget is determined by a computational model, often developed from analysis of historical data.	Are the relationships found in the model correct, and if so, will they apply in the future?

Creative strategy

The creative theme binds together the various parts of an advertising campaign. The choice of a successful creative strategy spells success for an advertising agency. Agencies, who receive 15 percent of gross billings by media to advertiser, are experts in the design of creative strategies. Possible strategies may range from copying the competition to unique themes designed to position a product or firm in some particular way. Consider, for example, the use of unknown people as the highlight of Dewar's Scotch whiskey advertisements in the late 1970s. The objective was to associate profiles of people in various successful roles who like Dewar's whiskey. Dewar's profile ads placed on the back covers of leading magazines, using an annual ad budget in 1978 of $3 million, helped to push the brand from fourth position in the United States to number two, right behind J&B.[9] The people whose profiles were placed in the ads each received five cases of Dewar's as compensation.

Let's examine the creative strategy used by Helen Curtis Industries to promote its Suave line of consumer hair-care products from an also-ran to a market leader.[10] The essence of the strategy was to offer lower-priced imitations of leading high-priced shampoos, aggressively promoted with ads comparing Suave to its competition. While one can question how creative the Curtis strategy really is, perhaps the best measure is how well it works. Gauged against a performance yardstick, Suave's sales and market share gains were impressive, moving from less than 1 percent of shampoo dollar sales in 1972 to the leading market position in volume by 1976. The theme of the campaign was simple, yet effective—"We do what theirs does for less than half the price," and competitors were either named or their brands shown in the ads. The choice of a creative strategy is often a vital determinant in the success or failure of an advertising strategy. Choosing the right theme for the marketing situation can make a major contribution to the success of a program. While tests can be used to evaluate creative approaches, the task is far more an art than a science.

Media/programming strategy

The experience and judgment of the advertising agency should guide media and programming decisions. The agency has the necessary experience and technical ability for matching media and programming to the target audience specified by the firm; often marketing management does not. Let's look at the media/programming strategy of a particular firm. Tootsie Roll Industries' 1980 advertising program is described:

During 1980 we had the most extensive advertising program we have had in our history. Television advertising accounted for the largest part of this advertising program. We have been increasing our advertising on national television since 1952. During 1980, we attained the heaviest TV coverage in our history. Tootsie Roll commercials appeared on television every week of the year.

Our programming is directed at a wide range of consumers and appeared on many types of television shows. We included in our programming variety shows, musicals, news, movies, sporting events, daytime and game shows.

During 1980, we used several different commercials for our television programs. We aired such commercials as: "Cow Fable" for Tootsie Pops; "Jingle" for Tootsie Rolls; "You're a Cool One" for Tootsie Mason Mints, and "Bird" for Tootsie Pop Drops. We also introduced our newest commercial "Give Your Tootsie a Tootsie" which was written to sell the "Tootsie Family Candy Store" program, a rack display promoting a variety of our Tootsie Roll products.

In addition to our TV commercials, we continued our successful program of offering cents-off coupons on Tootsie Roll products. An increasing number of coupons was distributed during this past year due to the fact that price conscious consumers are redeeming more coupons.[11]

Note the use of various media, types of shows, programming decisions, and the commercials used.

The choice of media, timing, and programming are influenced largely by two factors: (1) access to the target audience(s), and (2) costs of alternative ways of reaching target groups. Suppose that you are interested in reaching business executives through printed media. Possible publications and approximate costs for one-page advertisements are:

U.S. News & World Report (weekly)	$22,000
Fortune (monthly)	16,000
Harvard Business Review (6 per year)	4,000
The Wall Street Journal (daily)	4,000

Source: *Consumer Magazine and Farm Publication Rates and Data,* January 27, 1980, pp. 34, 86, 352, 355.

The cost differences are based upon circulation levels and type of publications. In making the media decision, the cost per exposure and the characteristics of subscribers should be evaluated.

To gain some idea as to the cost and scope of an advertising campaign, let's examine the promotion of Broadway stage shows. In recent years television has become a popular and effective means to promote shows. Budgeting for a typical musical is as follows:

> Mr. LeDonne recommends that his clients set aside $250,000 for pre-opening night publicity and $15,000 to $30,000 a week after the show opens. Commercials cost between $50,000 and $125,000 to produce including talent fees and often take the biggest chunk of pre-opening night publicity.
>
> After the initial campaign in which the commercial might be on the air 30 times a week, at a cost of between $10,000 and $25,000 for local network time, the frequency slows, and the time spots can be reduced to as little as 10 seconds.[12]

Television campaigns are normally used to promote musicals since they have larger budgets than other shows. News programs are favored for running commercials.

Implementation and management

The discussion of several issues in advertising by an industry veteran in Exhibit 9–8 offers some interesting insights about the industry, key issues in advertising strategy, and some recommended guidelines for management. Setting objectives is critical to determining the effect of advertising and deciding when to stop or alter a campaign. As illustrated by the Pert shampoo example, management should follow through with tracking methods to measure effectiveness. Another important point discussed in Exhibit 9–8 is knowing when to reduce and even stop advertising.

In concluding our discussion of advertising strategy, it is important to note that advertising is only one part of a marketing program, so the advertising program should be designed based on the role it is to play in marketing strategy. Also important is the fact that the *quality* of advertising can be as instrumental to getting results as is the *quantity* of advertising.

SELLING STRATEGY

An illustration of how a new company developed its selling strategy into a powerful marketing force will provide an overview of what selling strategy is all about. The company, unfamiliar to most people, has grown at a fantastic rate from the time its product line was first introduced in 1967. Sales should reach $200 million in 1983! U.S. Surgical's primary line of products consists of staplers, but they are not used to fasten two pieces of paper together. The product is used by a surgeon as

Exhibit 9–8
Industry veteran challenges conventional wisdom on ads

Fifty-five billion dollars was spent on advertising in the United States last year. A lot of it, says Gus Priemer, was spent wastefully and unscientifically, "polluting" consumers' minds and driving up advertising costs.

Mr. Priemer has spent 29 years and hundreds of millions of dollars buying advertising, first for Procter & Gamble and for the past 17 years at S. C. Johnson & Son, the consumer products company usually known as Johnson's Wax. His assessment of his profession: "Most advertising today is unproductive. It has become a kind of routine, a habit, a custom."

Five years ago TV commercial prices began climbing at unprecedented rates. Mr. Priemer, Johnson's advertising services director and overseer of its $50 million ad budget, began rethinking industry tradition. "We needed some new ground rules," he recalls. "I got tired of saying, 'Let's just cut the ads to a smaller size or run them less often.'"

He began to experiment with new approaches. "A lot of us just sit in ivory towers and hypothesize," says Jules Fine, executive vice president of Ogilvy & Mather, an ad agency for Johnson. "Gus goes out and does research."

Mr. Priemer's conclusions: Advertisers and their agencies have too much faith in advertising, use the wrong definitions of productivity, and offer little incentive to budget less—rather than more—for advertising. "Corporate managements need to act more responsibly," he says, "toward the investment of their advertising."

Most marketing executives agree that a causal link between advertising and sales never has been proven definitively. Thus, maintains Mr. Priemer, ad budgets are based largely on faith. "Executives go on the assumption that advertising is doing something," he says, "just like praying or going to church is doing something."

Often overlooked are the effects of distribution, sales promotion, product design, packaging, or pricing. A common belief, says Mr. Priemer, is: "If sales are okay, then advertising must be working. If sales are bad, the advertising must be bad."

Instead, he says, executives should ask: "What am I trying to make happen with this advertising that wouldn't happen without it? What evidence do I have that a campaign is working?"

Mr. Priemer says most companies accept "substitute evidence"; the number of consumers an ad reaches, the frequency with which they are reached, and the effect advertising has on their awareness of and attitudes toward the product. "Advertisers spend as much as they can afford to spend," he says. "They don't ask how much is needed to do the job."

Mr. Priemer contends that most ad executives—himself included—customarily have defined advertising productivity incorrectly as a gain in the number of consumer exposures per advertising dollar spent. "I'm one of the big wasters of the last two decades because I've bought more efficiently than most people," he acknowledges. "If I delivered 20 messages to a person, I counted them all as having value. I didn't count any of them as waste."

If there were specific goals for ads, says Mr. Priemer, companies would

Exhibit 9–8 *(concluded)*

know when to stop or change their campaigns. One of his studies of a competitor's product shows how to test when advertising reaches its goal.

Analyzing commercials for Procter & Gamble's Pert shampoo, which was introduced in test markets in Nashville and Milwaukee in 1979, he theorized that the company's goal was to familiarize women with the benefit Pert claimed—"bouncin' and behavin'" hair. From the day Pert commercials began women were polled regularly to determine if they could identify a shampoo that claimed to leave hair "bouncin' and behavin'."

Eventually the number of women familiar with Pert peaked, indicating to Mr. Priemer that the advertising had "completed its task." Procter & Gamble spent more on advertising in Nashville, but Pert's market share was higher in Milwaukee. His conclusion: "Higher spending wasn't productive."

Product performance, not advertising, counts when consumers make purchases; ads should tell shoppers what they might not know about a brand. If ads for an established product have "nothing new to say," Mr. Priemer suggests, they might be stopped altogether. "There'd be greater stimulus to find improvements for that product."

Johnson applies that standard to many of its own products, which include Pledge furniture polish, Glade air fresheners, Raid insecticides, and Edge shaving gel. Television commercials for Glade, for example, stopped in 1977, but Johnson has increased sales by introducing new scents.

Cutting budgets isn't always easy, Mr. Priemer says. Agencies haven't any incentive to spend less. And product managers and company ad executives often equate ad budgets with importance. "If someone recommends spending less money," says Mr. Priemer, "he's looked on as being not aggressive."

Even chief executives, he says, like to see advertising increase. "The CEO likes to see his commercials on TV and talk at cocktail parties about how much advertising he's doing."

Financial executives—frequently scorned as nitpickers by marketers— "often have an instinct that there's something wrong," says Mr. Priemer. "They can recognize a lot of the jargon for what it is, but they don't know how to cut through it."

Source: Bill Abrams, *The Wall Street Journal*, April 9, 1981, p. 31. Reprinted by permission. © Dow Jones & Co., Inc. 1981. All rights reserved.

an alternative to a needle and thread to close tissue openings in patients during and upon completion of an operation.

Perhaps what is most remarkable about this amazing success story is the intuition of the founder of the company and current president, Leon C. Hirsch, in recognizing the potential market for a surgical stapler. Hirsch's intuition is described in the following:

> Why not a disposable cartridge for the staples inside a reusable staple gun? That would make it far quicker and easier to use. He got the names

of three prominent U.S. surgeons who had used the old European "shille-lagh" staplers. He went down to the basement of his house and out of balsa wood made such a cartridge-loaded stapler with a few other refinements. It worked. Two Johns Hopkins surgery professors . . . showed keen interest in Hirsch's prototype and offered to test the stapler free when it was in finished form.[13]

U.S. Surgical offers 10 types of reusable surgical stapling instruments and 32 types of disposable loading units (DLU), or cartridges. The prices in 1981 for reusable surgical staplers ranged from $409 to $1,284 per instrument, and the disposable loading units ranged from $157 to $921 per dozen.[14]

While the product is expensive compared with needle and thread, the stapler represents a very attractive alternative on a cost-benefit basis. The mechanical application and the functional advantages reduce operating time as well as anesthesia time. The reduction of tissue handling and the reduction of blood loss also shortens the hospital stay.

After experiencing problems in getting surgeons to purchase and use surgical staples, Hirsch eventually realized the importance of developing corporate and marketing strategies for delivering customer satisfaction. The strategy that worked represented several trial-and-error attempts. At the heart of the problem was the fact that U.S. Surgical was not just marketing a new product but rather offering a completely new approach to tissue joining and closure. The company's challenge was in many ways similar to that of International Business Machines when the company first began producing and marketing computers. The marketing approach that was successful eventually is described below:

> U.S. Surgical's strength lies in its unique marketing methods. Proper use of the company's instruments requires detailed instructions and technical support. These functions are assigned to the company's sales force, which is given a 240-hour training program covering basic anatomy, physiology, surgical terminology, scrubbing and gowning, and operating room protocol, in addition to the operation of the company's products. Besides giving demonstrations to operating room personnel, a company salesperson often guides surgeons during initial operative procedures.[15]

Thus, we see the importance of understanding users' needs and wants and understanding how they use the product as well. Personal selling is the main part of U.S. Surgical's promotion strategy. Interestingly, it required nearly a decade of development to finally arrive at a successful and cost-effective selling strategy.

The major steps in developing a sales force strategy are shown in Exhibit 9–9. First, management must describe and analyze the people/organizations to be contacted by the sales force. U.S. Surgical's management aimed its sales force primarily at surgeons, and by failing

Exhibit 9-9
Steps in developing a sales force strategy

1. Describe and analyze the people/organizations to be contacted by the sales force.
2. Decide the role and scope of the sales force in the promotional mix.
3. Set sales force objectives.
4. Determine size and deployment of the sales force.
5. Recruit, train, and manage the sales force.

to recognize the importance of other medical personnel, allowed a competitor to gain a major position in the skin stapling market:

> Ethicon out-marketed USSC by focusing on operating room supervisors, who control noncritical purchasing—into which category skin products fall. USSC salesmen, by contrast, were focusing on surgeons, who alone control purchase of the less competitive internal stapling products. USSC's preoccupation was understandable, since its backorder problems in skin products made it more productive to concentrate on internals.[16]

Understanding the buyer provides the basis for deciding the role and scope of the sales force. Next, management must indicate exactly what the sales organization is expected to accomplish. This decision is followed by setting the size of the sales force and then deploying people to appropriate work units such as geographical sales territories. Finally, sales management's most demanding responsibility in terms of time consumption is recruiting, training, and managing the sales force. We turn now to a look at each of the decision areas shown in Exhibit 9-9.

Role and objectives

The role of personal selling in a firm can range from being the major component of marketing strategy, as in the case of U.S. Surgical, to a minor role, as in the case of many consumer products firms. The functions of salespeople span all the way from serving primarily as order takers to fulfilling major responsibilities as consultants to customers. While management has some flexibility in choosing the role of the sales force in the marketing mix, several factors often help to shape the role of selling. The factors include the size and importance of the purchase, complexity of the product, the buyer's information needs, and the number and location of buyers. Since these same factors affect decisions concerning the role of advertising, we shall delay further discussion until we consider selecting a promotion strategy later in the chapter.

The objectives assigned to salespeople frequently are concerned with sales results that are expected by management. Sales quotas are popular means of expressing sales expectations, and often incentive compensation is linked to quota achievement. There may be objectives other than sales that are also important in a particular organization. Examples include increasing the number of new accounts, providing services to customers and channel organizations, and obtaining market information. The objectives that are selected should be consistent with marketing program objectives, and they should be measurable so that sales performance can be evaluated.

Size and deployment decisions

Resource allocation decisions have an important influence upon the productivity of a sales organization. These decisions are similar to those made concerning equipment needed in production operations. The operations manager must decide how many machines are needed and where each will be placed. The sales manager must decide how many salespeople are needed and how they shall be deployed. The major distinction between the two decisions is that estimating the productivity of salespeople is far more complex than estimating the output of machines.

The problem in estimating sales force productivity is that often various factors not under the control of the salesperson are partially responsible for the results that are obtained in the work unit assigned to the salesperson. This is shown in Exhibit 9–10. Influences such as market potential, size and location of customers, intensity of competition, and

Exhibit 9–10
Illustrative impact of
salesperson upon the
results obtained in
the work unit

Portion of results due to salesperson (qualifications and effort)
Portion of results due to factors other than the salesperson

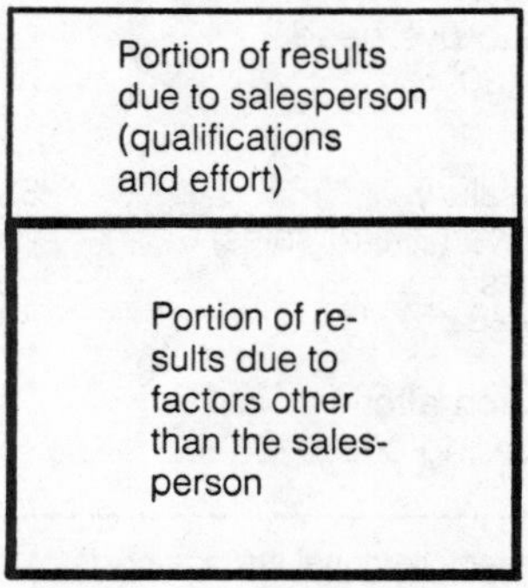

company market position may account for a substantial portion of sales results in a territory. Productivity analysis should take into account both the salesperson and uncontrollable factors.

There are several methods for analyzing sales force size and deployment. All fall into three categories: (1) revenue/cost analyses, (2) single-factor models, and (3) sales response models. Let's look at the three approaches to gain some idea of their features, strengths, and limitations. We are assuming that sales and/or costs are the basis for determining sales force size and allocation.

Revenue/cost analysis. Most of these techniques require information on sales and/or costs by individual salespeople, so if this informa-

Exhibit 9–11
**Illustrative revenue/cost methods of sales force
size/deployment analysis**

A. Break-even comparisons

Break-even
sales
volume
(average)

Territory number

B. Profit contribution of adding a salesperson

Estimated sales		$400,000
Contribution to overhead and profit (20%)		80,000*
Less:		
Base salary	35,000	
Incentive (2% of sales)	8,000	
Benefits	5,000	
Expenses	5,000	53,000
Net contribution after personal selling costs		27,000

*Before deducting direct personal sellings costs.

tion is not available, the techniques cannot be used. Two popular methods of sales force analysis are shown in Exhibit 9–11. Method A can be used to compare a sales force to an average break-even sales level. This is useful in spotting territories that are not profitable, thus directing management's attention to finding out why the territories are below break-even productivity levels. Method B can be used to analyze the profit performance of an existing work unit, to estimate the profit impact of adding one or more salespeople to an organization, or to determine how many people should be included in a new sales organization.

The major value of sales and cost analysis methods is to gauge existing or future productivity of salespeople. If the necessary information is available or can be collected, these techniques are very useful in locating high- and low-performance territories. Their main limitation is that the analyses do not indicate why one territory is doing better or worse than another. Management must provide this assessment using other available information plus judgment and experience.

Single-factor models. These approaches share one common feature. Each assumes that size and/or deployment is determined by one factor such as market potential, workload (e.g., number of calls required for customers and prospects), or other factors whose value can be used to determine required selling effort. An example will help to illustrate how these methods are used. Suppose that we have two territories, X and Y. Territory X has double the market potential (opportunity for business) that is in territory Y. Assuming selling effort is to be deployed according to market potential, X should be assigned double the selling effort that Y receives. Clearly, the emphasis here is upon the opportunity present in the work unit.

The single-factor models are easy to use, and when the proper factor is selected, they offer useful, although very rough, guides to effort allocation. Their main deficiency is that often several factors may be necessary to determine the amount of selling effort needed for a customer, product, territory, or other assigned work unit. For example, the use of only market potential fails to recognize other influences on sales results, such as the intensity of competition, composition of accounts and prospects, and market position.

Sales and effort models. Several promising models for aiding size and deployment decisions were developed during the last decade. One of their main strengths is the use of multiple determinants of sales response to guide effort allocation. The starting point is a model of market (sales) response to selling effort. This involves determining the relationship between sales and selling effort using historical data or subjective estimates of the sales force. Next, the response model is used with an effort allocation model to generate recommended deployment guidelines. This can be done for an existing sales force size, or alternative sizes above and below the present size can be examined to select an optimal size.

An illustrative output of these models is shown in Exhibit 9–12. The analysis indicates that Jones's territory requires only little more than one third of a person whereas Smith's territory can support about 2.36 people. Essentially, the way these models handle allocation is to increase selling effort in high-response areas and reduce effort where sales response is low. Note that Exhibit 9–12 includes only two members of a sales organization. A complete analysis of all territories would show that the sum of present effort is equal to the sum of recommended effort.

Of all the approaches to sales force size and deployment analysis, the sales and effort models are the most promising since they overcome many of the limitations of the other approaches we have been discussing. When you consider even modest allocation improvements in a sales force of 100 or more people, the payoffs from model applications can be substantial. Suppose that the use of a model leads to a 10 percent improvement in allocation of selling effort for a sales force of 100 people and that estimated total costs per salesperson are about $50,000.

Exhibit 9–12
Illustrative sales force decision model output for
Jones's and Smith's territories

	Trading area†	Present effort (percent)	Recommended effort (percent)	Estimated sales*	
				Present effort	Recommended effort
Jones:	1	10	4	19	13
	2	60	20	153	120
	3	15	7	57	50
	4	5	2	10	7
	5	10	3	21	16
Total		100	36	260	206
Smith:	1	18	81	370	520
	2	7	21	100	130
	3	5	11	55	65
	4	35	35	225	225
	5	5	11	60	70
	6	30	77	400	500
Total		100	236	1,210	1,510

*In $000.
†Each territory is made up of several trading areas.

Such an improvement could yield $500,000! We should note that the initial costs of model development are substantial although considerably less than the $500,000 saving cited above.

Sales force management and control

In our discussion of size and deployment, we assumed that, on the average, all salespeople are the same. This, of course, is not true. Nevertheless, it is useful to look at salespeople as if they are machines when making size and deployment decisions. After doing this, management has a basis for moving next to the important personnel management aspects of managing the sales force. These activities fall into the areas of:

☐ Finding and selecting salespeople.
☐ Training and development of sales and sales management personnel.
☐ Supervising and motivating salespeople.
☐ Evaluating and controlling selling operations.

Finding and selecting salespeople. Determining what criteria to use in selecting salespeople is one of the most debated issues among sales managers. The objective, of course, is to select people whose performance will be high while avoiding the hiring of overqualified people. There are many situation-specific factors that must be considered in the selection of salespeople. Exhibit 9–13 provides a useful overview of several characteristics that seem to have important ties to performance. Note that the characteristics vary considerably between different types of selling jobs, so management must first define the job to be performed. Churchill, Ford, and Walker comment upon criteria for selecting salespeople:

> . . . each sales executive must try to develop his or her own specifications concerning what to look for in new sales recruits. Those specifications should be developed after careful analysis and description of the tasks and activities involved in selling the firm's products to its target market. There should also be an evaluation of the characteristics and qualifications that new salespeople must have to perform those tasks and activities.[17]

Although there is a great amount of experience and judgment that guides the decision to hire a particular salesperson, several tools are used to assist management in the selection decision. These include application forms, personal interviews, rating forms, reference checks, and other tools. The personal interview is the single most important part of the selection process in most firms.

Exhibit 9–13

Characteristics related to sales performance in different types of sales jobs

Type of sales job	Characteristics that are relatively important	Characteristics that are relatively less important
Trade selling	Age, maturity, empathy, knowledge of customer needs and business methods	Aggressiveness, technical ability, product knowledge, persuasiveness
Missionary selling	Youth, high energy and stamina, verbal skill, persuasiveness	Empathy, knowledge of customers, maturity, previous sales experience
Technical selling	Education, product and customer knowledge—usually gained through training, intelligence	Empathy, persuasiveness, aggressiveness, age
New business selling	Experience, age and maturity, aggressiveness, persuasiveness, persistence	Customer knowledge, product knowledge, education, empathy

Source: Gilbert A. Churchill, Jr., Neil M. Ford, and Orville C. Walker, Jr., *Sales Force Management* (Homewood, Ill.: Richard D. Irwin, 1981), p. 290.

Training. Sales training is intended to accomplish one or more of the following objectives:

1. Increase productivity.
2. Improve morale.
3. Lower turnover.
4. Improve customer relations.
5. Produce better management of time and territory.[18]

Since the costs of training can be large, management should carefully evaluate training costs against benefits. In most firms, the importance of training is acknowledged, yet gauging its impact upon performance is difficult. Product training is probably more widespread than any other type of training.

Supervision and motivation. The prevailing position taken by sales management professionals is that financial compensation is by far the most important motivating force behind selling effort. Compensation is clearly a key element in motivating salespeople. However, recent research findings suggest that the linkage between motivation and possible determinants is not explained by money alone. Personal characteristics, environmental conditions, and company policies and procedures may also contribute directly and indirectly to the motivation of salespeople.[19]

Evaluation and control. It is necessary to have one or more yardsticks against which salesperson performance can be evaluated. Evaluation is most difficult when qualitative factors are used. For example, a regional food processor distributes through grocery wholesalers and large retail chains. The sales force devotes most of its selling effort to calling on retailers. The firm does not have information on sales of its products by individual retail outlet. Evaluation is made by a rating of several qualitative criteria by management. This type of evaluation is highly subjective and judgmental.

SELECTING A PROMOTION STRATEGY

Now that we have looked at advertising and personal selling strategies, we need to consider further the decision as to how each should be combined into a promotion strategy.

Several factors which may affect the design of a promotion strategy are shown in Exhibit 9–14. As you read the following description of

Exhibit 9–14
Factors affecting the design of promotion strategy

1. Number and characteristics of buyers.
2. The information needs of the target market.
3. Size and importance of the purchase.
4. Characteristics of the product.
5. The firm's resources.
6. Communications features of each promotion component.
7. Cost and effectiveness analysis.
8. Positioning against key competitors.

Zales's decision to become a national advertiser on television and radio, note how the factors in Exhibit 9–14 point heavily toward the promotion strategy adopted by Zales.

After debating the idea for years, the nation's biggest jewelry retailer decided to become a national advertiser on television and radio this fall. But before it did, Zales, the Dallas jewelry unit of Zale Corp., needed to know about people's perceptions of jewelry stores. From an extensive marketing study, it learned that a lot of people worry whether jewelers give them their money's worth.

"The thread of anxiety about purchasing jewelry ran through practically all interviews," says Robert McEnany, a vice president of Zales's outside advertising firm, The Bloom Agency. "We have to build an image of trust and confidence. We're aiming to be Middle America's authority on jewelry."

Zales's new ads reflect this image. As a globe spins in space in a television commercial, diamonds glint off various continents. A British-accented voice assures in soft tones that Zales keeps a close eye on its diamonds from the moment they are unearthed halfway around the world until they come to rest in local stores. Radio spot ads also are designed to soothe potential customers.

For Zales, which calls itself "The Diamond Store," national television and radio advertising is supposed to provide a way of getting more for its money. The company decided that a scattering of local TV, radio and newspaper ads wasn't sufficient for its more than 780 stores nationwide. The order went out to increase Zales's visibility and media advertising budget.

Zales and Bloom found that, with a 62 percent increase in the jeweler's annual media-advertising budget to $18.7 million, Zales could buy local television spots in 73 major markets, a 38 percent increase from the 53 markets allowed by the old budget. But by going to the national television networks, the same amount of money could buy 183 major market areas. "We can buy national coverage that converges on all markets for less than buying each market individually," says Donald Zale, vice chairman and chief executive officer of Zale Corp. "You just have to be in enough markets to make it worthwhile."[20]

The large number of buyers for jewelry, their information needs (anxiety about purchasing jewelry), the firm's ability to launch a national advertising campaign, and the capability of advertising to cost-effectively communicate with the target market all favor advertising as a major component of the promotion strategy used by Zales.

In contrast to Zales, the Boeing Co. uses high-level, executive selling as the primary means of promoting the firm's commercial aircraft. There are only a few customers (commercial airlines), orders are huge ($3 billion from Delta Air Lines for the new 757 jet), the product is complex, requiring the tailoring of communications to individual customers, and on a cost-effectiveness basis, personal selling ranks ahead of advertising. While Zales and Boeing represent two extremes, we should note that each utilizes both advertising and personal selling. Yet the two activities perform quite different roles in these firms. And we should recognize that there are several situations where neither selling nor advertising dominate promotion strategy, and instead they are balanced at about equal levels. Finally, there are many situations where management may find that advertising and personal selling are good substitutes for each other.

CONCLUDING NOTE

Promotion is the most visable part of marketing strategy since advertising, personal selling, and other promotional activities are the primary means of communication with customers and prospects in target markets. By 1981 the number of salespeople in the United States was approaching 10 million, and the combined expenditures for advertising and selling were $150 billion or more! In this chapter we have provided guidelines for determining the mix of promotional elements and for designing advertising and personal selling strategies. Our emphasis has been on the strategic aspects of promotion rather than managerial and tactical decision areas. Thus, there are many specific aspects of these important areas of marketing that we have not considered.

A manager's checklist for advertising and personal selling planning is shown in Exhibit 9–15.

Exhibit 9–15
Manager's checklist for advertising and personal selling planning

□ How does promotion fit into your marketing program plan?

□ What are the communications objectives assigned to promotion in your firm?

□ What objectives are assigned to:

    1. Advertising?
    2. Personal selling?
    3. Sales promotion?

□ Is there a plan spelling out how each promotion component is to meet its objectives?

□ Is your promotion program effective in carrying out the communications objectives?

□ Should resources be shifted between promotion components (e.g., spend more on sales force and less on advertising)?

□ Are promotion expenditures adequate for accomplishing the assigned objectives?

NOTES

1. This account is based, in part, upon Geoffrey Smith, "Phoenix," *Forbes*, April 14, 1980, pp. 122, 123, 125.
2. Ibid., pp. 123, 125.
3. Bill Abrams, "Firm Embarks on Risky Course with Ad Attack on Competition," *The Wall Street Journal*, December 11, 1980, p. 29.
4. This example is based upon discussions of Mercury's marketing strategy by Leonard Shane at various meetings held by the Savings Institutions Marketing Society of America.
5. Leonard Shane, "Marketing without Media—How Mercury's Done It," *Financial Marketing*, September/October 1979, p. 27.
6. Paul W. Farris and Robert D. Buzzell, "Why Advertising and Promotional Costs Vary: Some Cross-Sectional Analyses," *Journal of Marketing*, Fall 1979, p. 120.
7. "Brand Awareness Increases Market Share, Profits: Study," *Marketing News*, November 28, 1980, p. 5.
8. Gary L. Lilien, "Advisor 2: Modeling the Marketing Mix Decision for Industrial Products," *Management Science*, February 1979, pp. 191–204.
9. Ellen Graham, "The Dewar's Do-ers: Young, Ambitious, Instantly Famous," *The Wall Street Journal*, August 1, 1978, p. 1.
10. Gwen Kinkead, "A 'Me Too' Strategy That Paid Off," *Fortune*, August 27, 1979, pp. 86–88.
11. *1980 Annual Report*, Tootsie Roll Industries, Inc., p. 4.
12. Lydia Chavez, "New Hit on Broadway: Television Advertising to Promote the Shows," *The New York Times*, May 16, 1981, p. 31.
13. "The Guts to Say I Was Wrong," *Forbes*, May 28, 1979, p. 70.
14. "United States Surgical Corp.," *The Value Line OTC Special Situations Service* (New York: Arnold Bernhard & Co., April 28, 1980), pp. A–96, 97.
15. Ibid., p. A–97.
16. Kenneth S. Abramowitz, *United States Surgical Corporation* (New York: Sanford C. Bernstein & Co., September 15, 1980), p. 5.
17. Gilbert A. Churchill, Jr., Neil M. Ford, and Orville C. Walker, Jr., *Sales Force Management* (Homewood, Ill.: Richard D. Irwin, 1981), p. 292.
18. Ibid., p. 331.
19. Ibid., p. 394.
20. Lynda Schuster, "Zales Seeks Image as a Trusted Jeweler," *The Wall Street Journal*, September 18, 1980, p. 33.

10

Moving from plans to action

One of the most satisfying experiences in business practice is to see the management of a company in trouble diagnose its problems, take corrective action, and achieve a turnaround. Sherwin-Williams, the giant paint company, appeared to be on the brink of disaster in 1977 after attempting unsuccessfuly for several years to launch a new strategic marketing plan. The problem was a combination of incomplete planning and faulty implementation.[1] By 1980 recovery was apparent, with both sales and earnings reflecting impressive gains. Let's examine the firm's marketing strategy, its implementation, and the subsequent adjustments that were made to move the company toward profitable performance.

1. The strategic plan. In the late 1960s management decided to shift away from contractors and professional painters and instead to go after the do-it-yourself home decorating market as a primary target. This required an ambitious and costly store expansion program. This decision offered management an opportunity to reposition the paint segment of the business into the rapidly growing do-it-yourself market that other retail chains had found very attractive. Management reasoned that the main ingredient of the new strategy was a change in image in order to appeal to consumers interested in home decorating and remodeling.

2. Implementation. Launching the strategy involved far more than was anticipated. Many stores were in the wrong locations. All required major (and costly) upgrading and expansion to respond to the new home decorating theme. Product lines were expanded to provide a complete offering from floor coverings to fluorescent lights. At the time critics observed that Sherwin-Williams did not have the retail store management experience that was needed to carry out the strategy. Performance difficulties were compounded by the decision to pull Sherwin-Williams paint brand out of paint and hardware stores to avoid direct competition with company stores. It was replaced with another company brand that was not supported by a strong national advertising effort that would help to pull the brand through its distribution channels. Because of this limitation many dealers shifted to competing brands with established brand images.

3. Corrective action. Following two years of declining earnings, the company lost $8 million in 1977, and a new chairman and president, John G. Breen, was appointed. Under his leadership the company has experienced a strong turnaround. Obsolete plants and more than 100 of 1,500 retail stores have been closed. Half of the firm's top 100 managers have been replaced. Several of the new executives have extensive experience in retailing. New stores are smaller and are being located near suburban shopping malls. And the broad mix of decorating products is being pruned. Large increases have been made in advertising expenditures. To offer a strong brand to other retailers, in 1980 the Dutch Boy trademark was acquired. Profits for 1981 were $31 million and further improvement was expected in 1982 and 1983.

The Sherwin-Williams experience illustrates several important characteristics of successful marketing plans. First, a plan involves far more than coming up with a good idea. A sound concept has to be translated into a cohesive and complete plan of action. Second, proper implementation is crucial. Third, few plans remain constant over time. Although the modifications made by Sherwin-Williams' management were more drastic than most, corrective action is the rule rather than the exception, thus emphasizing the ongoing nature of strategic planning. Finally, the success of a marketing plan must be gauged by the results it achieves instead of how elaborate and innovative it may be.

Recall in Chapter 1 that Exhibit 1–2 spelled out the 10 steps in preparing the marketing plan. In Chapters 2 through 9 we considered the first seven steps of the plan. In this and the following chapter we shall examine the last three steps. In this chapter financial analysis for marketing plans and moving from plans to action are considered. Chapter 11 discusses tracking marketing performance.

FINANCIAL ANALYSIS

The purpose of Step 8 is to develop supporting financial analyses for marketing strategy in order to show the estimated impact of the strategy upon financial performance and to indicate marketing's financial requirements over the planning period. Since a complete discussion of financial analysis is beyond the scope of this discussion, we shall concentrate upon three topics: (1) marketing's influence on financial performance; (2) some analysis issues; and (3) some illustrative financial analyses.

Marketing's influence on financial performance

Marketing's strategy, once it is implemented, affects the financial performance of the corporation by generating sales and by incurring costs. An examination of a basic financial analysis system, widely known as the Du Pont investment model, will place into perspective marketing's impact upon financial performance. This model is shown in Exhibit 10–1, where the bold bordered boxes indicate that marketing has some effect on the area. By following the arrows you can trace marketing's influence upon revenues and costs all the way to return on investment. Exhibit 10–1 can be expanded to include more details. For example, the investment box can be broken down into fixed assets and current assets (cash, marketable securities, accounts receivable, and inventories). Likewise, selling, general, and administrative expenses can be divided into specific expense components.

The basic financial reports that are typically prepared for a company and its major subdivisions consist of the following:

1. *Balance sheet.* A statement of financial position at a particular time (e.g., December 31, 1984), indicating total assets by category, short- and long-term liabilities, and stockholder's equity.
2. *Income statement.* This report covers a period of time (e.g., year ending December 31, 1984). It indicates sales minus all relevant costs and the difference is net income.
3. *Cash flow statement.* This report starts with a beginning cash balance for a period (e.g., a quarter) plus all cash receipts minus all cash expenditures. It ends with a net cash balance for the period.

Since these reports and future forecasts (pro forma projections) are prepared for a company and its major parts or segments, the reports are normally not part of the strategic marketing plan. Nevertheless, it is important that marketing planners understand the composition and relationships among major financial reports for the enterprise. Let's turn now to look at the preparation of financial analyses and forecasts for the marketing plan.

Exhibit 10–1
Financial analysis model

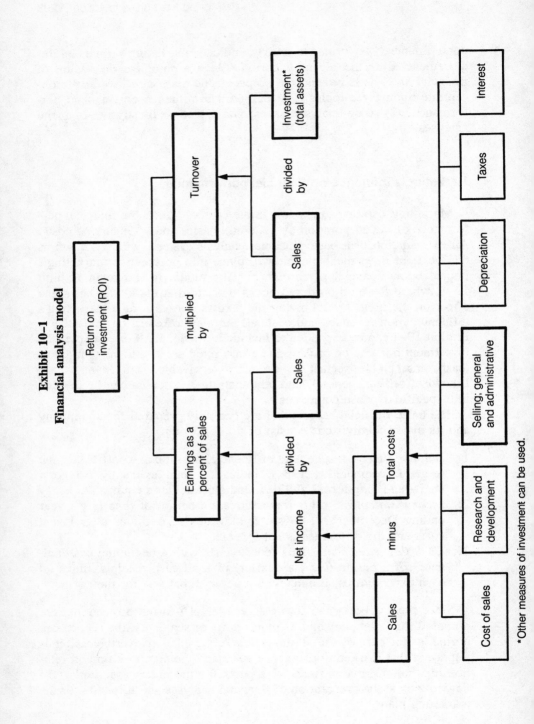

*Other measures of investment can be used.

Some analysis issues

Companies vary considerably as to how they gauge marketing performance. We will give some examples of profitability measures used by different firms:

☐ A diversified manufacturing company currently expects an operating margin on sales of at least 5 percent for all products.

☐ Management in a chemicals company now looks for ROI (return on investment) of at least 15 percent from each product line and considers an ROI figure of less than 11 percent as calling for close review and possible divestment.

☐ A consumer packaged goods company has the general objective that any product's marginal profit before advertising and promotional expenditures should be a minimum of 20 percent higher than fixed and variable costs.

☐ A manufacturer of capital equipment demands at least 25 percent ROI from each product or operating unit.

☐ Another capital goods producer, employing the ratio of direct costs to sales price as a means of measuring relative profit performance, classes a ratio of 60 percent as satisfactory and one over 70 percent as unsatisfactory.[2]

How exactly should management measure the financial performance of marketing operations? What criteria should be used—return on investment (ROI), sales, profit contribution, or what? Many firms use volume attainment and profitability as criteria although surprisingly those using ROI seem to be in the minority.[3] This may be due to several difficulties in attempting to apply the technique to gauge marketing performance:

> Because there are innumerable variations of profit levels, a proper question, initially, is *what return* is being used for the measure? Examples of profit levels are profit before royalties (including or excluding interest payments), profit before taxes, profit after taxes, cash flow, division profit contribution, factory contribution, or sales region or district contribution.
>
> Any of the above are useful, depending upon the investment base being used.
>
> Again, one could ask, "Return on *what investment?*" It may be total parent company investment, total investment of subsidiary, total assets, manipulative assets (excluding intangibles), funds employed (tangible working capital), or selected bases (receivables, inventories, cash, etc.).
>
> The remaining question is, *whose investment?* The investment of the stockholder differs in concept with the operating investment of the firm. Use of each may give startlingly different results, especially in the case

where tangible funds employed in a firm are contrasted with the stock-holder's investment if large amounts of good will have been capitalized.[4]

Once these questions are answered, ROI measures provide an important gauge of marketing performance. Some illustrative examples of its use will be provided in this chapter.

Choice of the proper unit of analysis is also an important consideration. There are several levels of analysis that are desirable depending upon the costs and feasibility of obtaining the information needed to conduct financial analysis. Marketing decision makers are interested in gauging past and estimating future performances from the SBU level to individual salespeople and for various organizational units. Geographic, product, and customer analyses are also of interest. The task then is to identify which units are appropriate and to examine the feasibility of obtaining the information.

Marketing's decision-making information needs often do not correspond to traditional managerial accounting reporting procedures, so some give-and-take negotiations may be necessary between top management, marketing, and accounting. Issues as to how to allocate revenues and costs, the extent of disaggregation of both revenues and costs, and many other questions must be resolved in order to obtain relevant information for financial analysis. Revenue and cost information has two dimensions, the past and the future. Accumulating past information and analyzing it are necessary in order to measure the effectiveness of past strategies. Developing future estimates is needed to evaluate proposed strategies.

Finally, the time period of analysis must be selected. Most strategic marketing decisions extend from a few to several years into the future, so financial analysis must take into account the time value of money and the flows of revenue and costs over the relevant time horizon. A high rate of inflation adds another complicating factor to financial projections for future periods.

Illustrative ROI analysis

We turn now to an illustrative analysis to show how several of the issues raised above can be handled in specific situations. Since our treatment of financial analysis of marketing operations is not intended to be exhaustive, you may want to consult other sources depending upon your interests and needs. The example pertains to the evaluation of a field sales district.[5]

Two units are required: the amount of the incremental contribution and of the incremental investment.

Sales reports showing volume and product mix can provide the sales input in the configuration shown below. Cost records showing the factory production mix on a variable cost basis provide the input for cost of goods manufactured. It is assumed that finished goods inventory policy is corporate and not incremental to the sales district.

DISTRICT ALPHA
Return on investment

Given:
Company Vega, aware that ROI techniques are used to evaluate overall performance, asks the controller why such techniques could not be used for evaluating the profitability of geographic areas and customers.
The configuration of District Alpha shows:

Sales		$3,500,000
Cost of goods manufactured		2,000,000
Gross margin		1,500,000
Less:		
Incremental district expenses:		
Sales and fringe benefits	$ 500,000	
Travel and entertainment	200,000	
Sales office and warehouse expense . .	40,000	740,000
Incremental district profit (before tax)		760,000
Profit after tax		380,000
Assets employed:		
Receivables	700,000	
Inventories (finished goods)	300,000	
Warehouse (net value)	300,000	
	$1,300,000	

$$\text{Return on investment} = \frac{\text{Profits}}{\text{Sales}} \times \frac{\text{Sales}}{\text{Investment}}$$

$$= \frac{\$ \ 380,000}{\$3,500,000} \times \frac{\$3,500,000}{\$1,300,000}$$

$$= 10.8\% \times 2.7\%$$

$$= 29.2\%$$

The illustration highlights how an ROI analysis can be made for a particular unit using as a measure of profit, incremental district profit. The investment base consists of receivables, inventories, and warehouse value. Although the analysis is for one period, the approach can accommodate estimates from multiple periods and into the future, using present value adjustments. Estimates can be made in current dollars or adjusted for the future effects of inflation.

Financial analyses and forecasts

The actual financial analyses and forecasts that are included in the marketing plan vary considerably from firm to firm. Those that are often placed in the financial analysis section of the plan include:

☐ Sales and market share analyses and forecasts by product, market segment, areas, and other categories.

☐ Budget projections for marketing operations.

☐ Break-even and profit contribution projections by marketing planning unit (e.g., market target, product line, market area, etc.).

☐ Return on investment projections by marketing planning unit.

☐ Capital requirements.

The choice of the financial information to be placed in the marketing plan will depend upon its relationship with the corporate or business unit strategic plan. Another important consideration is the selection of performance measures to be used in gauging strategic marketing performance. Our objective is to indicate the range of possibilities and to suggest some of the more frequently used financial analyses. Completion of financial analysis is the last step (Step 8) in actually preparing the strategic marketing plan. The remaining steps (9 and 10) are concerned with transforming the plan into short-term plans and the implementation of the plans.

AN ILLUSTRATION

A look at the marketing planning guidelines used by a particular company will be useful in illustrating how the planning steps we have considered so far fit into an actual plan. We shall present the planning approach used by the Grumman Corporation. Grumman produces carrier-based aircraft, transit buses, containers, canoes, yachts, and various other products and services. Sales in 1981 reached $2 billion. As you review Grumman's planning guidelines shown in Exhibit 10–2 note the similarity between them and the planning steps discussed in this book. As you might expect, there are some differences. This emphasizes that the steps provide a general guide which can be adopted to fit a particular company's needs. Exhibit 10–2 starts with a business area or segment.

In reviewing the Grumman planning guide, several of its characteristics stand out:

☐ There is a clear attempt to keep the plan as brief as possible.

☐ Note the concern with defining the product-market.

Exhibit 10–2
**Excerpts from marketing planning guidelines—
Grumman Corporation**

MARKET PLANNING FOR MAJOR BUSINESS AREAS

This phase proceeds from the gathering and analysis of facts to the setting of objectives and strategy for entire business areas. There is heavy marketing emphasis, although the other business functions of technical/R&D, manufacturing/operations, and finance are also covered. This phase sets the course for the more detailed product-oriented business planning that follows.

The steps are:

1. Market definition.
2. Situation analysis.
3. Problems and opportunities.
4. Objectives.
5. Market strategy.

The "market definition" step and the "situation analysis" step are separate items, but operate in parallel to collectively provide the total facts and information on the environment for analysis. The analysis results in a later statement of "problems and opportunities" (Step 3). The market definition is aimed at defining the broad potential marketplace for the business area. The situation analysis focuses on all aspects of our own historical performance which most probably has occurred only in a segment of the broader market definition.

A description of the requirements for each step follows:

Step 1. Market definition

The market definition addresses and examines the broad marketplace for a general line of business. Corporate goals, objectives, and guidelines should be used in determining the boundaries of these broad markets and businesses. We should be careful *not* to confine the market boundaries by our own existing or traditional product participation. The market definition analysis is purposely meant to create an outward awareness of the total surrounding market and its needs and trends that may offer opportunity or, on the other hand, challenges to our current or contemplated position.

The market definition should be approached as follows:

a. *General statement and description.* Write the statement in terms of the general categories of customers and users served and their needs. General, underlying motivations for customer and user needs should also be identified.

A second dimension that can be used in the general statement is a description of the generic family of products or services in the market served. Use of only this second dimension in the general statement is not good enough. Of the two dimensions, the customer/use oriented definition is most useful for market planning purposes.

A statement describing the relative maturity stage of the market should also be made.

Submittal Format: 1 page text

Exhibit 10–2 *(continued)*

b. *Quantification of market size.* The market described in (a) above must be sized in total and rate of growth or decline for the past, present, and future. Both dollars and units should be identified. Domestic and foreign information should be presented if pertinent and/or appropriate. The market forecast should be for at least a three- to five-year horizon and contain ranges (minimum, maximum, most likely, etc.) where possible.

    Submittal Format: 1 page of text/data
                             Chart optional

c. *Segmentation analysis.* The thought and creativity put into segmenting the market is key. There are no set categories into which the generally defined market must be segmented. However, customer and user categories are particularly important. Product characteristic categories such as price, size, weight, speed, and material are also common and useful. The segmentation may have many dimensions and combinations of dimensions. One should not retreat from trying unusual segmenting dimensions as these may reveal new insight and provide input to marketing strategy. Once the segmenting is complete, sales volumes should be identified and forecast for each segment. Needless to say, these sales forecasts are one of the most important elements in the entire business planning process.

    The segmentation analysis should address the history of the market as well as the forecast.

    Submittal Format: 1–2 pages of matrix charts
                             1 page forecast data

Step 2. Situation analysis

    The situation analysis presents the facts on "where the business has come from and where it stands." The situation analysis is necessary because it provides the basis for self-appraisal so that strengths can be built upon and weaknesses corrected. Internal performance and external impact factors are covered. The internal performance facts cover all the aspects of the business including marketing, technical/R&D, manufacturing/operations, and financial. In this sense, the situation analysis views and assesses the existing business as a whole.

    The external situation analysis provides information on (1) the market segments in which we are participating, and (2) those other segments identified in the segmentation analysis where we are not presently engaged.

    The information provided on the latter segments will most likely be briefer than the information provided for our own segments. However, judgment will have to be used to provide sufficient information depth to allow factual conclusions to be drawn relative to potential problems and opportunities.

    Submittal Format: 1/2 page summary text
                             1 page competition matrix
                             1 page trend data

Exhibit 10–2 *(continued)*

Step 3. Problems and opportunities

The market definition and the situation analysis must be critically and methodically analyzed and assessed in order to identify "problems and opportunities." Each problem and opportunity should be reduced to a concise statement. Avoid the obscuring of a problem or opportunity that may be caused by combining it in the statement of another.

A checklist to assist in identifying problems and opportunities during the analysis process follows:

a. *Internal problems and opportunities*
   1. Marketing.
   2. Technical/R&D.
   3. Manufacturing/operations.
   4. Financial.
   5. Other (e.g., corporate, personnel, organization).

b. *External problems and opportunities*
   1. Market.
   2. Specific market segments.
   3. Competition.
   4. Regulation.
   5. Economic.
   6. Political.
   7. Social.
   8. International.

After the statements of problems and opportunities have been completed, they should be ranked and prioritized according to criticality to the business.

Submittal Format: 1 page of "one liners"

c. *Planning for the unexpected.* Aside from the real problems and opportunities identified and ranked above, scenarios for unexpected events and trends (sometimes called "what-if's") should also be considered. Such events and trends might either have favorable or unfavorable impacts. "What-if" events that are particularly pertinent to the business area should be listed in brief. Later in the business planning process, contingency plans should be formulated to deal with the eventuality of "what-if" events.

Submittal Format: 1 page of "one-liners"

Note: Management review. At this point, a management review of the conclusions drawn in Steps 1–3 is appropriate.

Step 4. Objectives

As a result of the analysis and conclusions drawn from the market definition, situation analysis, and problems and opportunities steps, objectives for the business area are to be set. Obviously, the objectives must also be supportive and consistent with overall corporate goals, objectives, and guidelines.

212

Exhibit 10–2 *(concluded)*

Objectives should be stated concisely and precisely to "fit" the business area. They should not be lofty, generalized platitudes. Objectives might be stated in terms of any one or more of the following:

a. Market position—share, growth rate, competition, image, etc.
b. Financial rewards expected—profit, cash ROI, ROA, etc.
c. Long-term; near-term—state dates

Whatever the description, objectives should be stated in quantifiable terms and should be measurable.

Submittal Format: ½ page of "one-liners"

Step 5. Market strategy

The market strategy is the portion of the business planning process that states "how" the objectives for the business area will be met. The market strategy will govern not only the product-oriented marketing planning in this phase, but also the technical, manufacturing/operations, and financial planning functions. Market strategy is the mainstream guidance from which *all* subsequent planning functions flow. Market strategizing marks the point in the business planning process which is perhaps more pivotal to future profit success than any other phase. For this reason, strategy paths chosen must be entirely realistic with respect to resource capabilities.

The market strategy must address and describe, as appropriate, the following:

a. Market segments selected and targeted.
b. Positioning relative to competition.
c. Product-line requirements—including mix, maturity and life-cycle considerations, extensions, and protection (patents, etc.).
d. Penetration points—market segments and timing.
e. Channels of distribution—direct, distributors, dealers, reps, etc.
f. Demand creation—promotion, advertising, etc.
g. Personal selling.
h. Aftersale—warranty, service, etc.
i. Co-relationships—teaming, joint ventures, licensing, etc.

Submittal Format: 2–3 pages of text
(1 paragraph for each item *a* through *i*)

Note: Management approval. At this point, management should review and approve the objectives (Step 4) and the market strategy (Step 5).

Source: David S. Hopkins, *The Marketing Plan,* Report No. 801 (New York: Conference Board, 1981), pp. 119–23.

□ A three- to five-year time horizon is used, and a range of forecasts is prepared.

□ Market segmentation is highlighted in the planning process.

□ Grumman's situation analysis leads logically into a statement of problems and opportunities and contingencies.

□ Objectives are specified regarding market position and financial performance.

□ Finally, marketing strategy decisions are indicated and their pivotal role in business planning is emphasized.

One of the more interesting characteristics of the Grumman marketing planning guide is the fact that it serves as a kind of umbrella for technical, operations, and financial planning activities. While the guide represents only one of many ways of organizing and steering the planning process, it follows rather closely the approach advocated in this book and thus serves as a useful illustration of how the approach can be applied in a particular company.

SHORT-TERM PLANS AND IMPLEMENTATION

Step 9 is concerned with short-term programming of marketing activities and implementing the plan. The strategic marketing plan provides a basis for developing a short-term marketing plan which typically covers a one-year time span. At least two options exist. The strategic plan can include a detailed one-year plan as a portion of the stratetic plan. Alternatively, the short-term plan may be prepared as a separate entity. The important consideration is to provide a specific operational plan while avoiding unnecessary paperwork and overlapping coverage with the strategic marketing plan.

Planning cycle and frequency

The relationships between the strategic and short-term plans are shown in Exhibit 10–3. Notice that the planning cycle in which plans are implemented, evaluated, and adjusted is continuous. While the strategic plan establishes guidelines for action, day-to-day operations are guided by short-term plans. The frequency of various planning activities, in both strategic and short-term plans, is shown in Exhibit 10–4. These comparisons are illustrative in that variations will exist from one planning situation to another. Two important points are highlighted by Exhibit 10–4. First, the need for an annual planning period is clear since several of the activities shown require actions within a short-range time

Exhibit 10–3
Marketing planning cycle and relationships

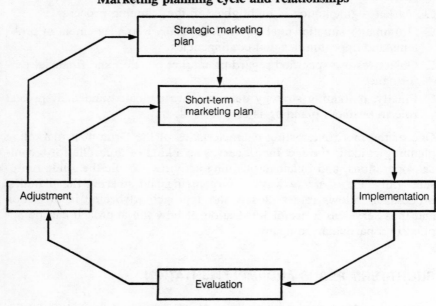

horizon of 12 months or less. Second, longer-range planning decisions emphasize the importance of looking ahead beyond a one-year period. Thus, we see the need for both short-term and strategic marketing plans.

The short-term marketing plan

As an illustration of a short-term planning situation, suppose that a new product introduction is scheduled for next year. The short-term plan for the introduction should include results, targets, actions, responsibilities, schedules, and dates. The plan should indicate details and deadlines, production plans, market introduction program, advertising and merchandising actions, employee training, and other aspects of launching the product (see Exhibit 10–5). The plan should answer the series of questions—what, when, where, who, how, and why—for each objective to be accomplished during the short-term planning period.

Implementation is an essential part of marketing planning. Once in operation, marketing strategy should be evaluated and updated on an annual basis via the short-term plan. People make things happen. Plans are only mechanisms for use by people in placing strategy and tactics

Exhibit 10–4
Illustrative frequency of planning activities

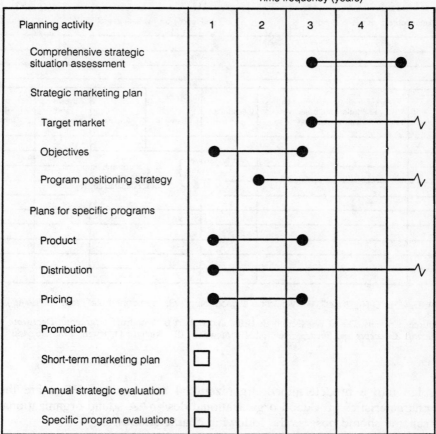

Time frequency (years)

Planning activity	1	2	3	4	5
Comprehensive strategic situation assessment			●		●
Strategic marketing plan					
Target market			●		
Objectives	●		●		
Program positioning strategy		●			
Plans for specific programs					
Product	●		●		
Distribution	●				
Pricing	●		●		
Promotion	☐				
Short-term marketing plan	☐				
Annual strategic evaluation	☐				
Specific program evaluations	☐				

into action. Without proper implementation plans are worthless, so implementation represents a crucial step in marketing planning. We conclude this chapter with a look in the next section at organizing the marketing team.

DESIGNING THE MARKETING ORGANIZATION

One basic rule in marketing organizational design is to build the organization around the marketing plan rather than to force the strategic

Exhibit 10–5
Marketing planning guide

Marketing objectives

- _____
- _____
- _____
- _____

Influences on marketing strategy

- _____
- _____
- _____
- _____

Priority*	Market/industry/customer targets (description and objectives, including sales targets)	Products/ services	Channels	Pricing	Advertising and promotion	Sales force
		Strategy and tactics }		{ Actions Responsibilities Deadlines Estimated costs		

*A, B, C, or D (A: "must"; B: "would be a good thing"; C: "can contribute"; and D: "defer").

Source: Cravens, David W., Gerald E. Hills, and Robert B. Woodruff. *Marketing Decision Making: Concepts and Strategy,* rev. ed. (Homewood, Ill.: Richard D. Irwin, 1980), p. 456.

plan into a predetermined organizational arrangement. What are the characteristics of a good organizational design? A sound organizational scheme should possess the following characteristics:

☐ The organization should correspond to the strategic marketing plan. For example, if the plan is structured around markets or products, then the marketing organizational structure should reflect this same emphasis.

☐ Coordination of activities is essential to successful implementation of plans, both within the marketing function and with other company and business unit functions. The more highly specialized marketing functions become, the more likely coordination and communications will be hampered.

☐ Specialization of marketing activities will lead to greater efficiency in performing the functions. As an illustration, a central advertising department may be more cost efficient than establishing an advertising

unit for each product category. Specialization can also provide technical depth. For example, product or application specialization in a
field sales force will enable salespeople to provide consultative type
assistance to customers.

☐ The organization should be structured so that responsibility for results will correspond with a manager's influence upon results. While
this objective is often difficult to fully achieve, it should be a prime
consideration in designing the marketing organization.

☐ Finally, one of the real dangers in a highly structured and complex
organization is the loss of flexibility. The organization should be
adaptable to changing conditions.

No doubt by now you have detected a flaw in this list of desirable
characteristics of a marketing organizational design. Some of them conflict with each other. For example, specialization can be expensive if
carried to extremes. The costs of having different sales specialists call
upon the same account must be weighed against the benefits obtained
from the overlapping coverage. Thus, organizational design represents
an assessment of priorities and a balancing of conflicting consequences.

Design considerations

Marketing functions always influence how an organization is structured. In fact, historically this factor has dominated design considerations. For certain functions that provide services to all markets or all
products, functional specialization is logical. Examples include advertising, administrative services, and research. Emphasis on functions may
be less appropriate when trying to organize activities around market
targets, products, and field sales operations. Target markets and products also have major influences upon organizational design. When two
or more targets and/or a mix of products exists, companies often depart
from organizational designs based on the functions of advertising, selling, research, and other supporting services. Similarly, distribution
channels and sales force considerations may influence the organizational
structure adopted by a firm. For example, marketing of home entertainment products for use as employee incentives and promotional gifts
might be placed in an organizational unit separate from one in which
marketing operations go through distributor and retailer-type distribution channels. Often, geographical factors have a heavy influence because of the need to make the field supervisory structure correspond to
sales force deployment.

We shall assume that the marketing organization is part of a business
segment or business unit unless the entire firm is comprised of a single

segment or unit. In this regard, two issues should be recognized. First, companies with multiple business activities may have corporate marketing organizations as well as business unit marketing components. Moreover, the extent of corporate involvement can range from primarily a coordination role to one in which the corporate staff has considerable influence upon business unit marketing operations. Second, the chief marketing executive (and staff) may participate in varying degrees in strategic planning for the enterprise and the business unit. For example, the chief marketing executive of the farm equipment division of a medium-sized, diversified manufacturer coordinates strategic planning and prepares the strategic plan for the division. We turn now to an examination of various approaches that are used in designing marketing organizations.

Functional organizations

In all companies, marketing functions influence organizational design to some degree. A marketing organization developed along functional lines consists of departments, groups, or individuals that are responsible for such functions as advertising and sales promotion, pricing, sales, marketing research, and marketing planning and services. All of these functions may not be included in an organization depending upon the size and scope of its marketing operations. This approach is often used as the primary basis of organizational design when a single product or closely related line is marketed to one market target. Snap-On Tools' business segment that markets hand tools to professional mechanics via independent dealers in vans fits such a situation. The conditions that may indicate a need for departing from a purely functional organizational structure include:

☐ The business unit is serving multiple market targets and/or substantial differences exist among end users in the target market according to their needs and because of the marketing activities used to serve the end users.

☐ The line or mix of products offered requires specialized expertise for particular products due to product complexity, type of application, and other factors.

☐ Special marketing situations call for a concentrated marketing effort to plan for and implement a new product, entry into a new market, development of a distribution channel, or some other new project or program that does not fit logically into the existing marketing organization.

Let's examine the major organizational approaches that have been developed to help respond to the above factors. As we do this, keep in mind that in nearly every marketing organization, functional considerations enter into the design to some degree. For example, any organization that assigns all salespeople to a single department is organizing according to the sales function regardless of how the sales force is deployed in the field.

Product organizations

There are several aspects of a product offering that may require special consideration in organizational design. One is the planning and coordination required for new products. Companies have found that new products do not receive the attention they need unless specific responsibility is designated for a new product. This problem can occur with existing products when a business unit offers several products and each involves technical and/or application differences. To assure that new and existing products receive sufficient management attention and coordination, companies have developed various organizational concepts.

The choice of a particular approach depends on the situation and management's preferences. Factors that often influence the decision are the nature and scope of products offered, the rate of new product development, amount of coordination necessary among functional areas, and types of management and technical problems encountered in the past with new products and existing products. For example, a firm with an existing functional organizational structure might choose to use a task force of people temporarily assigned to manage and coordinate a major new product being developed. Before or soon after commercial introduction, the responsibility for the product would be assigned to the functional organization. The purpose of the task force, in this instance, is to allocate enough direction and effort to the new product so that it will be properly launched.

Market organizations

When a business unit is serving more than one target market, customer considerations may influence the design of the marketing organization. If this situation occurs, it is most likely to affect the structuring of the field sales organization, although some firms have appointed market managers as well as specializing field sales coverage by type of customer. In these instances, the market manager operates much like a product manager with responsibility for market planning, research, advertising, and sales force coordination. One company, Quaker Chemical, has carried a market orientation in its organizational design down to the individual customer. Quaker, a manufacturer of specialty chemicals, serves its industrial customers using highly trained sales engineers. Each sales engineer has only a handful of accounts, working with each one on a consulting-type basis. Thus, each customer (and prospect) is a target market.

Market-oriented field organizations may be deployed according to industry, type of application, and in various other ways to achieve specialization according to end-user groups. For decades IBM has incorporated market considerations into its marketing organizational design. The conditions that may suggest a market-oriented design are:

☐ Multiple market targets are being served within a strategic business unit.

☐ Substantial differences in needs exist between end users in a given target market.

☐ Each customer or prospect purchases the product in large volume or dollar amounts.

Often, the situation is not clear-cut as to a functional, product, or market basis of building the marketing organization. Since many organizations represent a combination of the three factors, we shall complete our discussion of organizational design with an examination of these approaches.

Combination approaches

One of the more popular combination schemes is the matrix organization in which a cross-classification scheme is used to obtain emphasis upon two different factors, such as products and marketing functions. An illustration is shown in Exhibit 10–6. In this example note that field sales coverage is according to geography, whereas product emphasis is accomplished using product managers. In addition to working with salespeople, the product managers coordinate other marketing functions for their products, such as advertising and marketing research. Many other combination schemes are possible. For example, within the sales regions shown in Exhibit 10–6, salespeople could be organized by product category or customer group. Also, some of the marketing functions could be specialized by product category, such as an advertising supervisor for Product II.

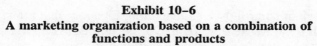

Exhibit 10–6
A marketing organization based on a combination of
functions and products

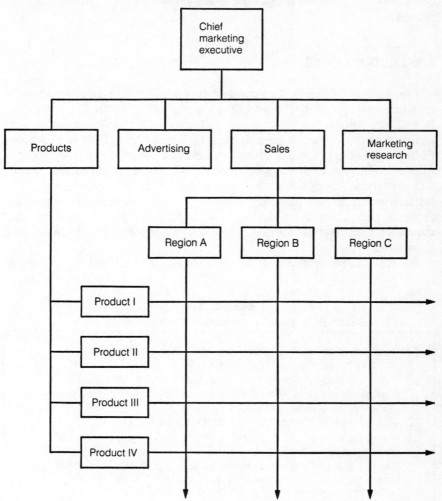

Combination approaches offer a lot of flexibility in responding to different influences in designing the organization. The major problem with these approaches is establishing lines of responsibility and authority. The matrix approaches, in particular, create overlaps in responsibility and gaps in authority. A frequent complaint of product and market managers is their lack of control over all marketing functions that affect the results for which they are held accountable. Nevertheless, matrix approaches continue to be popular, suggesting that their advantages exceed the limitations.

CONCLUDING NOTE

Preparation of the strategic marketing plan is one of the most demanding management responsibilities of the chief marketing executive. It requires folding together many different information gathering and analysis activities into a comprehensive and integrated plan of action. Following a step-by-step approach in building the strategic plan is a useful way to be sure each component of the plan is covered and that important interrelationships between the components are recognized. The starting point in the planning process is understanding the corporate strategic plan since the maketing plan is one of a bundle of functional strategies that must be combined to achieve corporate and business unit objectives.

Several characteristics of the marketing plan should be apparent.

Exhibit 10–7
Manager's guide to preparing the marketing plan

☐ Is our marketing plan based on a clear understanding of the corporate/business unit plan (Chapter 2)?

☐ Have we analyzed market opportunities to determine demand, customer characteristics, industry trends, and strengths and weaknesses of key competitors (Chapter 3)?

☐ Are our market targets clearly identified (Chapter 4)?

☐ Have we established measurable and realistic objectives for each market target (Chapter 5)?

☐ Does our marketing program positioning plan represent a coordinated combination of product/service, distribution, price, advertising, and sales force strategies (Chapters 5–9)?

☐ Do we have supporting financial analyses for our planned strategies (Chapter 10)?

☐ Is our organizational design appropriate for our planned marketing strategy (Chapter 10)?

☐ Have we translated our strategic marketing plans into short-term action plans (Chapter 10)?

☐ Have we set up a program to monitor the progress of our plans that will track marketing performance and spot problem areas (Chapter 11)?

First, a logical basis exists for developing a plan, as outlined in the manager's checklist for this chapter (Exhibit 10–7). This general approach can be implemented in any type of organization, as illustrated by the marketing planning guidelines followed in the Grumman Corporation (see Exhibit 10–2). Second, the planning process raises the questions; management must supply the answers thus emphasizing that decision makers must develop marketing plans. Third, marketing planning is a continuing activity that is adjusted and revised to take advantage of opportunities and threats. Finally, marketing planning, as we saw in the Grumman illustration, forms the leading edge of planning for the entire business unit, and so it is essential that marketing plans be closely coordinated with research and development, operations, financial, and other business functions.

NOTES

1. This account is based in part upon Susan Wagner Leisner, "Cleaning Up: Sherwin-Williams Co. Is Recovering from Its Spill," *Barron's*, November 24, 1980, pp. 35–36.
2. David S. Hopkins, *Business Strategies for Problem Products* (New York: The Conference Board, 1977), p. 11.
3. Sam R. Goodman, *Financial Analysis for Marketing Decisions* (Homewood, Ill.: Dow Jones-Irwin, 1972), p. 88.
4. Ibid., pp. 102–3.
5. The following example is drawn from ibid., pp. 112–13. This source provides an extensive discussion of financial analysis for marketing decisions.

11

Tracking marketing performance

Evaluation, or *tracking,* the last stage in marketing strategy, is more aptly designated as the starting point, except perhaps in new venture situations. Marketing planning requires information from various ongoing monitoring and performance evaluation activities. Discussion of evaluation has been delayed until now in order to first examine the marketing areas that require evaluation and to identify the kinds of information needed for assessing marketing performance in each area. Thus, the first 10 chapters serve as an essential foundation for building an evaluation program. Our objective in this chapter is to develop a step-by-step approach to monitoring and evaluating marketing performance, indicating the purposes and types of evaluation, and exploring the various sources of information used by management in keeping performance on track, solving problems, and finding new opportunities.

BUILDING AN EVALUATION PROGRAM

The essence of evaluation is obtaining relevant information for gauging performance, analyzing it, and then taking the actions that are necessary to keep performance on track. Marketing executives are continually monitoring performance, and often they must revise their strategies to cope with changing conditions. Consider, for example, the toothpaste illustration described in Exhibit 11–1. The 4 percent drop in P&G's market share for Crest in 1980 amounted to over $30 million! With the stakes so high it is not surprising that P&G's management is aggressively adjusting marketing strategy for the brand and developing new products in an attempt to stop the losses in market share. Keeping

Exhibit 11–1
P&G may give Crest a new look after failing to brush off rivals

Crest toothpaste, an undisputed leader for two decades, is one of the products that has built Procter & Gamble's reputation for invincibility. Recently, though, that record has been tarnished by P&G's cautious defense against two rivals that have discovered a weakness in Crest.

But don't count P&G out. It appears to be preparing a three-pronged counterattack to regain its lost ground in the $700 million dentrifice market. The Cincinnati concern's plans are likely to include a new brand name, Pace, a dark blue gel version of Crest, and a major change in the 25-year-old formula for the original aquamarine Crest.

To the average toothbrusher, such changes might seem ho-hum. But to companies that compete in the sale of consumer products, P&G's anticipated moves will offer insight into how the well-heeled, tightly-disciplined marketer reacts to a successful challenge.

When Crest was introduced in 1955, most toothpastes were sold for their ability to whiten teeth. Crest had a different story to tell: Its stannous fluoride ingredient, which P&G called Fluoristan, helped prevent cavities. To add credibility, P&G persuaded the American Dental Association in 1960 to make an unprecedented endorsement of the toothpaste. Crest quickly grabbed one third of the market.

Lever Brothers proved that consumers also were interested in flavor when it introduced Close-Up toothpaste in 1969 and Aim in 1975. Today the two translucent gels account for 17.3 percent of the toothpaste market. More recently, Beecham Products' Aqua-fresh—a striped combination of white paste and turquoise gel—has shown Crest's vulnerability. Borrowing the best features of Lever's and P&G's brands, it was introduced nationally in 1979 and already has 13.5 percent of the market.

Meanwhile, Crest's share fell to 36.2 percent in 1980 from 40.5 percent two years earlier. "Sometimes when you're king of the hill," says Hercules Segales, a consumer products analyst at Drexel Burnham Lambert and a former P&G executive, "you underestimate your competition."

To be sure, Crest isn't is mortal danger. Mr. Segales estimates that Crest provided $300 million in revenue to P&G last year and, along with Tide detergent and Pampers diapers, is one of its three most profitable products. Other companies envy Crest's market share.

But did P&G overlook the appeal of highly flavored gel toothpastes, which now account for nearly one third of the market? "P&G misread it," maintains Daniel Meade, a securities analyst at First Boston. "They thought the appeal of gels was largely to kids and was a fad that would pass." A P&G competitor agrees: "Procter felt impregnable on Crest."

Some observers believe P&G is weakest when it tries to respond to competitors that offer superficial, cosmetic advantages, such as flavor, rather than superior performance, such as cavity-prevention. Says Gordon Wade, a Park Hills, Kentucky, marketing consultant and a P&G alumnus: "Cosmetics don't sit well with the Calvinists at Sixth and Sycamore," the address of P&G's headquarters.

To protect Crest, P&G lately has been spending heavily on cents-off promotions to retailers and consumers. But the company hasn't increased its ad budget significantly, one conventional way to rebuff challenges. In

Exhibit 11-1 *(concluded)*

the first nine months of 1979, P&G spent $19.1 million to advertise Crest; in that period last year the outlay was $20.4 million.

The message of its Crest ads has become more aggressive, though. A new TV commercial talks about "those fancy stripes and gels," and a consumer says, "Toothpastes don't excite me. Good checkups. That excites me." Headlined "Presenting the checklist no other toothpaste would dare print," a magazine ad compares Crest with three unnamed rivals. And P&G, which rarely uses celebrities to tout its products, recently began running a magazine ad featuring Olympic skater Eric Heiden. The ads say he "has five gold medals on his chest. And Crest to help keep gold out of his teeth."

But P&G's biggest moves are its new products, the first of which is the revised formula Crest, now sold in limited areas. Instead of stannous fluoride, it contains sodium fluoride, which P&G calls Fluoristat. Industry experts say the new Crest costs P&G less to make, enabling the company to increase its profits from Crest or to spend more money marketing it.

Sodium fluoride toothpastes, which contain less tin than stannous fluoride brands, also taste better. But a P&G spokesman says flavor "isn't a major part" of the change. Instead, packages of the newer Crest call it an "advanced formula" product with "improved cavity protection."

Flavor is ballyhooed by the two other new P&G toothpastes. Crest gel, a dark blue dentifrice with a flavor a company spokesman describes as "sweet spice," has been test-marketed in Vermont since October. Its TV commercials talk about "the newest taste in toothpaste."

Pace, a green gel tested since September in Wisconsin, Illinois, and Maine, "leaves your teeth, your whole mouth, feeling remarkably clean and fresh," its package says. Pace also has a flip-top cap instead of a screw-on closure. The brand eventually may replace P&G's dying Gleem, which has only a 3.3 percent share.

After spending 20 years singing the virtues of stannous fluoride, P&G is taking risks by changing Crest's formula and introducing two gels with sodium fluoride. "They're giving up a lot of Crest's heritage to make aggressive moves quickly," says a competitor. He says P&G also must avoid "cannibalizing" Crest's market share—switching Crest loyalists to Crest gel or Pace.

Some say the new products, none of which is radically different from brands already on the market, are merely designed to protect P&G's share until the company can perfect a new generation of toothpastes based on a technological breakthrough comparable to Crest's introduction 25 years ago. Mr. Segales predicts that such an advance, perhaps a product that reduces or eliminates plaque, could occur as early as 1984.

Source: Bill Abrams, *The Wall Street Journal,* January 8, 1981, p. 21. Reprinted by permission. © Dow Jones & Co., Inc. 1981. All rights reserved.

marketing performance on track is the major reason why the marketing strategist needs an ongoing evaluation program. This activity consumes a high proportion of the chief marketing executive's time and energy.

The purposes and areas of strategic evaluation or tracking are shown in Exhibit 11–2. This classification represents the major evaluation activities that occur in any firm. As indicated, there are three reasons for evaluation. The types of evaluation listed in Exhibit 11–2 are accomplished in the areas of evaluation where Xs have been placed. The P&G Crest illustration is an example of keeping performance on track where possible evaluation activities might include analyses of consumer preferences and competition.

Exhibit 11–2
Purposes and areas of strategic evaluation

Area of evaluation	Finding new opportunities/ avoiding threats	Keeping performance on track	Problem solving
Environmental scanning	X		
Product-market analysis	X	X	
Marketing program performance analysis		X	X
Effectiveness of mix components		X	X

Purpose of evaulation

The major steps that must be taken in establishing an evaluation program are shown in Exhibit 11–3. Note that these activities are similar to those followed by P&G in the new product planning and management of Crest toothpaste. Management discovered an opportunity for a new toothpaste concept (prevention of cavities). Strategic plans were implemented in 1955 which resulted in the company gaining a dominant position for Crest. During the 1970s competition intensified and P&G's tracking program for Crest and its other toothpaste brands indicated the need for problem-solving actions to eliminate performance gaps (e.g., loss of market share). The actions called for in the counterattack began to appear in 1980 as we saw in Exhibit 11–1. Let's examine each of the steps shown in Exhibit 11–3.

THE MARKETING AUDIT

Since evaluation is essentially comparing results with expectations, it is necessary to lay some groundwork before setting up a tracking program. The starting point is a strategic marketing audit.

Exhibit 11–3
Establishing a strategic evaluation program

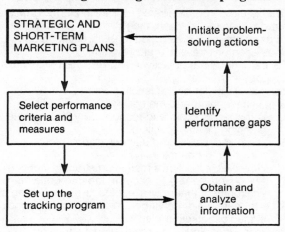

A guide to conducting the strategic marketing audit is shown in Exhibit 11–4. Although this guide is reasonably comprehensive, it can be expanded and adapted to meet the needs of a particular firm. For example, if channels of distribution are not utilized by a company or business unit, this section of the audit guide will require adjustment. Likewise, if

Exhibit 11–4
Guide to conducting the strategic marketing audit

I. Corporate mission and objectives
   A. Does the mission statement offer a clear guide to the product-markets of interest to the firm?
   B. Have objectives been established for the corporation?
   C. Is information available for the review of corporate progress toward objectives, and are the reviews conducted on a regular (quarterly, monthly, etc.) basis?
   D. Has corporate strategy been successful in meeting objectives?
   E. Are opportunities or problems pending that may require altering marketing strategy?
   F. What are the responsibilities of the chief marketing executive in corporate strategic planning?
II. Business composition and strategy
   A. What is the composition of the business (business segments, strategic planning units, and specific product-markets)?
   B. Have business strength and product-market attractiveness analyses been conducted for each planning unit? What are the results of the analyses?

Exhibit 11–4 *(continued)*

    C. What is the corporate strategy for each planning unit (e.g., growth, manage for cash, etc.)?
    D. What objectives are assigned to each planning unit?
    E. Does each unit have a strategic plan?
    F. For each unit what objectives and responsibilities have been assigned to marketing?

III. Marketing strategy (for each planning unit)
    A. Strategic planning and marketing:
        1. Is marketing's role and responsibility in corporate strategic planning clearly specified?
        2. Are responsibility and authority for marketing strategy assigned to one executive?
        3. How well is the firm's marketing strategy working?
        4. Are changes likely to occur in the corporate/marketing environment that may affect the firm's marketing strategy?
        5. Are there major contingencies that should be included in the strategic marketing plan?
    B. Marketing planning and organizational structure:
        1. Are annual and longer range strategic marketing plans developed, and are they being used?
        2. Are the responsibilities of the various units in the marketing organization clearly specified?
        3. What are the strengths and limitations of the key members of the marketing organization? What is being done to develop people? What gaps in experience and capabilities exist on the marketing staff?
        4. Is the organizational structure for marketing appropriate for implementing marketing plans?
    C. Target market strategy:
        1. Has each target market been clearly defined and its importance to the firm established?
        2. Have demand, industry, and competition in each target market been analyzed and key trends, opportunities, and threats identified?
        3. Has the proper target market strategy (mass, niche) been adopted?
        4. Should repositioning or exit from any product-market be considered?
    D. Objectives:
        1. Have objectives been established for each target market, and are these consistent with planning unit objectives and the available resources? Are the objectives realistic?
        2. Are sales, cost, and other performance information available for monitoring the progress of planned performance against actual results?
        3. Are regular appraisals made of marketing performance?
        4. Where do gaps exist between planned and actual results? What are the probable causes of the performance gaps?

Exhibit 11-4 (continued)

E. Marketing program positioning strategy:
   1. Does the firm have an integrated positioning strategy made up of product, channel, price, advertising, and sales force strategies? Is the role selected for each mix element consistent with the overall program objectives, and does it properly complement other mix elements?
   2. Are adequate resources available to carry out the marketing program? Are resources committed to target markets according to the importance of each?
   3. Are allocations to the various marketing mix components too low, too high, or about right in terms of what each is expected to accomplish?
   4. Is the effectiveness of the marketing program appraised on a regular basis?
IV. Marketing program activities
   A. Product strategy:
      1. Is the product mix geared to the needs that the firm wants to meet in each product-market?
      2. What branding strategy is being used?
      3. Are products properly positioned against competing brands?
      4. Does the firm have a sound approach to product planning and management, and is marketing involved in product decisions?
      5. Are additions to, modifications of, or deletions from the product mix needed to make the firm more competitive in the marketplace?
      6. Is the performance of each product evaluated on a regular basis?
   B. Channel of distribution strategy:
      1. Has the firm selected the type (conventional or vertically coordinated) and intensity of distribution appropriate for each of its product-markets?
      2. How well does each channel access its target market? Is an effective channel configuration being used?
      3. Are channel organizations carrying out their assigned functions properly?
      4. How is the channel of distribution being managed? What improvements are needed?
      5. Are desired customer service levels being reached, and are the costs of doing this acceptable?
   C. Price strategy:
      1. How responsive is each target market to price variations?
      2. What role and objectives does price have in the marketing mix?
      3. Should price play an active or passive role in program positioning strategy?
      4. How do the firm's price strategy and tactics compare to those of competition?

Exhibit 11–4 *(concluded)*

---

      5. Is a logical approach used to establish prices?
      6. Are there indications that changes may be needed in price strategy or tactics?

  D. Advertising and sales promotion strategies:
      1. Have a role and objectives been established for advertising and sales promotion in the marketing mix?
      2. Is the creative strategy consistent with the positioning strategy that is being used?
      3. Is the budget adequate to carry out the objectives assigned to advertising and sales promotion?
      4. Do the media and programming strategies represent the most cost-effective means of communicating with target markets?
      5. Do advertising copy and content effectively communicate the intended messages?
      6. How well does the advertising program measure up in meeting its objectives?

  E. Sales force strategy:
      1. Are the role and objectives of personal selling in the marketing program positioning strategy clearly specified and understood by the sales organization?
      2. Do the qualifications of salespeople correspond to their assigned roles?
      3. Is the sales force of the proper size to carry out its function, and is it efficiently deployed?
      4. Are sales force results in line with management's expectations?
      5. Is each salesperson assigned performance targets, and are incentives offered to reward performance?
      6. Are compensation levels and ranges competitive?

V. Implementation and management
  A. Have the causes of all performance gaps been identified?
  B. Is implementation of planned actions taking place as intended? Is implementation being hampered by marketing or other functional areas of the firm (e.g., operations, finance)?
  C. Has the strategic audit revealed areas requiring additional study before action is taken?

---

the sales force represents the major part of a marketing program, then this section should be expanded to include other aspects of sales force strategy. Notice how the audit corresponds to the strategic marketing plan. This should be expected since the main purpose of the audit is to appraise the effectiveness of strategic marketing operations. You should note that Exhibit 11–4 contains several questions about the performance of marketing operations. The answers to these questions will need to be incorporated into the design of the strategic tracking program.

Now that we have identified what should be audited, there are some additional aspects of conducting the audit that management must take into account. We shall briefly examine each aspect:

☐ *Who should conduct the audit?* Opinions are mixed on this issue; some advocate use of company personnel, and others recommend outside consultants. A combination approach can be used to gain the advantages of both company and external experience, capabilities, and perspectives. Objectivity and professional expertise are the two key prerequisites in selecting an individual or team to plan and conduct the audit.

☐ *Planning the audit.* Depending upon the size and scope of the business unit, proper attention should be given to planning the areas to be audited, defining scope of audit operations, scheduling activities, coordination of participation, and indicating desired results. Auditing costs and expected benefits should be estimated and priorities established regarding various aspects of the audit program.

☐ *Using the findings.* The results of the marketing audit should lead toward improved performance. Opportunities and problems that are identified should be incorporated into strategic plans.

There are reasons for conducting a strategic marketing audit other than its use in guiding the installation of a formal strategic marketing planning and evaluation program. Organizational changes may bring about a complete review of strategic marketing operations. Major shifts in business involvement, such as entry into new product and market areas, acquisitions, and other alterations in the composition of the business, may require strategic audits. While there is no norm as to how often a strategic audit should be conducted, the nature of the audit and costs involved suggest that the time span between audits should be at least three to five years and perhaps more depending upon the company situation.

Plans and performance criteria

As strategic and short-term marketing plans are developed, performance criteria should be specified for use in monitoring strategic performance. Needs for evaluation information should be identified and the needs gauged as to their relevance and importance in strategic evaluation. Specifying the information needed for marketing decision making is one of management's most important responsibilities. In the past, more than a few marketing executives were able to develop and manage successful marketing strategies relying primarily upon intuition, judgment, and experience. Successful executives of the future will combine judgment and experience with more formal approaches to planning for, acquiring, and analyzing marketing information for use in strategic planning and evaluation.

The key problem is selecting the information needed for decision making and then, once it is obtained, interpreting what it means. Too much information can be as dangerous as not having enough information. Since objectives indicate the results that are desired, they also serve as the basis for evaluating the success of a strategy that has been implemented. Objectives represent standards of performance.

In addition to information on objectives, management will require other kinds of information for use in performance evaluation. Some of this information will be incorporated into regular tracking activities (e.g., advertising expenditures). Other information can be obtained as the need first arises, such as a special study of consumer attitudes and opinions.

SETTING UP A TRACKING PROGRAM

After completion of the marketing audit and selection of performance standards, we are ready to set up the evaluation or tracking program (Exhibit 11-3). Determining the information that is needed is the starting point.

Due to the costs of acquiring, processing, and analyzing information, the potential benefits of needed information must be compared to costs. Then priorities should be established regarding information acquisition activities. The major parts of information planning are shown in Exhibit 11-5. Normally, needed information falls into two categories: (1) regularly scheduled information that is supplied on a continuing basis to marketing management from internal and external sources and (2) information that is obtained when it is required for a particular problem or

Exhibit 11-5
Information planning for strategic evaluation

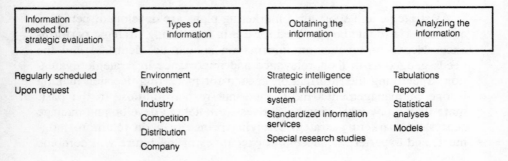

Information needed for strategic evaluation	Types of information	Obtaining the information	Analyzing the information
Regularly scheduled	Environment	Strategic intelligence	Tabulations
Upon request	Markets	Internal information system	Reports
	Industry	Standardized information services	Statistical analyses
	Competition	Special research studies	Models
	Distribution		
	Company		

situation. Examples of the former are sales and cost analyses, market share measurements, and customer analyses. Information from the latter category includes new product concept tests, brand preference studies, and studies of advertising effectiveness.

There are several types of information that may be needed by management as indicated in Exhibit 11–5. The importance of these categories of information will vary from one firm to another. Information for strategic planning and evaluation can be obtained as a part of four major information acquisition activities:

1. The firm's strategic intelligence system is concerned with monitoring and forecasting external, uncontrollable, factors that influence the product-markets of interest to a firm or business unit. These efforts range from formal information activities to very informal surveillance of the marketing environment. The product-markets that are monitored may be those currently served and those of potential interest to the company.
2. The internal information system is the backbone of any strategic evaluation program. These systems may consist primarily of sales and cost reports. Alternatively, an increasing number of firms are developing highly sophisticated marketing information systems for use in strategic and tactical planning and control activities.
3. A wide variety of standardized information services is available from information suppliers for purchase by subscription or on a one-time basis. Often the costs of these services are a small fraction of what they would cost if they were prepared for a single firm. Nielsen's TV rating data service is an example.
4. From time to time marketing decision makers require special research studies that may include one or a combination of the types of information shown in Exhibit 11–5. A study of distributor opinions concerning services provided by a manufacturer is an illustration of a research study.

Several ways of analyzing marketing information are shown on the right-hand side of Exhibit 11–5. Often simple tabulations of data are developed alone, or sometimes tabulations are included as a part of a formal report. Low information-processing costs by computer are leading to much greater use of statistical analyses and models by marketing executives than in the past.

INFORMATION, ANALYSIS, AND ACTION

Once the evaluation program is set up, management is concerned with two ongoing activities: (1) identifying opportunities or performance gaps and (2) initiating actions to take advantage of the opportunities or to correct existing and pending problems. Let's look at each of these important final aspects of strategic evaluation.

Opportunities and performance gaps

Strategic intelligence, internal reporting and analysis activities, standardized information services, and research studies should be developed to meet the information needs of marketing decision makers. The nature and scope of information gathering and analysis activities vary widely from firm to firm. Some companies have developed highly sophisticated marketing information systems. Others stick to basic internal financial reporting activities supplemented by special studies and standardized information services. Regardless of the approach that is adopted, the scheme should be carefully evaluated in terms of costs and benefits. With the impressive array of information-processing hardware and software available today, it is not difficult to fall into the trap of developing information-processing capabilities beyond management's needs.

The real challenge in strategic evaluation is to find opportunities and problems. Since these are the responsibilities of management, the best test of the marketing information system is whether it assists marketing management in meeting these responsibilities. In carrying out these actions, there are two critical factors that management should take into account in performing evaluation:

1. *Problem/opportunity definition.* Analysis should lead to a clear definition of an opportunity or problem since this will be needed to guide whatever strategic action may be taken. Often it is easy to confuse problem symptoms with problem causes.
2. *Interpreting information.* Management must also separate normal variations in performance from significant gaps in performance, since the latter are the ones requiring strategic action. For example, how much of a drop in market share is necessary to signal a strategic performance problem? Limits need to be set on the acceptable range of performance.

No matter how extensive the strategic information system may be, it cannot interpret the strategic importance of the information. This is the responsibility of management.

Determining strategic action

Many actions are possible, depending upon the situation. One objective of this book is to provide a guide to marketing action based upon the opportunity or problem at hand. Management's strategic needs may include divestment strategy, new product planning, target market strategy, adjustments in marketing strategy, or improvements in efficiency. The action must be matched with the situation.

Much of the actual work of managing involves strategic and tactical evaluation of marketing operations. Yet performing this function depends greatly upon management's understanding of the planning process. Evaluation is a continuing cycle of making plans, launching them, tracking performance, identifying performance gaps, and then initiating problem-solving actions. In accomplishing evaluation, management must select performance criteria and measures and then set up a tracking program to obtain the information needed to guide evaluation activities.

When first establishing an evaluation program (and periodically thereafter) a strategic marketing audit provides a useful basis for developing the program. In this chapter we developed a step-by-step approach to the strategic audit, followed by a discussion of how to plan for information needed in strategic evaluation. Finally, we overviewed the important activities of identifying performance gaps and initiating problem-solving actions. This completes our look at the steps in establishing a strategic evaluation program (Exhibit 11–3).

Managing in a changing environment is what marketing is all about. Keeping up with and even anticipating change is at the heart of marketing evaluation. Far too many executives develop innovative marketing strategies and then allow them to deteriorate by not monitoring their effectiveness and altering them due to changing conditions.

CONCLUDING NOTE

This final chapter is both an end and a beginning. It forms a vital link in a series of marketing planning activities. Moreover, it emphasizes that marketing is a continuing process of planning, implementing, evaluating, and adjusting strategies. Evaluation of marketing performance represents the first step in marketing planning and the last step after launching a strategy. Our objective has been to develop an approach to strategic evaluation, building on the marketing planning foundation established in Chapters 1 through 10. Evaluation is one of marketing management's most demanding and time-consuming responsibilities. While the activity lacks the glamour and excitement of new strategy development, effective evaluation often separates the winners from the losers.

We need to emphasize the important role played by the marketing audit in strategic evaluation. It is so easy for practicing managers to become preoccupied with day-to-day activities, neglecting to step back and review overall operations. Regular audits can prevent sudden shocks and can alert management to new opportunities. Building on the base of the findings of the marketing audit, we examined the major steps in planning for and acquiring information for strategic analysis. While the execution of the steps will vary by situation, they represent a useful framework for developing a strategic evaluation program in any type of firm. An important part of this process is setting standards for gauging marketing performance. These standards are useful guides for determining what information is needed to monitor performance. In this chapter we examined the various alternatives for obtaining information, including strategic intelligence, the internal information system, standardized information services, and special research studies. Information generated in these four categories forms the basis for identifying performance gaps and initiating problem-solving actions.

The manager's checklist for this chapter was provided earlier in Exhibit 11–4. It serves also as a consolidation of the checklists in the other chapters of the book.

Index

A

The AMBA Executive, 18
Abell, Derek F., 33, 41
Abramowitz, Kenneth S., 200
Abrams, Bill, 18, 172, 188, 200, 227
Adams, Bill, 131
Advertising, versus personal selling, 179, 181
Advertising budget, 183
Advertising objectives, 182, 186
  levels of, 182
  purchase decision in, 182
Advertising plans, 15
Advertising strategy, 180
  evaluation of effectiveness, 187
  quality in, 186
Adviser 2, 183
Anderson, M. J., Jr., 83
Anheuser-Busch, 67, 82
Axiom Market Research Bureau, 71

B

Bailey, Earl L., 107, 158, 160, 172
Barron's, 41, 83, 172, 223
Bell & Howell, 9
Benson, George, 131
Birnbaum, Jeffrey H., 18

Bonoma, Thomas V., 41
Boundaries, 29
Boyd, Harper W., 41
Brand awareness, 182
Brand product-market, 47
Branding strategy, 116
Breen, John G., 202
Briggs, Jean A., 172
Bristol-Myers, 124–25
Bronson, Gail, 125
Business planning
  guide to, 37
  overview of, 20
Business Strategies for Problem Products
  (Hopkins), 127, 128, 129, 223-
Business units, 9
Business Week, 18, 41, 131
Buyer's decision process, 54
  stages in, 176
Buzzell, Robert D., 200
Byrne, Harlan S., 151

C

Cadbury, N. D., 107
Carry, Bernard, 61
Caterpillar Tractor Co., 136–37

Channels of distribution; *see* Distribution channels
Chasin, Joseph, 131
Chavez, Lydia, 200
Chevalier, Michael, 61
Churchill, Gilbert A., Jr., 196, 200
Clark, J. L., Manufacturing Co., 22–23
Communications mix, 178
Communications objectives, 175
  informing buyers, 177
  need recognition, 177
  postpurchase communications, 178
  product choice, 177
  purchase decision, 177
Competitive advantage, 36
Competitors, 56
Composition of business, 28–29
  business segment, 28
  levels in, 28
Comtrex, 124–25
The Conference Board, Inc., 94, 95, 107
Consumer Magazine and Farm Publications Rates and Data, 185
Consumer studies, 4
Cooney, John E., 61
Core business, 24
Cost
  versus competition, 160
  experience and, 161
  volume and, 159
Cost analysis, 158
Cost structure, 159
Cravens, David W., 52, 83, 131, 172, 216
Creative strategy, 184
Crest, 226–27
Cumming, John W., 114
Customer profiles, 52, 154
Customer research, 103–5
Customer satisfaction, 3

D

Daimler-Benz, 78–79
Day, George S., 60
Deagon, John C., 137
Design and Marketing of New Products (Urban & Hauser), 107, 131
Development options, 24
Dewar's Scotch Whiskey, 184
Direct distribution, 135; *see also* End user
  control of, 138
  financial resources and, 138
  product characteristics in, 137

Distribution
  functions of, 139
  strategic role of, 134–35
Distribution channel strategy, 144–46
  analysis of, 146
  finances and, 149
  levels of, 149
  target market and, 146
Distribution channels, 14, 55, 139
  functions of, 146
  levels of, 144
  types of, 140
Distribution decisions, 134
Distribution intensity, 142
  target market and, 142–43
Distribution strategy, 133, 139
Diversification, 25–26
Donovan, Neil B., 18
Drucker, Peter F., 27, 41
du Pont de Nemours & Company, E. I., 157–58

E

El-Ansary, Adell F., 151
Eliminating products, 129–30
Ellis, Barbara, 83
End user, 49–50, 135–36; *see also* Direct distribution
Entenmann, Robert, 147
Entenmann, William, 147
Entenmann, William, Sr., 147
Entenmann's, Inc., 147–48
Evaluation, 225
  costs of, 234
  defined, 17
  information needed, 235
  interpreting information, 236
  on-going activities, 235
  problem/opportunity definition, 236
External influences, 54

F

Farris, Paul W., 200
Ferguson, James L., 30
Financial analysis, 202–3, 208
Financial Analysis for Marketing Decisions (Goodman), 223
Financial analysis model, 204
Financial forecast, 208
Financial Marketing, 200
Financial planning, 15
Financial reports, 203

Fine, Jules, 187
Fit of business units, 6
Flavin, Joseph B., 8
Folkerth, John, 173
Forbes, 60, 83, 107, 157, 172, 200
Ford, Neil M., 196, 200
Fortune, 200
Functional organization, 218

G

Garino, David P., 107
General Electric, 2
General Foods Corporation, 30
General Mills, Inc., 28
Generic product-market, 46
Gensamer, Blair, 154
Goodman, Sam R., 223
Graham, Ellen, 200
Gross, Irwin, 157, 158, 172
Grumman Corporation, 208–12
Guyon, Janet, 88

H

Hammermesh, R. G., 83
Hammond, John S., 33, 41
Hardee's Food Systems, Inc., 86–88
Harrell, Stephen G., 10, 39
Harris, J. E., 83
Harvard Business Review, 18, 83, 107
Hauser, John R., 107, 131
Heileman, G., Brewing Co., 21
Helene Curtis Industries, 184
Hills, Gerald E., 52, 83, 131, 172, 216
Hippel, Eric von, 131
Hirsch, Leon C., 188–89
Hopkins, David S., 95, 127, 128, 129, 212, 223
Hye, Thomas R., 45

I

Idea generation program, 120–21
Ike, Yokio, 53
Implementation plans, 16
Industry analysis, 55
Information acquisition, 235
Ingrassia, Lawrence, 22, 115
Integrating corporate and marketing strategies, 88–89
Intermediaries, 112, 135

J

Johnson, David, 148

Johnson, William E., 107
Journal of Marketing, 60, 61, 131, 200

K

K mart Corp., 63–64
Kalish, Samuel, 86
Keuffel & Esser Co., 45
Kinkead, Gwen, 200
Kikkoman International, 53–54, 57–58

L

Larreche, Jean-Claude, 41
Laughery, Jack A., 87
Leisner, Susan Wagner, 223
Lenox, Inc., 134–35
Life cycle, 116; *see also* Product-market life cycle
Lilien, Gary L., 200
Limited Stores, Inc., 43–44
Lippman, David, 124
Loctite Corp., 11
Long-term plans, 10
Lynch, Mitchell C., 83

M

MBA Executive, 41
McEnany, Robert, 198
Magid, James, 115
Maker's Mark Distillery, 100
Management Science, 200
Market
  defined, 45
  demographic characteristics of, 53
  socioeconomic characteristics of, 53
Market analysis, 59
Market information, 58
Market segment, 66
Market share, 81
Market targeting, 11
Marketing, as continuing activity, 3
Marketing audit; *see* Strategic marketing audit
Marketing Channels (Stern & El-Ansary), 151
Marketing Decision Making: Concepts and Strategy (Cravens, et al.), 52, 83, 131, 172, 216
Marketing mix, 106
Marketing News, 131, 200
Marketing organization design, 215–17
  considerations affecting, 217–18
  customer effect on, 219–20
  determinants of success, 216–17
  product effect on, 219

Marketing orientation, 2–3, 5
Marketing performance
  criteria to measure, 205
  levels of analysis, 206
  ROI analysis, 206–7
  time period of analysis, 206
The Marketing Plan (Hopkins), 95, 212
Marketing planning, 10, 216
Marketing planning guide, 209–12, 216
Marketing strategy, 57
Mass strategy, 65, 66–67
Matrix organization, 220–22
Matsushita Electric, 109–10
Mayers, Frank K., 125
The Maytag Co., 48, 114
Meade, Daniel, 226
Media, choice of, 185
Media/programming strategy, 184
Mercury Savings and Loan Association,
  178–79
Methods of analysis, 31–34
Mission, 9, 26–27
  determination, 22
  planning, 27
Monroe, Kent B., 169, 172
Multiple niche strategy, 67; *see also* Niche(s)

N

New markets, 25
New product(s), 25, 117–19
  pricing, 170
New product ideas, 120
  from customers, 121
  evaluation of, 121
New product planning, 119–20, 123
  methods of, 122
  organization for, 122–23
The New York Times, 200
Niche(s), 64, 66, 75–77, 79, 105
  attractiveness of, 77
  describing, 74–75
  financial analysis of, 77–78
  forming, 69
  worth of, 68–69
Niche strategy, 65, 67–69
  advantages of, 68
Nonprice factors, in buying decision, 157

O

Objectives, 12, 89–96
  components of, 94
  consistency among, 90–91

Objectives—*Cont.*
  criteria of achieving, 93
  defined, 90
  levels of, 91
  long-range, 27
  and people, 94
  range of, 13
  responsibility for meeting, 96
  specific versus general, 27
Opportunity, 55, 236

P

Packard, David, 6
Paul, Ronald N., 18
Perceptual maps, 72, 73–74
Performance criteria, 233
Personal selling, 190
PIMS; *see* Profit impact of marketing strategy
Planning cycle, 213
Points of influence, 180
Polk, Sol, 115
Position analysis, 102–6
Positioning, 12–13; *see also* Product
  positioning strategy
Positioning research, 72–73
Positioning strategies, 96–97
  judging, 100
  overview, 101
Predetermined niche analysis, 72
Prestbo, John A., 18
Price, 14
  as communication with buyer, 164
  competition and, 164–65
  components of, 158
  flexibility of, 170
  product life cycle and, 170
  product mix and, 169
  role in marketing mix, 165
Price analysis, 156
  product-market and, 157
  sales force in, 158
Price elasticity, 157
Price strategy, 164
  active versus passive, 166–67
  versus competitors, 161
  defined, 154
  distribution and, 156
  flexibility in, 163
  legal issues in, 162
  product strategy and, 156
  responsibility for, 154–55
  target return methods for, 165

Price structure, 169
  demand and competition in, 169
Pricing: Making Profitable Decisions
  (Monroe), 172
Pricing objectives, 167–68
Pricing Practices and Strategies (Bailey ed.),
  107, 158, 160, 172
Priemer, Gus, 187
Procter & Gamble, 2, 3–5, 188, 226–27
Product(s)
  matching to needs, 110
  priorities for, 117
Product analysis form, 128
Product improvement, 127
Product-market, 11, 44–49
  boundaries of, 47–49
  characteristics of, 79
  defined, 45
  levels of, 46
Product-market analysis, 52
  information from, 51
  limitations, 58–59
  strengths, 58
Product-market life cycle, 98–99; *see also*
  Life cycle
Product mix, 113, 137
Product objectives, 116
Product performance, 126
Product planning, 13, 111–12
Product positioning strategy, 97; *see also*
  Positioning
Product strategy, 112–13, 115
Profit impact of marketing strategy (PIMS),
  31
Profitability, measures of, 205
Program strategy, 98
Programming decisions, 97
Promotion, as communication, 173
Promotion strategy, 174, 197
  developing, 175

Q–R

Quick Metal, 11–12, 14–15
Ralston Purina, 154
Rawls, Leonard, 87
Relevant objectives, 90
Restaino, Philip C., 124
Revenue/cost analysis, 192–93
Revlon, Inc., 85–86
Revson, Charles, 102–3
Role of marketing, 38–40
Risks of new products, 121

Ruckert, David, 125

S

Sales force
  criteria for selecting, 195
  distribution, 191
  management of, 195–97
  methods of analyzing, 192
  motivation of, 195
  size of, 191
  training of, 196
Sales Force Management (Churchill et al.),
  196, 200
Sales objectives, 191
Sales response, determinants of, 193–94
Salesperson performance
  determinants of, 196
  evaluation of, 197
Schuster, Lynda, 200
Segmentation criteria, 69
Selling, analysis of, 192
Selling strategy, 186
  as product education, 189
Service-market, 66
Setting objectives; *see also* Objectives
  guidelines, 93
  top-down approach, 93
Shane, Leonard, 178–79, 200
Sherman, Richard, 87
Sherwin-Williams, 201–2
Shocker, Allan D., 60
Shopsmith, Inc., 173–74
Short-term marketing plan, 10, 213–14
  implementation of, 214–15
Singer Company, 5–9
Single-factor analysis, 193
Situation assessment, 19–20
Slom, Stanley H., 107
Smith, Frederick W., 66
Smith, Geoffrey, 200
Snap-On Tools, 67
Specialization, versus flexibility, 16
Specific product-market, 47
Srivastava, Rajendra K., 60
Stern, Louis W., 151
Strategic action, 236–37
Strategic business units, 30
Strategic marketing, 105
Strategic marketing audit, 228–33, 237
  main purpose, 232
Strategic Marketing Planning (Abell &
  Hammond), 33, 41

Strategic options, 127
Strategic planning, steps in, 9
Strategic Planning Institutue, 31, 182
The Structure of New Product Organization (Benson & Chasin), 131

T

Tannenbaum, Jeffrey A., 172
Target Group Index, 71
Target market, 12, 64, 96, 98, 135
  evaluation of alternative, 75
Target market strategy, 78–81
Tassie, John, 135
Taylor, James W., 18
Test marketing, 105–6
  limitations of, 105
Tharp, Mike, 131
Tootsie Roll Industries, 24, 184–85, 200
Toys 'R' Us, 168
Tracking product performance, 16, 126–27;
  see also Evaluation
Troxell, Thomas N., Jr., 83

U–V

U.S. Surgical, 186, 188–89
United States Surgical Corporation (Abramowitz), 200

Urban, Glen L., 107, 131
Valspar Corp., 20–22
The Value Line OTC Special Situations Service, 200
Variety strategy, 68
Vertical marketing systems
  characteristics of, 140
  concessions in, 141–42

W

Wade, Gordon, 226
Waldholz, Michael, 148
Walker, Orville, C., Jr., 196, 200
The Wall Street Journal, 18, 22, 60, 61 83, 88, 107, 115, 123, 131, 148, 151, 172, 188, 200, 227
Warner-Lambert, 147
Woodruff, Robert B., 52, 60, 83, 131, 172, 216
Wurtele, C. Angus, 21

Z

Zahn, Joachim, 78
Zale, Donald, 198
Zales, 197–98
Zaltman, Gerald, 41

This book has been set on a Quadex-Compugraphic 8400 phototypesetting system in 10 and 9 point Times Roman, leaded 2 points. Chapter numbers are set in 48 point Times Roman and chapter titles are set in 24 point Helvetica. The size of the type page is 27 by 46½ picas.